CARING

CARING

A Feminine Approach To Ethics

&

Moral Education

NEL NODDINGS

UNIVERSITY OF CALIFORNIA PRESS

Berkeley   Los Angeles   London

University of California Press
Berkeley and Los Angeles, California

University of California Press, Ltd.
London, England

Copyright © 1984 by The Regents of the University of California

Library of Congress Cataloging in Publication Data

Noddings, Nel.
  Caring, a feminine approach to ethics and moral
education.

  Includes bibliographical references and index.
  1. Caring—Moral and ethical aspects.   2. Ethics.
3. Women—Psychology.   4. Moral education.   I. Title.
BJ1475.N62 1984   170   83-18223
ISBN 0-520-05043-6

Printed in the United States of America

1 2 3 4 5 6 7 8 9

To my husband, Jim, who has
never stopped caring.

CONTENTS

ACKNOWLEDGMENTS

AMONG THOSE WHO helped greatly in the initial stages of this project by making constructive suggestions on my first "caring" papers are Nick Burbules, William Doll, Bruce Fuller, Brian Hill, William Pinar, Mary Anne Raywid, Gerald Reagan, and, in general, the California Association for Philosophy of Education. For steady encouragement throughout the process, I would like to thank Elliot Eisner, Julius Moravcsik, and David Tyack. For careful reading of the final draft and useful editorial comments, I thank Donald Arnstine, Shirley Warren, and Walter Rosenauer. For constant support and encouragement, I thank John Miles, Karen Reeds, and Laurie Taylor of the University of California Press. Finally, very special thanks are given to Denis Phillips, who read early drafts with meticulous care and offered many valuable criticisms.

I would also like to thank Margaret Rausch, for her efficient typing, and my secretary, Jane Wassam, for her typically intelligent handling of details, corrections, and correspondence.

INTRODUCTION

Ethics, the philosophical study of morality, has concentrated for the most part on moral reasoning. Much current work, for example, focuses on the status of moral predicates and, in education, the dominant model presents a hierarchical picture of moral reasoning. This emphasis gives ethics a contemporary, mathematical appearance, but it also moves discussion beyond the sphere of actual human activity and the feeling that pervades such activity. Even though careful philosophers have recognized the difference between "pure" or logical reason and "practical" or moral reason, ethical argumentation has frequently proceeded as if it were governed by the logical necessity characteristic of geometry. It has concentrated on the establishment of principles and that which can be logically derived from them. One might say that ethics has been discussed largely in the language of the father: in principles and propositions, in terms such as justification, fairness, justice. The mother's voice has been silent. Human caring and the memory of caring and being cared for, which I shall argue form the foundation of ethical response, have not received attention except as outcomes of ethical behavior. One is tempted to say that ethics has so far been guided by Logos, the masculine spirit, whereas the more natural and, perhaps, stronger approach would be through Eros, the feminine spirit. I hesitate to give way to this temptation, in part because the terms carry with them a Jungian baggage that I am unwilling to claim in its totality. In one sense, "Eros" does capture the flavor and spirit of what I am attempting here; the notion of psychic relatedness lies at the heart of the ethic I shall propose. In another sense, however, even "Eros" is masculine in its roots and fails to capture the receptive rationality of caring that is characteristic of the feminine approach.

When we look clear-eyed at the world today, we see it wracked with fighting, killing, vandalism, and psychic pain of all sorts. One of the saddest features of this picture of violence is that the deeds are so often done in the name of principle. When we establish a principle forbidding kill-

1

ing, we also establish principles describing the exceptions to the first principle. Supposing, then, that we are moral (we are principled, are we not?), we may tear into others whose beliefs or behaviors differ from ours with the promise of ultimate vindication.

This approach through law and principle is not, I suggest, the approach of the mother. It is the approach of the detached one, of the father. The view to be expressed here is a feminine view. This does not imply that all women will accept it or that men will reject it; indeed, there is no reason why men should not embrace it. It is feminine in the deep classical sense—rooted in receptivity, relatedness, and responsiveness. It does not imply either that logic is to be discarded or that logic is alien to women. It represents an alternative to present views, one that begins with the moral attitude or longing for goodness and not with moral reasoning. It may indeed be the case that such an approach is more typical of women than of men, but this is an empirical question I shall not attempt to answer.

It seems to me that the view I shall try to present would be badly distorted if it were presented in what I have referred to as the "language of the father." Several theorists in education—among them, William Pinar, Madeleine Grumet, Dwayne Huebner, Elliot Eisner—have suggested that our pictures of the world are unduly cramped and narrowed by reliance on a restricted domain of language. Pinar and Grumet, in particular, have looked at this problem in the context of gender studies. I agree with their assessment. But we must realize, also, that one writing on philosophical/educational problems may be handicapped and even rejected in the attempt to bring a new voice to an old domain, particularly when entrance to that domain is gained by uttering the appropriate passwords. Whatever language is chosen, it must not be used as a cloak for sloppy thinking; that much is certain. This part of what I am doing, then, is not without risk.

Women, in general, face a similar problem when they enter the practical domain of moral action. They enter the domain through a different door, so to speak. It is not the case, certainly, that women cannot arrange principles hierarchically and derive conclusions logically. It is more likely that we see this process as peripheral to, or even alien to, many problems of moral action. Faced with a hypothetical moral dilemma, women often ask for more information. We want to know more, I think, in order to form a picture more nearly resembling real moral situations. Ideally, we need to talk to the participants, to see their eyes and facial expressions, to receive what they are feeling. Moral decisions are, after all, made in real situations; they are qualitatively different from the solution of geometry problems. Women can and do give reasons for their acts, but the reasons often point to feelings, needs, impressions, and a sense of personal ideal rather than to universal principles and their application. We shall see that, as a result of this "odd" approach, women have often been judged inferior to men in the moral domain.

Because I am entering the domain through a linguistic back door of sorts, much of what I say cannot be labeled "empirical" or "logical." (Some of it, of course, can be so labeled.) Well, what is it then? It is language that attempts to capture what Wittgenstein advised we "must pass over in silence." But if our language is extended to the expressive—and, after all, it is beautifully capable of such extension—perhaps we can say something in the realm of ethical feeling, and that something may at least achieve the status of conceptual aid or tool if not that of conceptual truth. We may present a coherent and enlightening picture without *proving* anything and, indeed, without claiming to present or to seek moral *knowledge* or moral *truth*. The hand that steadied us as we learned to ride our first bicycle did not provide propositional knowledge, but it guided and supported us all the same, and we finished up "knowing how."

This is an essay in practical ethics from the feminine view. It is very different from the utilitarian practical ethics of, say, Peter Singer. While both of us would treat animals kindly and sensitively, for example, we give very different reasons for our consideration. I must resist his charge that we are guilty of "speciesism" in our failure to accord rights to animals, because I shall locate the very wellspring of ethical behavior in human affective response. Throughout our discussion of ethicality we shall remain in touch with the affect that gives rise to it. This does not mean that our discussion will bog down in sentiment, but it is necessary to give appropriate attention and credit to the affective foundation of existence. Indeed, one who attempts to ignore or to climb above the human affect at the heart of ethicality may well be guilty of romantic rationalism. What is recommended in such a framework simply cannot be broadly applied in the actual world.

I shall begin with a discussion of caring. What does it mean to care and to be cared for? The analysis will occupy us at length, since relation will be taken as ontologically basic and the caring relation as ethically basic. For our purposes, "relation" may be thought of as a set of ordered pairs generated by some rule that describes the affect—or subjective experience—of the members.

In order to establish a firm conceptual foundation that will be free of equivocation, I have given names to the two parties of the relation: the first member is the "one-caring" and the second is the "cared-for." Regular readers of "existentialist" literature will recognize the need for such terminology—bothersome as it is. One may recall Sartre's use of for-itself and in-itself, Heidegger's being-in-the-world, and Buber's I-Thou and I-It. There are at least two good reasons for invoking this mechanism. First, it allows us to speak about our basic entities without explaining the entire conceptual apparatus repeatedly; second, it prevents us from smuggling in meanings through the use of synonyms. Hence, even though hyphenated entities offend the stylist, they represent in this case an attempt to achieve both economy and rigor. Another matter of style in connection with "one-caring" and "cared-for" should be mentioned here. In order to maintain balance and avoid confusion, I have consistently associated the generic "one-caring" with the universal feminine, "she," and "cared-for" with the masculine, "he." Clearly, however, when actual persons are substituted for "one-caring" and "cared-for" in the basic relation, they may be both male, both female, female-male, or male-female. Taking *relation* as ontologically basic simply means that we recognize human encounter and affective response as a basic fact of human existence. As we examine what it means to care and to be cared for, we shall see that both parties contribute to the relation; my caring must be somehow completed in the other if the relation is to be described as caring.

This suggests that the ethic to be developed is one of reciprocity, but our view of reciprocity will be different from that of "contract" theorists such as Plato and John Rawls. What the cared-for gives to the caring relation is not a promise to behave as the one-caring does, nor is it a form of "consideration." The problem of reciprocity will be, possibly, the most important problem we shall discuss, and facets of the problem will appear in a spiral design throughout the book. When we see what it is that the cared-for contributes to the relation, we shall find it possible to separate human infants from nonhuman animals (a great problem for those who insist on some form of rationality in those we should treat ethically), and we shall do this without recourse to notions of God or some other external source of "sanctity" in human life.

The focus of our attention will be upon how to meet the other morally. Ethical caring, the relation in which we do meet the other morally, will be described as arising out of natural caring—that relation in which we respond as one-caring out of love or natural inclination. The relation of natural caring will be identified as the human condition that we, consciously or unconsciously, perceive as "good." It is that condition toward which we long and strive, and it is our longing for caring—to be in that special relation—that provides the motivation for us to be moral. We want to be *moral* in order to remain in the caring relation and to enhance the ideal of ourselves as one-caring.

It is this ethical ideal, this realistic picture of ourselves as one-caring, that guides us as we strive to meet the other morally. Everything depends upon the nature and strength of this ideal, for we shall not have absolute principles to guide us. Indeed, I shall reject ethics of principle as ambiguous and unstable. Wherever there is a principle, there is implied its exception and, too often, principles function to separate us from each other. We may become dangerously self-righteous when we perceive ourselves as holding a precious principle not held by the other. The other may then be devalued and treated "differently." Our ethic of caring will not permit this to happen. We recognize that in fear, anger, or hatred we will treat the other differently, but this treatment is never conducted ethically. Hence, when we must use violence or strategies on the other, we are already diminished ethically. Our efforts must, then, be directed to the maintenance of conditions that will permit caring to flourish. Along with the rejection of principles and rules as the major guide to ethical behavior, I shall also reject the notion of universalizability. Many of those writing and thinking about ethics insist that any ethical judgment—by virtue of its *being* an ethical judgment—must be universalizable; that is, it must be the case that, if under conditions X you are required to do A, then under sufficiently similar conditions, I too am required to do A. I shall reject this emphatically. First, my attention is not on judgment and not on the particular acts we perform but on how we meet the other morally. Second, in recognition of the feminine approach to meeting the other morally—our insistence on caring for the other—I shall want to preserve the uniqueness of human encounters. Since so much depends on the subjective experience of those involved in ethical encounters, conditions are rarely "sufficiently similar" for me to declare that you must do what I must do. There is, however, a fundamental universality in our ethic, as there must be to escape relativism. The caring attitude, that attitude which expresses our earliest memories of being cared for and our growing store of memories of both caring and being cared for, is universally accessible. Since caring and the commitment to sustain it form the universal heart of the ethic, we must establish a convincing and comprehensive picture of caring at the outset.

Another outcome of our dependence on an ethical ideal is the emphasis upon moral education. Since we are dependent upon the strength and sensitivity of the ethical ideal—both our own and that of others—we must nurture that ideal in all of our educational encounters. I shall claim that we are dependent on each other even in the quest for personal goodness. How good *I* can be is partly a function of how *you*—the other—receive and respond to me. Whatever virtue I exercise is completed, fulfilled, in you. The primary aim of all education must be nurturance of the ethical ideal.

To accomplish the purposes set out above, I shall strike many contrasts between masculine and feminine approaches to ethics and education and, indeed, to living. These are not intended to divide men and women into opposing camps. They are meant, rather, to show how great the chasm is that already divides the masculine and feminine in each of us and to suggest that we enter a dialogue of genuine dialectical nature in order to achieve an ultimate transcendence of the masculine and feminine in moral matters. The reader must keep in mind, then, that I shall use the language of both father and mother; I shall have to argue for the positions I set out expressively.

An important difference between an ethic of caring and other ethics that give subjectivity its proper place is its foundation in relation. The philosopher who begins with a supremely free consciousness—an aloneness and emptiness at the heart of existence—identifies *anguish* as the basic human affect. But our view, rooted as it is in relation, identifies *joy* as a basic human affect. When I look at my child—even one of my grown children—and recognize the fundamental relation in which we are each defined, I often experience a deep and overwhelming joy. It is the recognition of and longing for relatedness that form the foundation of our ethic, and the joy that accompanies fulfillment of our caring enhances our commitment to the ethical ideal that sustains us as one-caring.

In the final chapter on moral education, we shall explore how all this may be brought to bear on recommendations for the reorganization of schooling. The specific suggestions made there are not intended as fully developed plans for action but, rather, as illustrations of an approach, of a mode of thinking and feeling about education. They are an invitation to dialogue and not a challenge to enter battle.

1

WHY CARE ABOUT CARING?

THE FUNDAMENTAL NATURE OF CARING

T HE MAIN TASK in this chapter is a preliminary analysis of caring. I want to ask what it means to care and to lay down the lines along which analysis will proceed in chapters two and three. It seems obvious in an everyday sense why we should be interested in caring. Everywhere we hear the complaint "Nobody cares!" and our increasing immersion in bureaucratic procedures and regulations leads us to predict that the complaint will continue to be heard. As human beings we want to care and to be cared for. *Caring* is important in itself. It seems necessary, however, to motivate the sort of detailed analysis I propose; that is, it is reasonable in a philosophical context to ask: Why care about caring?

If we were starting out on a traditional investigation of what it means to be moral, we would almost certainly start with a discussion of moral judgment and moral reasoning. This approach has obvious advantages. It gives us something public and tangible to grapple with—the statements that describe our thinking on moral matters. But I shall argue that this is not the only—nor even the best—starting point. Starting the discussion of moral matters with principles, definitions, and demonstrations is rather like starting the solution of a mathematical problem formally. Sometimes we can and do proceed this way, but when the problematic situation is new, baffling, or especially complex, we cannot start this way. We have to operate in an intuitive or receptive mode that is somewhat mysterious, internal, and nonsequential. After the solution has been found by intuitive methods, we may proceed with the construction of a formal demonstration or proof. As the mathematician Gauss put it:

"I have got my result but I do not know yet how to get (prove) it."[1]

A difficulty in mathematics teaching is that we too rarely share our fundamental mathematical thinking with our students. We present everything ready-made as it were, as though it springs from our foreheads in formal perfection. The same sort of difficulty arises when we approach the teaching of morality or ethical behavior from a rational-cognitive approach. We fail to share with each other the feelings, the conflicts, the hopes and ideas that influence our eventual choices. We share only the justification for our acts and not what motivates and touches us.

I think we are doubly mistaken when we approach moral matters in this mathematical way. First, of course, we miss sharing the heuristic processes in our ethical thinking just as we miss that sharing when we approach mathematics itself formally. But this difficulty could be remedied pedagogically. We would not have to change our approach to ethics but only to the teaching of ethical behavior or ethical thinking. Second, however, when we approach moral matters through the study of moral reasoning, we are led quite naturally to suppose that ethics is necessarily a subject that must be cast in the language of principle and demonstration. This, I shall argue, is a mistake.

Many persons who live moral lives do not approach moral problems formally. Women, in particular, seem to approach moral problems by placing themselves as nearly as possible in concrete situations and assuming personal responsibility for the choices to be made. They define themselves in terms of *caring* and work their way through moral problems from the position of one-caring.[2] This position or attitude of caring activates a complex structure of memories, feelings, and capacities. Further, the process of moral decision making that is founded on caring requires a process of concretization rather than one of abstraction. An ethic built on caring is, I think, characteristically and essentially feminine—which is not to say, of course, that it cannot be shared by men, any more than we should care to say that traditional moral systems cannot be embraced by women. But an ethic of caring arises, I believe, out of our experience as women, just as the traditional logical approach to ethical problems arises more obviously from masculine experience.

One reason, then, for conducting the comprehensive and appreciative investigation of caring to which we shall now turn is to capture conceptually a feminine—or simply an alternative—approach to matters of morality.

WHAT DOES IT MEAN TO CARE?

Our dictionaries tell us that "care" is a state of mental suffering or of engrossment: to care is to be in a burdened mental state, one of anxiety, fear, or solicitude about something or someone. Alternatively, one cares for something or someone if one has a regard for or inclination toward that something or someone. If I have an inclination toward mathematics, I may willingly spend some time with it, and if I have a regard for you, what you think, feel, and desire will matter to me. And, again, to care may mean to be charged with the protection, welfare, or maintenance of something or someone.

These definitions represent different uses of "care" but, in the deepest human sense, we shall see that elements of each of them are involved in caring. In one sense, I may equate "cares" with "burdens"; I have cares in certain matters (professional, personal, or public) if I have burdens or worries, if I fret over current and projected states of affairs. In another sense, I *care* for someone if I feel a stir of desire or inclination toward him. In a related sense, I *care* for someone if I have regard for his views and interests. In the third sense, I have the care of an elderly relative if I am charged with the responsibility for his physical welfare. But, clearly, in the deep human sense that will occupy us, I cannot claim to care for my relative if my caretaking is perfunctory or grudging.

We see that it will be necessary to give much of our attention to the one-caring in our analysis. Even though we sometimes judge caring from the outside, as third-persons, it is easy to see that the essential elements of caring are located in the relation between the one-caring and the cared-for. In a lovely little book, *On Caring,* Milton Mayeroff describes caring largely through the view of one-caring. He begins by saying: "To care for another person, in the most significant sense, is to help him grow and actualize himself."[3]

I want to approach the problem a bit differently, because I think emphasis on the actualization of the other may lead us to pass too rapidly over the description of what goes on in the one-caring. Further, problems arise in the discussion of reciprocity, and we shall feel a need to examine the role of the cared-for much more closely also. But Mayeroff has given us a significant start by pointing to the importance of constancy, guilt, reciprocation, and the limits of caring. All of these we shall consider in some detail.

Let's start looking at caring from the outside to discover the limitations of that approach. In the ordinary course of events, we expect some action from one who claims to care, even though action is not all we expect. How are we to determine whether Mr. Smith cares for his elderly mother, who is confined to a nursing home? It is not enough, surely, that Mr. Smith should say, "I care." (But the possibility of his saying this will lead us onto another path of analysis shortly. We shall have to examine caring from the inside.) We, as observers, must look for some action, some manifestation in Smith's behavior, that will allow us to agree that he cares. To care, we feel, requires some action in behalf of the cared-for. Thus, if Smith never visits his mother, nor writes to her, nor telephones her, we would be likely to say that, although he is charged formally with her care—he pays for her confinement—he does not really care. We point out that he seems to be lacking in regard, that he is not troubled enough to see for himself how his mother fares. There is no desire for her company, no inclination toward her. But notice that a criterion of action would not be easy to formulate from this case. Smith, after all, does perform some action in behalf of his mother: he pays for her physical maintenance. But we are looking for a qualitatively different sort of action.

Is direct, externally observable action necessary to caring? Can caring be present in the absence of action in behalf of the cared-for? Consider the problem of lovers who cannot marry because they are already committed to satisfactory and honorable marriages. The lover learns that his beloved is ill. All his instincts cry out for his presence at her bedside. Yet, if he fears for the trouble he may bring her, for the recriminations that may spring from his appearance, he may stay away from her. Surely, we would not say in such a case that the lover does not care. He is in a mental state of engrossment, even suffering; he feels the deepest regard and, charged by his love with the duty to protect, he denies his own need in order to spare her one form of pain. Thus, in caring, he chooses not to act directly and tenderly in response to the beloved's immediate physical pain. We see that, when we consider the action component of caring in depth, we shall have to look beyond observable action to acts of commitment, those acts that are seen only by the individual subject performing them.

In the case of the lover whose beloved has fallen ill, we might expect him to express himself when the crisis has passed. But even this might not happen. He might resolve never to contact her again, and his caring could then be known only to him as he renews his resolve again and again. We do not wish to deny that the lover cares, but clearly, something is missing in the relationship: caring is not completed in the cared-for. Or, consider the mother whose son, in young adulthood, leaves home in anger and rebellion. Should she act to bring about reconciliation? Perhaps. Are we sure that she does not care if she fails to act directly to bring him into loving contact with his family? She may, indeed, deliberately abstain from acting in the belief that her son must be allowed to work out his problem alone. Her regard for him may force her into anguished and carefully considered inaction. Like the lover, she may eventually express herself to her son—when the crisis has passed—but then again, she may not. After a period of, say, two years, the relationship may stabilize, and the mother's caring may resume its usual form. Shall we say, then, that she "cares again" and that for two years she "did not care"?

There are still further difficulties in trying to formulate an action criterion for caring. Suppose that I learn about a family in great need, and suppose that I decide to help them. I pay their back rent for them, buy food for them, and supply them with the necessities of life. I do all this cheerfully, willingly spending time with them. Can it be doubted that I care? This sort of case will raise problems also. Suppose both husband and wife in this family want to be independent, or at least have a latent longing in this direction. But my acts tend to suppress the urge toward independence. Am I helping or hindering?[4] Do I care or only seem to care? If it must be said that my relation to the needy family is not, properly, a caring relation, what has gone wrong?

Now, in this brief inspection of caring acts, we have already encountered problems. Others suggest themselves. What of indirect caring, for example? What shall we say about college students who engage in protests for the blacks of South Africa or the "boat people" of Indochina or the Jews of Russia? Under what conditions would we be willing to say that they care? Again, these may be questions that can be answered only by those claiming to care. We need to know, for example, what motivates the protest. Then, as we shall see, there is the recurring problem of "completion." How is the caring conveyed to the cared-for? What sort of meeting can there be between the one-caring and the cared-for?

We are not going to be able to answer all of these questions with certainty. Indeed, this essay is not aiming toward a systematic exposition of criteria for caring. Rather, I must show that such a systematic effort is, so far as the system is its goal, mistaken. We expend the effort as much to show what is not fruitful as what is. It is not my aim to be able to sort cases at the finish: A cares, B does not care, C cares but not about D, etc. If we can understand how complex and intricate, indeed how subjective, caring is, we shall perhaps be better equipped to meet the conflicts and pains it sometimes induces. Then, too, we may come to understand at least in part how it is that, in a country that spends billions on caretaking of various sorts, we hear everywhere the complaint, "Nobody cares."

In spite of the difficulties involved, we shall have to discuss behavioral indicators of caring in some depth, because we will be concerned about problems of entrusting care, of monitoring caretaking and assigning it. When we consider the possibility of institutional caring and what might be meant by the "caring school," we shall need to know what to look for. And so, even though the analysis will move us more and more toward first- and second-person views of caring, we shall examine caring acts and the "third-person" view also. In this initial analysis, we shall return to the third-person view after examining first- and second-person aspects.

So far, we have talked about the action component of caring, and we certainly have not arrived at a determinate set of criteria. Suppose, now, that we consider the engrossment we expect to find in the one-caring. When Mr. Smith, whose "caring" seems to us to be at best perfunctory, says, "I care," what can he mean? Now, clearly we can only guess, because Mr. Smith has to speak for himself on this. But he might mean: (1) I *do* care. I think of my mother often and worry about her. It is an awful burden. (2) I *do* care. I should see her more often, but I have so much to do—a houseful of kids, long working hours, a wife who needs my companionship. . . . (3) I *do* care. I pay the bills, don't I? I have sisters who could provide company. . . .

These suggested meanings do not exhaust Mr. Smith's possibilities, but they give us something to work with. In the first case, we might rightly conclude that Mr. Smith does not care for his mother as much as he does for himself as caretaker. He is burdened with cares, and the focus of his attention has shifted inward to himself and his worries. This, we shall see, is a risk of caring. There exists in all caring situations the risk that the one-caring will be overwhelmed by the responsibilities and duties of the task and that, as a result of being burdened, he or she will cease to care for the other and become instead the object of "caring." Now, here— and throughout our discussion on caring—we must try to avoid equivocation. There are, as we have noted, several common meanings of "to care," but no one of them yields the deep sense for which we are probing.

When it is clear that "caring" refers to one of the restricted senses, or when we are not yet sure to what it refers, I shall enclose it in quotes. In the situation where Mr. Smith is *burdened with cares,* he is the object of "caring."

In the third case, also, we might justifiably conclude that Mr. Smith does not care. His interest is in equity. He wants to be credited with caring. By doing something, he hopes to find an acceptable substitute for genuine caring. We see similar behavior in the woman who professes to love animals and whisks every stray to the animal shelter. Most animals, once at the shelter, suffer death. Does one who cares choose swift and merciful death for the object of her care over precarious and perhaps painful life? Well, we might say, it depends. It depends on our caretaking capabilities, on traffic conditions where we live, on the physical condition of the animal. All this is exactly to the point. What we do depends not upon rules, or at least not wholly on rules—not upon a prior determination of what is fair or equitable—but upon a constellation of conditions that is viewed through both the eyes of the one-caring and the eyes of the cared-for. By and large, we do not say with any conviction that a person cares if that person acts routinely according to some fixed rule.

The second case is difficult. This Mr. Smith has a notion that caring involves a commitment of self, but he is finding it difficult to handle the commitments he has already made. He is in conflict over how he should spend himself. Undergoing conflict is another risk of caring, and we shall consider a variety of possible conflicts. Of special interest to us will be the question: When should I attempt to remove conflict, and when should I resolve simply to live with the conflict? Suppose, for example, that I care for both cats and birds. (I must use "care for" at this stage without attempting to justify its use completely.) Having particular cats of my own and *not* having particular birds of my own at the same time are indications of my concern for each. But there are wild birds in my garden, and they are in peril from the cats. I may give the matter considerable thought. I feed the cats well so that they will not hunt out of hunger. I hang small bells on their collars. I keep bird cages ready for victims I am able to rescue. I keep bird baths and feeders inaccessible to the cats. Beyond this, I live with the conflict. Others might have the cats declawed, but I will not do this. Now, the point here is not whether I care more for cats than birds, or whether Ms. Jones (who declaws her cats) cares more for birds than I do. The point lies in trying to discern the kinds of things I must think about when I am in a conflict of caring.

When my caring is directed to living things, I must consider their natures, ways of life, needs, and desires. And, although I can never accomplish it entirely, I try to apprehend the reality of the other.

This is the fundamental aspect of caring from the inside. When I look at and think about how I am when I care, I realize that there is invariably this displacement of interest from my own reality to the reality of the other. (Our discussion now will be confined to caring for persons.) Kierkegaard has said that we apprehend another's reality as *possibility*.[5] To be touched, to have aroused in me something that will disturb my own ethical reality, I must see the other's reality as a possibility for my own. This is not to say that I cannot try to see the other's reality differently. Indeed, I can. I can look at it objectively by collecting factual data; I can look at it historically. If it is heroic, I can come to admire it. But this sort of looking does not touch my own ethical reality; it may even distract me from it. As Kierkegaard put it:

> Ethically speaking there is nothing so conducive to sound sleep as admiration of another person's ethical reality. And again ethically speaking, if there is anything that can stir and rouse a man, it is a possibility ideally requiring itself of a human being.[6]

But I am suggesting that we do not see only the direct possibilities for becoming better than we are when we struggle toward the reality of the other. We also have aroused in us the feeling, "I must do something." When we see the other's reality as a possibility for us, we must act to eliminate the intolerable, to reduce the pain, to fill the need, to actualize the dream. When I am in this sort of relationship with another, when the other's reality becomes a real possibility for me, I care. Whether the caring is sustained, whether it lasts long enough to be conveyed to the other, whether it becomes visible in the world, depends upon my sustaining the relationship or, at least, acting out of concern for my own ethicality as though it were sustained.

In this latter case, one in which something has slipped away from me or eluded me from the start but in which I strive to regain or to attain it, I experience a genuine caring for self. This caring for self, for the *ethical* self, can emerge only from a caring for others. But a sense of my physical self, a knowledge of what gives me pain and pleasure, precedes my caring for others. Otherwise, their realities as possibilities for my own reality would mean nothing to me. When we say of someone, "He cares only for himself," we mean that, in our deepest sense, he does not care at all. He has only a sense of that physical self—of what gives him pain and pleasure. Whatever he sees in others is pre-selected in relation to his own needs and desires. He does not see the reality of the other as a possibility for himself but only as an instance of what he has already determined as self or not-self. Thus, he is ethically both zero and finished. His only "becoming" is a physical becoming. It is clear, of course, that I must say more about what is meant by "ethical reality" and "ethical self," and I shall return to this question.

I need not, however, be a person who cares only for myself in order to behave occasionally as though I care only for myself. Sometimes I behave this way because I have not thought through things carefully enough and because the mode of the times pushes the thoughtless in its own direction. Suppose, for example, that I am a teacher who loves mathematics. I encounter a student who is doing poorly, and I decide to have a talk with him. He tells me that he hates mathematics. *Aha,* I think. *Here is the problem. I must help this poor boy to love mathematics, and then he will do better at it.* What am I doing when I proceed in this way? I am not trying to grasp the reality of the other as a possibility for myself. I have not even asked: *How would it feel to hate mathematics?* Instead, I project my own reality onto my student and say, *You will be just fine if only you learn to love mathematics.* And I have "data" to support me. There is evidence that intrinsic motivation is associated with higher achievement. (Did anyone ever doubt this?) So my student becomes an object of study and manipulation for me. Now, I have deliberately chosen an example that is not often associated with manipulation. Usually, we associate manipulation with trying to get our student to achieve some learning objective that we have devised and set for him. Bringing him to "love mathematics" is seen as a noble aim. And so it is, if it is held out to him as a possibility that he glimpses by observing me and others; but then I shall not be disappointed in him, or in myself, if he remains indifferent to mathematics. It is a possibility that may not be actualized. What matters to me, if I care, is that he find some reason, acceptable in his inner self, for learning the mathematics required of him or that he reject it boldly and honestly. How would it feel to hate mathematics? What reasons could I find for learning it? When I think this way, I refuse to cast about for rewards that might pull him along. He must find his rewards. I do not begin with dazzling performances designed to intrigue him or to change his attitude. I begin, as nearly as I can, with the view from his eyes: Mathematics is bleak, jumbled, scary, boring, boring, boring. . . . What in the world could induce me to engage in it? From that point on, we struggle together with it.

Apprehending the other's reality, feeling what he feels as nearly as possible, is the essential part of caring from the view of the one-caring. For if I take on the other's reality as possibility and begin to feel its reality, I feel, also, that I must act accordingly; that is, I am impelled to act as though in my own behalf, but in behalf of the other. Now, of course, this feeling that I must act may or may not be sustained. I must make a commitment to act. The commitment to act in behalf of the cared-for, a continued interest in his reality throughout the appropriate time span, and the continual renewal of commitment over this span of time are the essential elements of caring from the inner view. Mayeroff speaks of devotion and the promotion of growth in the cared-for. I wish to start with engrossment and motivational displacement. Both concepts will require elaboration.

PROBLEMS ARISING IN THE ANALYSIS OF ONE-CARING

As I think about how I feel when I care, about what my frame of mind is, I see that my caring is always characterized by a move away from self. Yet not all instances of caring are alike even from the view of one-caring. Conditions change, and the time spanned by caring varies. While I care for my children throughout our mutual lifetimes, I may care only momentarily for a stranger in need. The intensity varies. I care deeply for those in my inner circles and more lightly for those farther removed from my personal life. Even with those close to me, the intensity of caring varies; it may be calm and steady most of the time and desperately anxious in emergencies.

The acts performed out of caring vary with both situational conditions and type of relationship. It may bother me briefly, as a teacher, to learn that students in general are not doing well with the subject I teach, but I cannot really be said to care for each of the students having difficulty. And if I have not taken up a serious study of the difficulties themselves, I cannot be said to care about the problem qua problem. But if one of my own students is having difficulty, I may experience the engrossment and motivational displacement of caring. Does this caring spring out of the relationship I have formed with the student? Or, is it possible that I cared in some meaningful way before I even met the particular student?

The problems arising here involve time spans, intensity, and certain formal aspects of caring. Later, I shall explore the concept of chains of caring in which certain formal links to known cared-fors bind us to the possibility of caring. The construction of such formal chains places us in a state of readiness to care. Because my future students are related (formally, *as* students) to present, actual students for whom I do care, I am prepared to care for them also.

As we become aware of the problems involving time, intensity, and formal relationships, we may be led to reconsider the requirement of engrossment. We might instead describe caring of different sorts, on different levels and at varying degrees of intensity. Although I understand why several writers have chosen to speak of special kinds of caring appropriate to particular relationships, I shall claim that these efforts obscure the fundamental truth. At bottom, all caring involves engrossment. The engrossment need not be intense nor need it be pervasive in the life of the one-caring, but it must occur. This requirement does not force caring into the model of romantic love, as some critics fear,[7] for our engrossment may be latent for long periods. We may say of caring as Martin Buber says of love, "it endures, but only in the alternation of actuality and latency."[8] The difference that this approach makes is significant. Whatever roles I assume in life, I may be described in constant terms as one-caring. My first and unending obligation is to meet the other as one-caring. Formal constraints may be added to the fundamental requirement, but they do not replace or weaken it. When we discuss pedagogical caring, for example, we shall develop it from the analysis of caring itself and not from the formal requirements of teaching as a profession.[9]

Another problem arises when we consider situations in which we do not naturally care. Responding to my own child crying in the night may require a physical effort, but it does not usually require what might be called an ethical effort. I naturally want to relieve my child's distress. But receiving the other as he feels and trying to do so are qualitatively different modes. In the first, I am already "with" the other. My motivational energies are flowing toward him and, perhaps, toward his ends. In the second, I may dimly or dramatically perceive a reality that is a repugnant possibility for me. Dwelling in it may bring self-revulsion and disgust. Then I must withdraw. I do not "care" for this person. I may hate him, but I need not. If I do something in his behalf—defend his legal rights or confirm a statement he makes—it is because I care about my own ethical self. In caring for my ethical self, I grapple with the question: Must I try to care? When and for whom? A description of the ethical ideal and its construction will be essential in trying to answer these questions.

There are other limitations in caring. Not only are there those for whom I do not naturally care—situations in which engrossment brings revulsion and motivational displacement is unthinkable—but there are, also, many beyond the reach of my caring. I shall reject the notion of universal caring—that is, caring for everyone—on the grounds that it is impossible to actualize and leads us to substitute abstract problem solving and mere talk for genuine caring. Many of us think that it is not only possible to care for everyone but morally obligatory that we should do so. We can, in a sense that will need elaboration, "care about" everyone; that is, we can maintain an internal state of readiness to try to care for whoever crosses our path. But this is different from the caring-for to which we refer when we use the word "caring." If we are thoughtful persons, we know that the difference is great, and we may even deliberately restrict our contacts so that the caring-for of which we are capable does not deteriorate to mere verbal caring-about. I shall not try to maintain this linguistic distinction, because it seems somewhat unnatural, but we should keep in mind the real distinction we are pointing at: in one sense, "caring" refers to an actuality; in the other, it refers to a verbal commitment to the possibility of caring.

We may add both guilt and conflict to our growing list of problems in connection with the analysis of caring. Conflict arises when our engrossment is divided, and several cared-fors demand incompatible decisions from us. Another sort of conflict occurs when what the cared-for wants is not what we think would be best for him, and still another sort arises when we become overburdened and our caring turns into "cares and burdens." Any of these conflicts may induce guilt. Further, we may feel guilty when we fall short of doing what the cared-for wants us to do or when we bring about outcomes we ourselves did not intend to bring about. Conflict and guilt are inescapable risks of caring, and their consideration will suggest an exploration of courage.

The one-caring is, however, not alone in the caring relationship. Sometimes caring turns inward—as for Mr. Smith in his description of worries and burdens—because conditions are intolerable or because the cared-for is singularly difficult. Clearly, we need also to analyze the role of the cared-for.

THE CARED-FOR

We want to examine both the effects of caring on the cared-for and the special contributions that the cared-for makes to the caring relation. The first topic has received far more attention, and we shall start there also. We shall see that for (A, B) to be a caring relation, both A (the one-caring) and B (the cared-for) must contribute appropriately. Something from A must be received, completed, in B. Generally, we characterize this something as an attitude. B looks for something which tells him that A has regard for him, that he is not being treated perfunctorily.

Gabriel Marcel characterizes this attitude in terms of "disposability (disponibilité), the readiness to bestow and spend oneself and make oneself available, and its contrary, indisposability."[10] One who is disposable recognizes that she has a self to invest, to give. She does not identify herself with her objects and possessions. She is present to the cared-for. One who is indisposable, however, comes across even to one physically present as absent, as elsewhere. Marcel says: "When I am with someone who is indisposable, I am conscious of being with someone for whom I do not exist; I am thrown back on myself."[11]

The one-caring, in caring, is *present* in her acts of caring. Even in physical absence, acts at a distance bear the signs of presence: engrossment in the other, regard, desire for the other's well-being. Caring is largely reactive and responsive. Perhaps it is even better characterized as receptive. The one-caring is sufficiently engrossed in the other to listen to him and to take pleasure or pain in what he recounts. Whatever she does for the cared-for is embedded in a relationship that reveals itself as engrossment and in an attitude that warms and comforts the cared-for.

The caring attitude, this quality of disposability, pervades the situational time-space. So far as it is in my control, if we are conversing and if I care, I remain present to you throughout the conversation. Of course, if I care and you do not, then I may put my presence at a distance, thus freeing you to embrace the absence you have chosen. This is the way of dignity in such situations. To be treated as though one does not exist is a threatening experience, and one has to gather up one's self, one's presence, and place it in a safer, more welcome environment. And, of course, it is the way of generosity.

The one cared-for sees the concern, delight, or interest in the eyes of the one-caring and feels her warmth in both verbal and body language. To the cared-for no act in his behalf is quite as important or influential as the attitude of the one-caring. A major act done grudgingly may be accepted graciously on the surface but resented deeply inwardly, whereas a small act performed generously may be accepted nonchalantly but appreciated inwardly. When the attitude of the one-caring bespeaks caring, the cared-for glows, grows stronger, and feels not so much that he has been given something as that something has been added to him. And this "something" may be hard to specify. Indeed, for the one-caring and the cared-for in a relationship of genuine caring, there is no felt need on either part to specify what sort of transformation has taken place.

The intangible something that is added to the cared-for (and often, simultaneously, to the one-caring) will be an important consideration for us when we discuss caring in social institutions and, especially, in schools. It may be that much of what is most valuable in the teaching-learning relationship cannot be specified and certainly not prespecified. The attitude characteristic of caring comes through in acquaintance. When the student associates with the teacher, feeling free to initiate conversation and to suggest areas of interest, he or she is better able to detect the characteristic attitude even in formal, goal-oriented situations such as lectures. Then a brief contact of eyes may say, "I am still the one interested in you. All of this is of variable importance and significance, but you still matter more." It is no use saying that the teacher who "really cares" wants her students to learn the basic skills which are necessary to a comfortable life; I am not denying that, but the notion is impoverished on both ends. On the one extreme, it is not enough to want one's students to master basic skills. I would not want to choose, but if I had to choose whether my child would be a reader or a loving human being, I would choose the latter with alacrity. On the other extreme, it is by itself too much, for it suggests that I as a caring teacher should be willing to do almost anything to bring my students to mastery of the basic skills. And I am not. Among the intangibles that I would have my students carry away is the feeling that the subject we have struggled with is both fascinating and boring, significant and silly, fraught with meaning and nonsense, challenging and tedious, and that whatever attitude we take toward it, it will not diminish our regard for each other. The student is infinitely more important than the subject.

So far in this discussion of the cared-for, I have emphasized the attitude of the one-caring and how its reception affects the cared-for. But we are interested also in the unique contribution of the cared-for to the relation. In chapter three, where we shall discuss the role of the cared-for in some detail, we shall encounter the problem of *reciprocity*. What exactly does the cared-for give to the relation, or does he simply receive? What responsibility does he have for the maintenance of the relation? Can he be blamed for ethical deterioration in the one-caring? How does he contribute to the construction of the ethical ideal in the one-caring?

AESTHETICAL CARING

I am going to use the expression "aesthetical caring" for caring about things and ideas, and I shall justify that use a bit later. Caring about things or ideas seems to be a qualitatively different form of caring. We do use "care about" and "care for" in relation to objects. We say, "Mr. Smith really cares about his lawn," and "Ms. Brown cares more for her kitchen than for her children." But we cannot mean by these expressions what we have been talking about in connection with caring for persons. We may be engrossed in our lawn or kitchen, but there is no "other" toward whom we move, no other subjective reality to grasp, and there is no second person to whom an attitude is conveyed. Such "caring" may be related to caring for persons other than ourselves and, of course, it is related to the ways in which we care for ourselves, but it may also distract us from caring about persons. We can become too busy "caring" for things to care about people.

We shall encounter challenging anomalies in this area of caring also. Most of us commonly take as pejorative, "He cares only about money"; but we have mixed feelings when we hear, "He cares only about mathematics," or "She cares only about music." In part, we react this way because we feel that a person who cares only about money is likely to hurt others in his pursuit of it, while one who cares only about mathematics is a harmless and, perhaps, admirable person who is denying himself the pleasures of life in his devotion to an esoteric object. But, again, our attitude may be partially conditioned by a traditional respect and regard for the intellectual and, especially, the aesthetic, here interpreted as a sort of passionate involvement with form and nonpersonal content. It will be a special problem for us to ask about the relation between the ethical and the aesthetic and how caring, which we shall take to be the very foundation of the ethical, may be enhanced, distorted, or even diminished by the aesthetic. From the writing of T. E. Lawrence on his Arabian adventures[12] to Kierkegaard's disinterested and skeptical "Mr.

A,"[13] we see the loss of the ethical in a highly intellectualized aesthetic. To be always apart in human affairs, a critical and sensitive observer, to remain troubled but uncommitted, to be just so much affected or affected in just such a way, is to lose the ethical in the aesthetic.

And yet we feel, perhaps rightly, that the receptivity characteristic of aesthetic engagement is very like the receptivity of caring. Consciousness assumes a similar mode of being—one that attempts to grasp or to receive a reality rather than to impose it. Mozart spoke of hearing melodies in his head,[14] and the mathematician Gauss was "seized" by mathematics.[15] Similarly, one who cares for another is seized by the other's projects or plight and often "hears" without words having been spoken by the other. Further, the creative artist, in creating, is present to the work of art as it is forming: listening, watching, feeling, contributing. This exchange between artist and work, this sense of an apprehended or received reality that is nevertheless uniquely one's own, was attested to by Mozart when he asked: "Now, how does it happen that, while I am at work, my compositions assume the form or style which characterize Mozart and are not like anybody else's?"[16]

The sense of having something created through one and only incidentally by one is reported frequently by artists. In an interview celebrating his eighty-sixth birthday, Joan Miró tried to explain his creativity to questioning interviewers. He said such things as, "The paper has magnetism," "My hand is guided by a magnetic force," "It is like I am drunk."[17] Yet when we discuss creativity in schools our focus is almost invariably on the activity, the manipulation, the freedom. And, similarly, when we talk about caring, our emphasis is again on the action, on what might properly be called the caretaking. But the caring that gives meaning to the caretaking is too often dismissed as "sentiment." In part, our approaches to creativity and caring are induced by the dominating insistency on objective evaluation. How can we emphasize the receptivity that is at the core of both when we have no way of measuring it? Here we may ultimately decide that some things in life, and in education, must be undertaken and sustained by faith and not by objective evaluation.

Even though the receptivity characteristic of artistic creation resembles that of caring, we shall find important differences, and we are by no means convinced that artistic receptivity is correlated (in individual human beings) with the receptivity of caring. After all, we have known artistic monsters (Wagner comes to mind); men who have loved orchids and despised human life (Conan Doyle's fictional "Moriarty"); people such as some in the Nazi high command, who loved music and art and yet performed unbelievable cruelty on humans. And, of course, we are acquainted with those who care passionately for their families, tribes, or nations and tear the heads off enemies with gusto. We do not expect, then, to find a simple formula that will describe what our children should learn to care about in order to care meaningfully for persons. But we shall see, again, the great importance of the cared-for in contributing to caring relations. Perhaps some people find ideas and things more responsive than the humans they have tried to care for.

Finally, in our discussion of education, we shall be interested in aesthetical caring in its own right. Schools and teachers may, if they wish to do so, exercise some control over the nature and responsiveness of the potential "cared-fors" presented to students as subject matter, and there may be reasonable ways in which to give perceptive/creative modes an appropriate place alongside judgmental/evaluative modes.

CARING AND ACTING

Let's return briefly to the issue of action. Perhaps, with a better notion of what constitutes the first- and second-person aspects of caring, we can now say something more determinate about acts of caring. Our motivation in caring is directed toward the welfare, protection, or enhancement of the cared-for. When we care, we should, ideally, be able to present reasons for our action/inaction which would persuade a reasonable, disinterested observer that we have acted in behalf of the cared-for. This does not mean that all such observers have to agree that they would have behaved exactly as we did in a particular caring situation. They may, on the contrary, see preferred alternatives. They may experience the very conflicts that caused us anxiety and still suggest a different course of action; or they may proceed in a purely rational-objective way and suggest the same or a different course. But, frequently, and especially in the case of inaction, we are not willing to supply reasons to an actual observer; our ideal observer is, and remains, an abstraction. The reasons we would give, those we give to ourselves in honest subjective thinking, should be so well connected to the objective elements of the problem that our course of action clearly either stands a chance of succeeding in behalf of the cared-for, or can have been engaged in only with the hope of effecting something for the cared-for.

Caring involves stepping out of one's own personal frame of reference into the other's. When we care, we consider the other's point of view, his objective needs, and what he expects of us. Our attention, our mental engrossment is on the cared-for, not on ourselves. Our reasons for acting, then, have to do both with the other's wants and desires and with the objective elements of his problematic situation. If the stray cat is healthy and relatively safe, we do not whisk it off to the county shelter; instead, we provide food and water and encourage freedom. Why condemn it to death when it might enjoy a vagabond freedom? If our minds are on ourselves, however—if we have never really left our own a priori frame of reference—our reasons for acting point back at us and not outward to the cared-for. When we want to be thought of as caring, we often act routinely in a way that may easily secure that credit for us.

This gives us, as outsiders to the relation, a way, not infallible to be sure, to judge caretaking for signs of real caring. To care is to act not by fixed rule but by affection and regard. It seems likely, then, that the actions of one-caring will be varied rather than rule-bound; that is, her actions, while predictable in a global sense, will be unpredictable in detail. Variation is to be expected if the one claiming to care really cares, for her engrossment is in the variable and never fully understood other, in the particular other, in a particular set of circumstances. Rule-bound responses in the name of caring lead us to suspect that the claimant wants most to be credited with caring.

To act as one-caring, then, is to act with special regard for the particular person in a concrete situation. We act not to achieve for ourselves a commendation but to protect or enhance the welfare of the cared-for. Because we are inclined toward the cared-for, we want to act in a way that will please him. But we wish to please him for his sake and not for the promise of his grateful response to our generosity. Even this motivation—to act so that the happiness and pleasure of the cared-for will be enhanced—may not provide a sure external sign of caring. We are sometimes thrown into conflict over what the cared-for wants and what we think would be best for him. As caring parents, for example, we cannot always act in ways which bring immediate reactions of pleasure from our children, and to do so may bespeak a desire, again, to be credited with caring.

The one-caring desires the well-being of the cared-for and acts (or abstains from acting—makes an internal act of commitment) to promote that well-being. She is inclined to the other. An observer, however, cannot see the crucial motive and may misread the attitudinal signs. The observer, then, must judge caring, in part, by the following: First, the action (if there has been one) either brings about a favorable outcome for the cared-for or seems reasonably likely to do so; second, the one-caring displays a characteristic variability in her actions—she acts in a nonrule-bound fashion in behalf of the cared-for.

We shall have to spend some time and effort on the discussion of non-rule-bound, caring behavior. Clearly, I do not intend to advocate arbitrary and capricious behavior, but something more like the inconsistency advocated long ago by Ralph Waldo Emerson,[18] the sort of behavior that is conditioned not by a host of narrow and rigidly defined principles but by a broad and loosely defined ethic that molds itself in situations and has a proper regard for human affections, weaknesses, and anxieties. From such an ethic we do not receive prescriptions as to how we must behave under given conditions, but we are somewhat enlightened as to the kinds of questions we should raise (to ourselves and others) in various kinds of situations and the places we might look for appropriate answers. Such an ethic does not attempt to reduce the need for human judgment with a series of "Thou shalts" and "Thou shalt nots." Rather, it recognizes and calls forth human judgment across a wide range of fact and feeling, and it allows for situations and conditions in which judgment (in the impersonal, logical sense) may properly be put aside in favor of faith and commitment.

We establish funds, or institutions, or agencies in order to provide the caretaking we judge to be necessary. The original impulse is often the one associated with caring. It arises in individuals. But as groups of individuals discuss the perceived needs of another individual or group, the imperative changes from "I must do something" to "Something must be done." This change is accompanied by a shift from the nonrational and subjective to the rational and objective. What should be done? Who should do it? Why should the persons named do it? This sort of thinking is not in itself a mistake; it is needed. But it has buried within it the seed of major error. The danger is that caring, which is essentially nonrational in that it requires a constitutive engrossment and displacement of motivation, may gradually or abruptly be transformed into abstract problem solving. There is, then, a shift of focus from the cared-for to the "problem." Opportunities arise for self-interest, and persons entrusted with caring may lack the necessary engrossment in those to be cared-for. Rules are formulated and the characteristic variation in response to the needs of the cared-for may fade away. Those entrusted with caring may focus on satisfying the formulated requirements for caretaking and fail to be present in their interactions with the cared-for. Thus caring disappears and only its illusion remains.

It is clear, of course, that there is also danger in failing to think objectively and well in caring situations. We quite properly enter a rational-objective mode as we try to decide exactly what we will do in behalf of the cared-for. If I am ill informed, or if I make a mistake, or if I act impetuously, I may hurt rather than help the cared-for. But one may argue, here, that the failure is still at the level of engrossment and motivational displacement. Would I behave so carelessly in my own behalf?

It would seem, then, that one of the greatest dangers to caring may be premature switching to a rational-objective mode. It is not that objective thinking is of no use in problems where caring is required, but it is of limited and particular use, and we shall have to inquire deeply into what we shall call "turning points." If rational-objective thinking is to be put in the service of caring, we must at the right moments turn it away from the abstract toward which it tends and back to the concrete. At times we must suspend it in favor of subjective thinking and reflection, allowing time and space for *seeing* and *feeling*. The rational-objective mode must continually be re-established and redirected from a fresh base of commitment. Otherwise, we find ourselves deeply, perhaps inextricably, enmeshed in procedures that somehow serve only themselves; our thoughts are separated, completely detached, from the original objects of caring.

Now, before turning to a closer look at the one-caring, perhaps we should consider where we are headed through our analysis of caring.

ETHICS AND CARING

It is generally agreed that ethics is the philosophical study of morality, but we also speak of "professional ethics" and "a personal ethic." When we speak in the second way, we refer to something explicable—a set of rules, an ideal, a constellation of expressions—that guides and justifies our conduct. One can, obviously, behave ethically without engaging in ethics as a philosophical enterprise, and one can even put together an ethic of sorts—that is, a description of what it means to be moral—without seriously questioning what it means to be moral. Such an ethic, it seems to me, may or may not be a guide to moral behavior. It depends, in a fundamental way, on an assessment of the answer to the question: What does it mean to be moral? This question will be central to our investigation. I shall use "ethical" rather than "moral" in most of our discussions but, in doing so, I am assuming that to behave ethically is to behave under the guidance of an acceptable and justifiable account of what it means to be moral. To behave ethically is not to behave in conformity with just any description of morality, and I shall claim that ethical systems are not equivalent simply because they include rules concerning the same matters or categories.

In an argument for the possibility of an objective morality (against relativism), anthropologist Ralph Linton makes two major points that may serve to illuminate the path I am taking. In one argument, he seems to say that ethical relativism is false because it can be shown that all societies lay down rules of some sort for behavior in certain universal categories. All societies, for example, have rules governing sexual behavior. But Linton does not seem to recognize that the content of the rules, and not just their mere existence, is crucial to the discussion of ethicality. He says, for example: "... practically all societies recognize adultery as unethical and punish the offenders. The same man who will lend his wife to a friend or brother will be roused to fury if she goes to another man without his permission."[19] But, surely, we would like to know what conception of morality makes adultery "wrong" and the lending of one's wife "right." Just as surely, an ethical system that renders such decisions cannot be equivalent to one that finds adultery acceptable and wife lending unacceptable.

In his second claim, Linton is joined by a substantial number of anthropologists. Stated simply, the claim is that morality is based on common human characteristics and needs and that, hence, an objective morality is possible. That morality is rooted somehow in common human needs, feelings, and cognitions is agreed. But it is not clear to me that we can move easily or swiftly from that agreement to a claim that objective morality is possible. We may be able to describe the moral impulse as it arises in response to particular needs and feelings, and we may be able to describe the relation of thinking and acting in relation to that impulse; but as we tackle these tasks, we may move farther away from a notion of objective morality and closer to the conviction that an irremovable subjective core, a longing for goodness, provides what universality and stability there is in what it means to be moral.

I want to build an ethic on caring, and I shall claim that there is a form of caring natural and accessible to all human beings. Certain feelings, attitudes, and memories will be claimed as universal. But the ethic itself will not embody a set of universalizable moral judgments. Indeed, moral judgment will not be its central concern. It is very common among philosophers to move from the question: What is morality? to the seemingly more manageable question: What is a moral judgment? Fred Feldman, for example, makes this move early on. He suggests:

> Perhaps we can shed some light on the meaning of the noun "morality" by considering the adjective "moral." Proceeding in this way will enable us to deal with a less abstract concept, and we may thereby be more successful. So instead of asking "What is morality?" let us pick one of the most interesting of these uses of the adjective "moral" and ask instead, "What is a moral judgment?"[20]

Now, I am not arguing that this move is completely mistaken or that nothing can be gained through a consideration of moral judgments, but such a move is not the only possibility. We might choose another interesting use of the adjective and ask, instead, about the moral impulse or moral attitude. The choice is important. The long-standing emphasis on the study of moral judgments has led to a serious imbalance in moral discussion. In particular, it is well known that many women—perhaps most women—do not approach moral problems as problems of principle, reasoning, and judgment. I shall discuss this problem at length in chapter four. If a substantial segment of humankind approaches moral problems through a consideration of the concrete elements of situations and a regard for themselves as caring, then perhaps an attempt should be made to enlighten the study of morality in this alternative mode. Further, such a study has significant implications, beyond ethics, for education. If moral education, in a double sense, is guided only by the study of moral principles and judgments, not only are women made to feel inferior to men in the moral realm but also education itself may suffer from impoverished and one-sided moral guidance.

So building an ethic on caring seems both reasonable and important. One may well ask, at this point, whether an ethic so constructed will be a form of "situation ethics." It is not, certainly, that form of act-utilitarianism commonly labeled "situation ethics."[21] Its emphasis is not on the consequences of our acts, although these are not, of course, irrelevant. But an ethic of caring locates morality primarily in the pre-act consciousness of the one-caring. Yet it is not a form of agapism. There is no command to love nor, indeed, any God to make the commandment. Further, I shall reject the notion of universal love, finding it unattainable in any but the most abstract sense and thus a source of distraction. While much of what will be developed in the ethic of caring may be found, also, in Christian ethics, there will be major and irreconcilable differences. Human love, human caring, will be quite enough on which to found an ethic.

We must look even more closely at that love and caring.

2

THE ONE-CARING

RECEIVING

C ARING INVOLVES, FOR the one-caring, a "feeling with" the other. We might want to call this relationship "empathy," but we should think about what we mean by this term. *The Oxford Universal Dictionary* defines *empathy* as "The power of projecting one's personality into, and so fully understanding, the object of contemplation." This is, perhaps, a peculiarly rational, western, masculine way of looking at "feeling with." The notion of "feeling with" that I have outlined does not involve projection but reception. I have called it "engrossment." I do not "put myself in the other's shoes," so to speak, by analyzing his reality as objective data and then asking, "How would I feel in such a situation?" On the contrary, I set aside my temptation to analyze and to plan. I do not project; I receive the other into myself, and I see and feel with the other. I become a duality. I am not thus caused to see or to feel—that is, to exhibit certain behavioral signs interpreted as seeing and feeling—for I am committed to the receptivity that permits me to see and to feel in this way. The seeing and feeling are mine, but only partly and temporarily mine, as on loan to me.

Although receptivity is referred to by mystics, it is not a mystical notion. On the contrary, it refers to a common occurrence, something with which we are all familiar. It does not have to be achieved by meditation, although many persons do enter a receptive state in this way. We are interested here in the reception of persons, however, and we do not receive persons through meditation. Yet a receptive state is required. It can happen by chance when our manipulative efforts are at rest. Suppose, for example, that I am having lunch with a group of colleagues. Among them is one for whom I have never had much regard and for whom I have little professional respect. I do not "care" for him. Somewhere in the light banter of lunch talk, he begins to talk about an experience in the

30

wartime navy and the feelings he had under a particular treatment. He talks about how these feelings impelled him to become a teacher. His expressions are unusually lucid, defenseless. I am touched—not only by sentiment—but by something else. It is as though his eyes and mine have combined to look at the scene he describes. I know that I would have behaved differently in the situation, but this is in itself a matter of indifference. I feel what he says he felt. I have been invaded by this other. Quite simply, I shall never again be completely without regard for him. My professional opinion has not changed, but I am now prepared to care whereas previously I was not.

Mothers quite naturally feel with their infants. We do not project ourselves into our infants and ask, "How would I feel if I were wet to the ribs?" We do this only when the natural impulse fails. Naturally, when an infant cries, we react with the infant and feel that something is wrong. *Something is wrong.* This is the infant's feeling, and it is ours. We receive it and share it. We do not begin by trying to interpret the cry, although we may learn to do this. We first respond to the feeling that something is the matter. It is not foolishness to begin talking to our child as we respond to the cry. We say, "I'm here, sweetheart," and "I hear you, darling," as we move physically toward the child. And, usually, we comfort first, saying, "There, there. Everything is all right," before we begin to analyze what is the matter. We do not begin by formulating or solving a problem but by sharing a feeling. Even when we move into the problem identification stage, we try to retain alternating phases of receptivity. We say, "Do you have a pain?" or its equivalent in baby talk. We do not expect, certainly, that the infant will respond verbally, but the question and its tone impel us to attentive quietude. We await an answer of some sort. We watch for a knee to be drawn up, the head to be tossed, a fist to be sucked.

Now it is just nonsense to say that a feeling response to my infant's cry will "reinforce his crying behavior." To begin with, I am not sure what is meant by "to reinforce," and I suspect that, if it has any meaning in the real world, I cannot know what is being reinforced without being inside the one whose behavior is being so affected. But the sort of empathy we are discussing does not first penetrate the other but receives the other. Hence I do not "reinforce." I receive, I communicate with, I work with. If by "reinforce" we mean simply that the likelihood of the behavior's being continued is increased, then, in the case we are discussing, the claim is quite simply and demonstrably false.

There is another point to be made here. When we consider reinforcement strategies, we are obviously in a manipulative mode. We want to change the other's behavior. The mother as one-caring, however, wants first and most importantly to relieve her child's suffering. But, the philosopher asks, suppose the child is not suffering? Suppose it has merely acquired a bothersome habit of crying at the same hour every night? For that matter, how can you even know that you are actually "receiving the other"?

How can I know? We must move cautiously here. The entire program I am trying to establish hangs on the answer to this question. If I respond that I cannot be mistaken in a basic act of receptivity, I fall into the trap that has already snared the phenomenologist when he speaks of the infallibility of basic intuitions. He asserts his position and presents it as right by definition. Surely, I do not want to respond in this way. Gently, gently, I must resist my colleague's efforts to bring me into the standard mode of argumentation. I am not claiming that I know either in my receptivity itself or in my description of it. It is not at bottom a matter of knowledge but one of feeling and sensitivity. Feeling is not *all* that is involved in caring, but it is essentially involved.

When I receive the other, I am totally with the other. The relation is for the moment exactly as Buber has described it in *I and Thou*.[1] The other "fills the firmament." I do not think the other, and I do not ask myself whether what I am feeling is correct in some way. When I have a sudden, severe pain in my mouth, for example, I may complain of a toothache. I cannot be wrong in responding to what I feel as a pain. It is not a matter of knowledge at all. Later, when the pain has gone and I think back on it, however, I may say, "Well, I guess it was not a toothache after all. It's gone. Perhaps it was a bit of neuralgia caused by the cold or altitude." I do not say, "Well, I guess I did not have a pain." Of course I had a pain. My error, if one occurred, lay in assessing the pain as a toothache. Similarly, I may, in looking back, become aware that there was a failure somewhere in my movement from feeling to assessment. But in the receptive mode itself, I am not thinking the other as object. I am not making claims to knowledge. There can be failures to receive, and we shall discuss such cases, but these are not matters of faulty claims to knowledge.

But am I not making claims to knowledge as I describe the state of one-caring in moments of caring? What is offered is not a set of knowledge claims to be tested but an invitation to see things from an alternative perspective. When I describe the one-caring in particular situations, we should not infer that one who behaves or feels differently in similar situations is necessarily one who does not care. To begin with, I am denying the sort of generalizability that would be required to make such a judgment. Situations of relatedness are unique, and it is my purpose to build a picture of one-caring from a collection of concrete and unique situations. There is, I think, a logic of the caring relation, and there is empirical support for much of what I shall say, but the program under construction does not evolve inevitably out of the "logic of the concept" nor out of a catalog of what is known about persons caring. Both require a move to abstraction that tends to destroy the uniqueness of the caring itself. This must be captured in the caring moment—in the one-caring and in the cared-for.

When I care, when I receive the other in the way we have been discussing, there is more than feeling; there is also a motivational shift. My motive energy flows toward the other and perhaps, although not necessarily, toward his ends. I do not relinquish myself; I cannot excuse myself for what I do. But I allow my motive energy to be shared; I put it at the service of the other. It is clear that my vulnerability is potentially increased when I care, for I can be hurt through the other as well as through myself. But my strength and hope are also increased, for if I am weakened, this other, which is part of me, may remain strong and insistent. When this displacement occurs in the extreme form, we sometimes hear parents speak of "living for" their children. Clearly, both parents and children are at risk of losing themselves under such conditions, and I shall say more about this when we discuss the cared-for in detail.

Now, just what is the place of emotion or affect in caring, and how is it related to the motivational shift just described? I have claimed that the one-caring is engrossed in the other. But this engrossment is not completely characterized as *emotional* feeling. There is a characteristic and appropriate mode of consciousness in caring. When we are in problem solving situations, the characteristic and appropriate mode of consciousness is, usually, one of rational objectivity. It is a thinking mode that moves the self toward the object. It swarms over the object, assimilates it. When this mode breaks down under pressure, we respond emotionally. Suppose that I am trying to open a window that is stuck. As I push, one side goes up and the other side goes down. I move very carefully trying to prevent this lopsided movement. No luck. I examine the parts of the window. I hypothesize. I may examine a window that is working properly in the hope of understanding its mechanism. I experiment.

Then, suddenly, I deteriorate. I beat and curse the window. Consciousness has entered a mode in which it meets its objects with emotion.

Jean-Paul Sartre calls this a "degradation of consciousness,"[2] a condition in which the higher consciousness of rationality gives way to the lower, nonreflective consciousness of emotion. At least his use of "degradation" leads us to infer a movement from higher to lower. In the case I have described, "degradation" seems to be the right word, for my beating and cursing the window seem indicators of an attempt to influence the window as though it had an obstinate will. But, perhaps, in most cases, it would be more fruitful to think in terms of a movement from appropriate and/or effective to inappropriate and/or ineffective, for there is an appropriate change in modes even in problem solving. We can switch from an assimilatory mode to a receptive-intuitive mode which, by a process we do not understand well, allows us to receive the object, to put ourselves quietly into its presence. We enter a feeling mode, but it is not necessarily an emotional mode. In such a mode, we receive what-is-there as nearly as possible without evaluation or assessment. We are in the world of relation, having stepped out of the instrumental world; we have either not yet established goals or we have suspended striving for those already established. We are not attempting to transform the world, but we are allowing ourselves to be transformed. This is, clearly, not a degradation of consciousness, although it may be accompanied by an observable change in energy pattern.

It is a lateral move of some sort. We mentioned earlier Mozart hearing music, Gauss being seized by mathematics, and Miró having his hand guided when he painted. An affective-receptive mode of this kind cannot be thought of as a "degradation" of consciousness. Indeed, emotion may be absent or, at least, the one-receiving may be unaware of it. But it is, clearly, qualitatively different from the analytic-objective mode in which we impose structure on the world. It is a precreative mode characterized by outer quietude and inner voices and images, by absorption and sensory concentration. The one so engrossed is listening, looking, feeling.

The receptive mode seems to be an essential component of intellectual work. We do not pass into it under stress, and this is further evidence that it is not a degradation of consciousness. Indeed, we must settle ourselves, clear our minds, reduce the racket around us in order to enter it. If we are unable to do this, we may remain in an unproductive assimilative mode. Sometimes, for example, mathematics students get "stuck" in an analytic mode. They persist in trying to force a particular structure upon an unyielding problem. They are usually tense, frowning—on the edge of a genuine degradation. Then, the teacher may say, "Wait. Just sit still for a minute. Stop thinking and just look at the problem." Humor, patience, and quiet enter. The student may say, "What kind of mathematics teacher would tell a person to 'stop thinking'?" Teacher and student receive each other. Then the student relaxes and receives the problem. Often the result is quite remarkable. Over and over, I have heard students say, as they looked at what was in front of them, "For goodness sake! Why didn't I see that before?"

The receptive or relational mode seems to be essential to living fully as a person. In caring, a permanent or untimely move from feeling and affective engrossment to abstract problem solving would be a "degradation," a movement from the appropriate to something qualitatively different and less appropriate. Again, this is not to say that a lateral or temporary move into objective thinking is necessarily a "degradation." What seems to be crucial is that we retain the ability to move back and forth and to invest the appropriate mode with dominance. When we give over control to the inappropriate mode, we may properly speak of a degradation of consciousness; in the one case we become irrational and in the other unfeeling and unseeing.

THINKING AND FEELING: TURNING POINTS

The receptive mode is at the heart of human existence. By "existence" or "existing," I mean more than merely living or subsisting. When existentialist philosophers refer to "existence," they mean to include an awareness of and commitment to what we are doing, what we are living, and I am using the term in this way. Existence involves, then, living with heightened awareness. A receptive mode may be both reflexive and reflective; that is, instead of receiving the world or the other, I may receive myself, and I may direct my attention to that which I have already received. It is in this subjective-receptive mode that I see clearly what I have received from the other, and then I must decide whether to proceed in a state of truth or to deny what I have received and talk myself into feeling comfortable with the denial.

Instrumental thinking may, of course, enhance caring; that is, I may use my reasoning powers to figure out what to do once I have committed myself to doing something. But clearly, rationality (in its objective form) does not of necessity mark either the initial impulse or the action that is undertaken. If I care enough, I may do something wild and desperate in behalf of the other—something that has only the tiniest probability of success, and that only in my own subjective view. Hence, in caring, my rational powers are not diminished but they are enrolled in the service of my engrossment in the other. What I will do is subordinate to my commitment to do something.

I have suggested that we can make lateral moves—that is, moves which are neither up nor down—in modes of consciousness. Clearly we cannot remain perpetually in the receptive mode. Mozart moved to the piano, to pen and paper. Gauss produced proofs. Miró perfected what his hand sketched out. And we, in caring, must respond: we express ourselves, we make plans, we execute. But there, are, properly, turning points. As we convert what we have received from the other into a problem, something to be solved, we move away from the other. We clean up his reality, strip it of complex and bothersome qualities, in order to think it. The other's reality becomes data, stuff to be analyzed, studied, interpreted. All this is to be expected and is entirely appropriate, provided that we see the essential turning points and move back to the concrete and the personal. Thus we keep our objective thinking tied to a relational stake at the heart of caring. When we fail to do this, we can climb into clouds of abstraction, moving rapidly away from the caring situation into a domain of objective and impersonal problems where we are free to impose structure as we will. If I do not turn away from my abstractions, I lose the one cared-for. Indeed, I lose myself as one-caring, for I now care about a problem instead of a person.

As an ethical theory develops out of this analysis of caring, we shall consider a process of concretization that is the inverse of abstraction, and we shall explore the possibility that this process is one preferred by women faced with moral dilemmas. Instead of proceeding deductively from principles superimposed on situations, women seek to "fill out" hypothetical situations in a defensible move toward concretization. Suppose, for example, that we are considering appropriate punishment for one who has committed a particular crime. The traditional approach, that of the father, is to ask under what principle the case falls. But the mother may wish to ask more about the culprit and his victims. She may begin by thinking, "What if this were my child?" Neither position is fairly put forth and examined by merely identifying its first move but, clearly, the approaches are different: The first moves immediately to abstraction where its thinking can take place clearly and logically in isolation from the complicating factors of particular persons, places, and circumstances; the second moves to concretization where its feeling can be modified by the introduction of facts, the feelings of others, and personal histories. The father might sacrifice his own child in fulfilling a principle; the mother might sacrifice any principle to preserve her child. This is far too simplistic to be considered a summary or definitive description of positions, but it is indicative and instructive. It underscores the sort of difference that places the present approach in opposition to traditional ethics.

GUILT AND COURAGE

The one-caring is in a unique position with respect to the caring. I can be aware of myself caring, and I can think about and doubt my caring. If the cared-for receives my caring and completes it, I may never turn inward (except in wonder) to examine my own state or to question it. I *care,* and that means that my consciousness is turned to the cared-for. I have little need to reflect on this consciousness, and I may be but dimly aware of a euphoria, ranging from a mild "all's well" to ecstasy, that accompanies my activity with the cared-for.

But if the cared-for does not complete my caring by receiving and acknowledging it, I may examine myself and ask, "Do I really care?" In some cases, an affirmative answer comes through clearly and honestly. I do care. I shall always care. The situation may be such that I just have to wait for my caring to be completed in the other and, if it never is, I see clearly that the attempt to care will nonetheless go on. This is a source of wonder when I see it. However, a negative answer may come through. If it does, I may accept it honestly and study it, or I may reject it in horror and begin to talk myself out of it. Let's say that I have the courage to accept it. My caring for this other has turned into "cares and burdens." When I see this, I know that I have become the object of my own "caring." I need my pity, compassion, and sympathy. "Wallowing in self-pity" is not a bad thing if I intend to help myself as I would another. So, perhaps, I dwell on my troubles for a while, let them lead and chase themselves into an enhanced state of despair at which I draw back sheepishly and say, "Well, now, it is not that bad." Then I can climb out. I recognize that I do not care at this time, that I am weary, but I recognize, also, that this mood may pass. It may be that I must still do certain things in behalf of the cared-for. I resolve to do them as though I care. This is very dangerous, and I must monitor the situation in a way that is completely unnecessary when I do care. I am not really prepared to care. I am in a deliberate state of neutrality, waiting and watching. I run a dreadful risk in this decision for, if the potential cared-for turns on me and says, "You don't really care!" I may become stricken with guilt. I do not really care, and yet I "care" enough to be bothered by this accusation.

What I care about is crucial at this point. If I care about the other, if I am stricken by his belief that I do not care—that is, if I am stricken as he is by disappointment and desperation—then I do care, and things will mend naturally. But if this accusation strikes me as a threat, as a reprimand that triggers no sympathy for the other but only a massive resistance, I will feel guilt. Here am I, one who cared, who does not now care, and the other sees it. I can summon reason to my defense: Look at this other! What has he done to encourage or to appreciate me? What a mess he is. How I have tried.... I can go on and on and guilt comes right along like my shadow.

Can I avoid this? Can I be free of guilt? I do not think it is possible. Paul Tillich describes the anxiety of guilt as ontological. It transcends the subjective and objective. It is a constant threat in caring. In caring, I am turned both outward (toward the other) and inward (my engrossment may be reflected upon); when caring fails, I feel its loss. I want to care, but I do not. I feel that I ought to behave as though I care, but I do not want to do this. Of someone in this kind of situation, Tillich says:

> A profound ambiguity between good and evil permeates everything he does, because it permeates his personal being as such. Non-being is mixed with being in his moral self-affirmation as it is in his spiritual and ontic self-affirmation. The awareness of this ambiguity is the feeling of guilt.[3]

Contrary to many of the messages from some schools of modern psychology, we cannot be free of this guilt. There is something to be said for "not wasting time on guilt," if by this we mean suffering guilt and letting our guilt color all we do in the world. Clearly, if that which has induced guilt can be partially remedied by action, then it makes sense to act. This does not mean to avoid. We might, of course, refuse the guilt and engage in frenetic activity to avoid looking at it, but I am not suggesting this. I am saying what we all know, that some action which may remove the reason for the other's accusation will tend to alleviate the guilt. In such cases we act out of regard for our own ethical or, perhaps, psychical selves, but the reaction of the other may enable us to recover the caring that has lapsed. Caring is, by its nature, filled out in the other.

There are, however, occasions upon which no action can relieve guilt. These are not necessarily situations in which caring has lapsed. There are situations in which caring is sustained but something has gone wrong. Something terrible has happened. In caring we risk guilt, either through accidents while caring is sustained or through the lapse of caring. In the former case, nothing can undo what has been done. Atonement is not required, because forgiveness was freely given at the outset. To be free of the guilt, the one-caring would do *anything* for the cared-for. Yet this "anything" would be a mockery, because there is nothing that could restore what has been lost to the cared-for. So here is this reality, this thing of which I can never be free. Courage requires that I accept it. I do not dwell on it so that it cripples me and provides an excuse (which I can never have) for my lapsed projects. But I accept it. When it comes to me I accept it as mine-that-I-would-not-have-chosen but mine nonetheless. I live it through as often as it comes to me. There is a double requirement of courage in caring: I must have the courage to accept that which I have had a hand in, and I must have the courage to go on caring. Might it not be easier to escape to the world of principles and abstractions? These cared-fors under whose gaze I fall—whose real eyes look into mine—are related to me. I can be hurt through them and by them. Intermittently, they are I and I they. The possibilities for both pain and joy are increased in my world, but I need courage to grasp the possibilities.

The question raised by mistaken psychologies, "Why should I feel guilty?" suggests that I may reject the possibility—and, of course, I may, if I am willing to reject my self, that part of my finite self which is embedded in an infinite that I cannot entirely grasp. But I do know, if I look with open eyes upon it, that any movement out of a stagnant self-as-it-is risks this guilt which is existential, which accompanies an awareness of lived experience. It is a risk I always run when I care.

The risk of guilt is present in all caring. But its likelihood is greater in caring that is sustained over time. Here we experience the "ups and downs" of close contact in normal living. Not all caring is sustained over lengthy periods. When we care for a stranger in immediate need, we care for the interval of need and, afterward, forget. A stranger needs to use our telephone, or we stop to help a stranded motorist. There is no demand in these cases that we care either intensely or for a prolonged

period of time. There is a temporal aspect to caring. From the view of the
one-caring, the engrossment characteristic of caring and the typical motivational shift must span the interval whether that be, properly, a few
moments or a lifetime. Martin Buber says: "Love is responsibility of an I
for a Thou:* in this consists what cannot consist in any feeling."* Caring,
too, although it is not necessarily accompanied by love, is partly responsibility for the other—for the cared-for. As we care, we hear the "I
ought"—direct and primitive—and the potential for suffering guilt is
ever present. What "I ought" to respond to, I may ignore or reject; what
I decide to do in genuine response to the other and to the internal "I
ought" may go awry, bringing pain to the cared-for and guilt to me.

To spare ourselves guilt, we may prefer to define our caring in terms of
conformity and/or regard to principle. If the other does not respond, we
are still quite safe from criticism. We are righteous. We act in obedience
to some great principle—I must defend my country! I must execute the
law! I must be fair!—and from the potential cared-for we avert our eyes.
We do not care for him any longer.

WOMEN AND CARING

We have already noted that women often define themselves as both persons and moral agents in terms of their capacity to care. When we move
from natural caring to an ethic of caring, we shall consider the deep psychological structures that may be responsible for this mode of definition.
Here I wish to concentrate on the caring itself—on particular examples of
feminine courage in relating and remaining related and on the typical differences between men and women in their search for the ethical in human
relationships.

We may find the sorts of examples and contrasts we seek in legend,
Biblical accounts, biography, and fiction. I shall do no more than sample
the possibilities here. The legend of Ceres, for example, can be interpreted beautifully to illustrate the attitude and conflicts of one-caring.[5]
Recall that Ceres was the goddess who cared for the earth. It was she who
made the fields fertile and watched over the maturation and harvest of
crops. She had a daughter, Proserpine, whom she dearly loved. One day,

---

*Kaufman translates *du* as You, but because this usage is unfamiliar to many readers, I
have substituted the more familiar Thou.

Pluto, god of the underworld, crazed by love from Cupid's arrow, snatched Proserpine from her play and abducted her to his underground kingdom. Ceres searched the world for her daughter without success and was grief-stricken. Next something happens in the legend that is especially instructive for the one-caring: Ceres, in all her misery, is approached by an old man, Celeus, and his little girl. They respond to her grief and invite her to visit their cottage; indeed, they respond by weeping with her. Ceres is moved by this show of compassion and accompanies them. Here is a concrete illustration of the power of the cared-for in contributing to the caring relation. Ceres knows that she is the one-caring, that she has the power to confer good or ill on these passersby. But, in her misery, she needs the active response of the cared-for to maintain herself as one-caring. Typical of one-caring who would be one-caring, she answers Celeus by saying: "Lead on, . . . I cannot resist that appeal."[6]

Arriving at the cottage, Ceres finds a little boy very ill, probably dying. She is received, however, by the child's mother, Metanira, and moved to pity, Ceres cures the child with a kiss. Later, when Ceres tries to make the child immortal by tempering his body in flaming ashes, Metanira snatches the child fearfully from her. Ceres chides the mother for depriving her son of immortality but, still, she assures Metanira that he will nevertheless be "great and useful." The boy, Triptolemus, will someday teach humankind the secrets of agriculture as revealed to him by Ceres. Here, then, is a second facet of the ideal for one-caring. The cared-for shall be blessed not with riches, luck, and power but with the great gift of *usefulness*. The conversation between Ceres intending immortality for Triptolemus and Metanira afraid to risk her son in the flames is illustrative, again, of the feminine striving for an attainable ideal. It stands in bold contrast to the story we shall consider next—that of Abraham's willingness to sacrifice his son to divine command.

Eventually, Ceres finds the place where Proserpine was swallowed up by the earth, but she mistakenly supposes that the earth itself did this terrible thing. She is stricken by a double grief. Not only has she lost her beloved Proserpine but another cared-for, her fruitful earth, has turned against her. Now Ceres does not fly into a destructive rage and visit the earth with lightning, fire and flood. She merely ceases to care; she withdraws as one-caring, and the earth dries up in mud and weeds and brambles. Ceres, the one-caring, has nothing to sustain her in caring. Here, we see foreshadowed the power of the cared-for in maintaining the caring relationship.

Finally, Ceres learns the truth and entreats Jove to intercede on her behalf with Pluto. As you may recall, Pluto, in fear of losing his kingdom entirely, agrees to return Proserpine but induces her to eat some pomegranate seeds so that she will be unable to spend more than half of each year with her mother. When Proserpine returns each spring, Ceres bestows great fruitfulness on the earth and, when she leaves each fall, Ceres is overcome by grief and allows winter to settle on the earth.

This story is widely understood as an allegory of the seasons, of sleeping grain and awakening fruitfulness, but it may be interpreted also as a fable of caring and being cared-for.[7] It illustrates the vulnerability of the one-caring, her reception of the proximate stranger, her generosity upon being herself received, and the munificent displacement of motivation that occurs when she is sustained as one-caring.

Now, someone is sure to point out that, in contrast to the legend of one-caring as the pinnacle of feminine sensibility, feminine skullduggery lies at the root of the problem described in the legend.[8] It was, after all, Venus who prompted her son, Cupid, to shoot Pluto with the arrow of love. I am not denying the reality of this dark side of feminine character,[9] but I am rejecting it in my quest for the ethical. I am not, after all, suggesting a will to power but rather a commitment to care as the guide to an ethical ideal.

This commitment to care and to define oneself in terms of the capacity to care represent a feminine alternative to Kohlberg's "stage six" morality.[10] At stage six, the moral thinker transcends particular moral principles by appealing to a highest principle—one that allows a rearrangement of the hierarchy in order to give proper place-value to human love, loyalty, and the relief of suffering. But women, as ones-caring, are not so much concerned with the rearrangement of priorities among principles; they are concerned, rather, with maintaining and enhancing caring. They do not abstract away from the concrete situation those elements that allow a formulation of deductive argument; rather, they remain in the situation as sensitive, receptive, and responsible agents. As a result of this caring orientation, they are perceived by Kohlberg as "being stuck" at stage three—that stage in which the moral agent wants to be a "good boy or girl." The desire to be good, however, to be one-caring in response to these cared-fors here and now, provides a sound and lovely alternative foundation for ethical behavior. Like Ceres, the one-caring will not turn from the real human beings who address her. Her caring is the foundation of—and not a mere manifestation of—her morality.

In contrast to the story of Ceres, who could not abandon her child even for the sake of her beloved Earth, we may consider Abraham. In obedience to God, Abraham traveled with his son, Isaac, to Moriah, there to offer him as a sacrifice: "And they came to the place which God had told him of; and Abraham built an altar there, and laid the wood in order, and bound Isaac his son, and laid him on the altar upon the wood. And Abraham stretched forth his hand, and took the knife to slay his son."[11]

Kierkegaard interprets Abraham's action as supra-ethical, that is, as the action of an individual who is justified by his connection to God, the absolute. For him, as for us, the individual is higher than the universal, but for him that "higher" status is derived from "absolute duty toward God." Hence a paradox is produced. Out of duty to God, we may be required to do to our neighbor what is ethically forbidden. The ethical is, for Kierkegaard, the universal, and the individual directly obedient to God is superior to the universal. He says: "In the story of Abraham we find such a paradox. His relation to Isaac, ethically expressed, is this, that the father should love the son. This ethical relation is reduced to a relative position in contrast with the absolute relation to God."[12]

But for the mother, for us, this is horrendous. Our relation to our children is not governed first by the ethical but by natural caring. We love not because we are required to love but because our natural relatedness gives natural birth to love. It is this love, this natural caring, that makes the ethical possible. For us, then, Abraham's decision is not only ethically unjustified but it is in basest violation of the supra-ethical—of caring. The one-caring can only describe his act—"You would kill your own son!"—and refuse him forgiveness. Abraham's obedience fled for protection under the skirts of an unseeable God. Under the gaze of an abstract and untouchable God, he would destroy *this* touchable child whose real eyes were turned upon him in trust, and love, and fear. I suspect no woman could have written either *Genesis* or *Fear and Trembling,* but perhaps I should speak only for myself on that. The one-caring, male or female, does not seek security in abstractions cast either as principles or entities. She remains responsible here and now for this cared-for and this situation and for the forseeable futures projected by herself and the cared-for.

Now, of course, the scholar may argue that I have interpreted the story too literally, and even that Kierkegaard did so in an agony of faith against ethical reason. He will point out that, on another interpretation,

God used Abraham and Isaac to teach His people that human sacrifice was unacceptable to Him and, henceforth, forbidden. This interpretation will not satisfy the mother. The mother in Abraham's position would respond to the fear and trust of her child—not to the voice of abstraction. The Mother-as-God would not use a parent and child so fearfully and painfully to teach a welcome lesson to her other children. The Mother-God must respond caringly to Abraham as cared-for and to Isaac as cared-for, and she must preserve Abraham as one-caring in relation to Isaac.

Everything that is built on this sacrificial impulse is anathema to woman. Here, says woman, is my child. I will not sacrifice him for God, or for the greatest good, or for these ten others. Let us find some other way.

The devotion to "something beyond" that is revealed in traditional, masculine ethics is often devotion to deity, but sometimes it is devotion to principle. Recall the story of Manlius, a Roman commander who laid down harsh laws for the conduct of his legions. One of the first to disobey a rule about leaving camp to engage in individual combat was his own son. In compliance with the rules, Manlius ordered the execution of his son. A principle had been violated; for this violation, X must be executed. That "X" was replaced by "my son" gave Manlius no release from obedience to the principle. Why, then, did he not think concretely before establishing the rule? Why do men so often lay out their own clear paths to tragedy? The one-caring would want to think carefully about the establishment of rules and even more carefully about the prescription of penalties. Indeed, she would prefer to establish a climate of cooperative "we-ness" so that rules and penalties might be kept to a minimum. For her, the hypothetical is filled with real persons, and, thus, her rules are tempered a priori with thoughts of those in her inner circle. A stranger might, then, be spared death because she would not visit death upon her own child. She does not, in whatever personal agony, inflict death upon her child in devotion to either principle or abstract entity.

History, legend, and biography might profitably be reinterpreted in light of feminine experience. Both men and women may participate in the "feminine" as I am developing it, but women have suffered acutely from its lack of explication. They have felt and suffered and held fast, but they have—as a result—been accused of deficiency in abstract reasoning, of capricious behavior, of emotional reaction. Even in parenting, perhaps especially in parenting, the typical differences between concrete and abstract, between here-and-now and here-and-after, between flesh-and-blood and spirit, stand out in life and literature. In Robert Frost's "Home Burial," the conflict between man and woman in the loss of their child is dramatic. He tries to relieve his grief by speaking of ordinary things; she is convinced because of this that he feels no grief. He makes matters worse by saying:

> What was it brought you up to think it the thing
> To take your mother-loss of a first child
> So inconsolably—in the face of love.
> You'd think his memory might be satisfied—[13]

What is the man doing here? He is not callous, and he has not escaped suffering, but he has not met his wife on the level of feeling. He accuses her of thinking "it the thing" to grieve deeply; he speaks of "mother-loss" and "first child," but he avoids the child's name and any concrete reference to him. He speaks of "his memory" but not of the small, warm body his wife nurtured. It is this difference in language and direction of reference that forms the difference between an ethic of caring and an ethic of principle.

Examples appear in real life as well as in poetry and fiction. Pearl Buck describes the difference in her own parents.

> The fascinating thing about Andrew and Carie was that from the two of them we always got entirely different stories about the same incident. They never saw the same things or felt the same way about anything, and it was as though they had not gone to the same place or seen the same people.[14]

Andrew was spirit—all heaven and abstraction; Carie was completely human. He was a preacher, a missionary in China, and cared for the souls of his parishioners. Carie cared for them as persons, ministering to their bodies and earthly minds. She had no preconceived notion of what her children should be; she did not cast them in the image of a catechism-produced God. Rather, she loved their warm bodies, cherished their laughter and childish pranks, nurtured their earthly courage and compassion for each other. The greatest joy in her life came through her children, and her greatest suffering was incurred by their loss. When Andrew was seventy years old, some time after Carie had died, he wrote the story of his life. The record fit into twenty-five pages. His daughter remarks:

It was the story of his soul, his unchanging soul. Once he mentioned the fact of his marriage to Carie, his wife. Once he listed the children he had had with her, but in the listing he forgot entirely a little son who lived to be five years old and was Carie's favorite child, and he made no comment on any of them.[15]

Yet all of her life Carie was made to feel spiritually inferior to her husband and, as she lay near death, he expressed concern about her soul!

Today we are asked to believe that women's "lack of experience in the world" keeps them at an inferior stage in moral development. I am suggesting, to the contrary, that a powerful and coherent ethic and, indeed, a different sort of world may be built on the natural caring so familiar to women.

CIRCLES AND CHAINS

We find ourselves at the center of concentric circles of caring. In the inner, intimate circle, we care because we love. In particularly trying situations we may act out of ethical sense even here. After all, sometimes we are tired, the other has behaved abominably, and our love is frayed. Then we remind ourselves of the other's location in our system of circles: He is (was) my friend; she is my child; he is my father. The engrossment remains, although its color changes, and we may vacillate between the once natural caring for other to growing concern for ourselves.

As we move outward in the circles, we encounter those for whom we have personal regard. Here, as in the more intimate circles, we are guided in what we do by at least three considerations: how we feel, what the other expects of us, and what the situational relationship requires of us. Persons in these circles do not, in the usual course of events, require from us what our families naturally demand, and the situations in which we find ourselves have, usually, their own rules of conduct. We are comfortable in these circles if we are in compliance with the rules of the game. Again, these rules do not compel us, but they have an instrumental force that is easily recognized. I listen with a certain ready appreciation to colleagues, and I respond in a polite, acceptable fashion. But I must not forget that the rules are only aids to smooth passage through unproblematic events. They protect and insulate me. They are a reflection of someone's sense of relatedness institutionalized in our culture. But they do not put me in touch; they do not guarantee the relation itself. Thus rules will not be decisive for us in critical situations, but they will be acknowledged as economies of a sort. As such they will be even less important than the "illuminative maxims" described by Joseph Fletcher.[16] For us, the destructive role of rules and principles must be clarified and acknowledged.

Beyond the circles of proximate others are those I have not yet encountered. Some of these are linked to the inner circle by personal or formal relations. Out there is a young man who will be my daughter's husband; I am prepared to acknowledge the transitivity of my love. He enters my life with potential love. Out there, also, are future students; they are linked formally to those I already care for and they, too, enter my life potentially cared-for. Chains of caring are established, some linking unknown individuals to those already anchored in the inner circles and some forming whole new circles of potential caring. I am "prepared to care" through recognition of these chains.

But what of the stranger, one who comes to me without the bonds established in my chains of caring? Is there any sense in which I can be prepared to care for him? I can remain receptive. As in the beginning, I may recognize the internal "I must," that natural imperative that arises as I receive the other, but this becomes more and more difficult as my world grows more complex. I may be bombarded with stimuli that arouse the "I must," and I learn to reduce the load. As we have seen, a standard fashion of controlling what comes in is to rely on situational rules. These protect me. What, under normal circumstances, I must do for a colleague is different from what I must do for my child. I may come to rely almost completely on external rules and, if I do, I become detached from the very heart of morality: the sensibility that calls forth caring. In an important sense, the stranger has an enormous claim on me, because I do not know where he fits, what requests he has a formal right to make, or what personal needs he will pass on to me. I can meet him only in a state of wary anticipation and rusty grace, for my original innocent grace is gone and, aware of my finiteness, I fear a request I cannot meet without hardship. Indeed, the caring person, one who in this way is prepared to care, dreads the proximate stranger, for she cannot easily reject the claim he has on her. She would prefer that the stray cat not appear at the back door—or the stray teenager at the front. But if either presents himself, he must be received not by formula but as individual.

The strain on one who would care can be great. Literature is filled with descriptions of encounters of this sort: the legitimate dread of the one-caring and the ultimate acceptance or rejection of the internal "I must."

One thinks of John Steinbeck's Carl Tiflin and Mr. Gitano in *The Red Pony*.[17] In defiance of a loud and insistent "I must," Tiflin diminishes his ethical ideal and turns the old man away. In contrast, Robert Frost has the farm wife, Mary, express the one-caring as she accepts the "hired man" into her home:

> Yes, what else but home? It all depends on
> what you mean by home.
> Of course he's nothing to us, any more
> Than was the hound that came a stranger to us
> Out of the woods, worn out upon the trail.
> Home is the place where, when you have to go there,
> They have to take you in.[18]

Both imperatives expressed here, the "have to's" of the one-caring and the cared-for, are internal imperatives. An observer can see alternatives clearly, but the "I must" suggests itself as binding upon the one in whom it occurs. We are both free and bound in our circles and chains.

ASYMMETRY AND RECIPROCITY IN CARING

Clearly, the cared-for depends upon the one-caring. But the one-caring is also oddly dependent upon the cared-for. If the demands of the cared-for become too great or if they are delivered ungraciously, the one-caring may become resentful and, pushed hard enough, may withdraw her caring. Each of us is dependent upon the other in caring and moral relationships. The very goodness I seek, the perfection of ethical self is, thus, partly dependent on you, the other. And this peculiar dependence holds beyond caring relationships into antagonistic and adversarial relations. If you are unscrupulous enough, you can deprive me not only of life and fortune but of the ethical ideal for which I am striving. You can push me to betray my principles, deny my loves, sacrifice my ethical self. How hard it is for you to do this depends upon the strength of my commitment to the ethical ideal, but that you can do it is scarcely questionable. You may recall the denial and betrayal of Orwell's Winston Smith in *Nineteen Eighty-Four* when he was threatened by that which he feared most in Room 101. With the caged rats against his face, he cried out to betray the one he loved: "Do it to Julia! Do it to Julia! Not me! Julia! I don't care what you do to her. Tear her face off, strip her to the bones. Not me! Julia! Not me!"[19]

In all we discuss here, we shall be reminded of our fundamental relatedness, of our dependence upon each other. We are both free—that which I do, *I* do—and bound—I might do far better if you reach out to help me and far, far worse if you abuse, taunt, or ignore me. As we build an ethic on caring and as we examine education under its guidance, we shall see that the greatest obligation of educators, inside and outside formal schooling, is to nurture the ethical ideals of those with whom they come in contact.

THE ETHICAL IDEAL AND THE ETHICAL SELF

What is this "ethical ideal" I have referred to? When I reflect on the way I am in genuine caring relationships and caring situations—the natural quality of my engrossment, the shift of my energies toward the other and his projects—I form a picture of myself. This picture is incomplete so long as I see myself only as the one-caring. But as I reflect also on the way I am as cared-for, I see clearly my own longing to be received, understood, and accepted. There are cases in which I am not received, and many in which I fail to receive the other, but a picture of goodness begins to form. I see that when I am as I need the other to be toward me, I am the way I want to be—that is, I am closest to goodness when I accept and affirm the internal "I must." Now it is certainly true that the "I must" can be rejected and, of course, it can grow quieter under the stress of living. I can talk myself out of the "I must," detach myself from feeling and try to think my way to an ethical life. But this is just what I must not do if I value my ethical self.

This "goodness" to which I have referred is an assessment of the state of natural caring. I am not arguing that what *is* is of necessity *good*. I am arguing that natural caring—some degree of which each of us has been dependent upon for our continued existence—is the natural state that we inevitably identify as "good." This goodness is felt, and it guides our thinking implicitly. Our picture of ourselves as ethical inevitably involves a consideration of this goodness.

The ethical self is an active relation between my actual self and a vision of my ideal self as one-caring and cared-for. It is born of the fundamental recognition of relatedness; that which connects me naturally to the other, reconnects me through the other to myself. As I care for others and am cared for by them, I become able to care for myself. The characteristic "I must" arises in connection with this other in me, this ideal self, and I respond to it. It is this caring that sustains me when caring for the other fails, and it is this caring that enables me to surpass my actual uncaring self in the direction of caring.

As my receiving the other enables the "I must" to arise with respect to the other, so receiving the vision of what I might be enables the "I must" to arise with respect to the ethical self. I see what I might be, and I see also that *this* vision of what I might be is the genuine product of caring. My acceptance and affirmation of this caring for self will not tell me exactly what to do, of course. Neither does caring in and of itself tell me what to do in behalf of the other. But as caring for another engrosses me in the other and redirects my motivational energy, so caring for my ethical self commits me to struggle toward the other through clouds of doubt, aversion, and apathy.

There are many problems that need to be explored in connection with the ethical ideal and its construction. As I shall use the expression, it refers to a personal construct, although there is a sense in which groups, too, may have an ethical ideal. I shall require that the ethical ideal be—in a way I must describe—realistic, attainable. It is constrained by what I have been and done and not fully described by what I am striving to be and do. If, for example, I have been jealous once, my ethical ideal reflects the image of a once-jealous woman striving to remain only-once jealous. An ethical ideal that is not constrained cannot be diminished but only discarded and replaced.

We may now anticipate two questions with which we shall wrestle a bit later. In response to the question why I should behave morally toward one about whom I do not care, we shall see that interest in, caring for, my ethical self induces the characteristic "I must." This interest in ethical self is not merely self-interest, although interest in the physical self is surely involved in the development of caring for the ethical self. If I did not care for my physical well-being, I would be unable to appreciate the efforts of those who care for me. I would have no vision of my own needs, fears, and desires by which to interpret the plight of the other and evaluate the accompanying "I must." Indeed, the "I must" might be pathologically afflicted in the absence of normal self-interest. But, clearly, interest in the ethical self surpasses self-interest. Caring for others does not arise out of it, but it arises out of caring for others.

Am I, then, suggesting that the answer to the question, "Why should I behave morally?" is "Because I am or want to be a moral person"? Roughly, this is the answer and can be the only one, but I shall try to show how this interest in moral behavior arises out of our natural impulse to care. At every level, in every situation, there are decisions to be made, and we are free to affirm or to reject the impulse to care. But our relatedness, our apprehension of happiness or misery in others, comes through immediately. We may reject what we feel, what we see clearly, but at the risk of separation not only from others but from our ideal selves.

It seems to me that a large part of the anguish that existentialist philosophers associate with our apprehension of freedom springs from our awareness of obligation and the endless claims that can be, and will be, made upon us. We feel that we are, on the one hand, free to decide; we know, on the other hand, that we are irrevocably linked to intimate others. This linkage, this fundamental relatedness, is at the very heart of our being. Thus I am totally free to reject the impulse to care, but I enslave myself to a particularly unhappy task when I make this choice. As I chop away at the chains that bind me to loved others, asserting my freedom, I move into a wilderness of strangers and loneliness, leaving behind all who cared for me and even, perhaps, my own self. I am not naturally alone. I am naturally in a relation from which I derive nourishment and guidance. When I am alone, either because I have detached myself or because circumstances have wrenched me free, I seek first and most naturally to reestablish my relatedness. My very individuality is defined in a set of relations. This is my basic reality.

RULES AND CONFLICTS

How can I meet the endless demands of caring? Here, interestingly, standards of behavior, of custom, come to my rescue. While we often suppose that rules of behavior are laid down for the benefit of the cared-for —that is, for others—it is clear that rules of behavior make it easier for those-who-would-care to fulfill the minimum requirements of caring. So long as I behave according to the general rules of the group I find myself in (and so long as those rules are not somehow offensive themselves), I am not likely to hurt those around me. But as we noted earlier, if I behave consistently and automatically by rule, I cannot be said to care. My interest seems to be focused on obtaining credit for caring. I want to be considered a "polite" person. Thus while the rules are instituted for the sake of gentle and pleasant interpersonal relations, and they are an enormous boon to the one-caring whose energies are, after all, finite, I must know when to abandon rules and receive the cared-for directly. The rules of general conduct are accepted by one who is prepared to care out of regard for others but also in recognition of their time and energy saving usefulness.

I am also aided in meeting the burdens of caring by the reciprocal efforts of the cared-for. When my infant wriggles with delight as I bathe or feed him, I am aware of no burden but only a special delight of my own. Similarly, when I spend time in dialogue with my students, I am rewarded not only with appreciation but also with all sorts of information and insights. I could as easily, and properly, say, "I am receiving" as, "I am giving." Thus, many of the "demands" of caring are not felt as demands. They are, rather, the occasions that offer most of what makes life worth living. This, of course, does not surprise us. Caring, when it is the result of easy obedience to the natural impulse and to the state of engrossment already established, is not burdensome. But when we move beyond the natural circles of caring, we may begin to feel burdened. And even within the inner circle, conflicts of caring may arise. They are of several kinds.

In a very common—and sometimes deceptively simple—dilemma, we fall into conflict over the needs or wants of two different persons for whom we care. Consider Ms. Brown, who has promised to attend the symphony with her husband, and then their child comes down with an illness. Sometimes the decision is easy: the child is obviously too ill to leave, or the child is hardly ill at all and happily engaged in some activity. But often the dilemma is real, and we struggle with it. There is fever and, while there is no clear danger, the child keeps asking, "Mother, *must* you go?" The solution to this sort of conflict cannot be codified. Slogans such as "Put your husband (child) first!" are quite useless. There are times when he must come first; there are times when he cannot.

Is this problem a "moral" problem? In the important sense that it involves the needs and wants of others in relation or in conflict with our own, it certainly is and, without doubt, it is a problem of caring. When Ms. Brown looks at her child, she feels the immediate impulse to stay at home. The "I must" tells her to respond to the child's expressed need. When she looks at her husband and listens to him, she adds thinking to feeling; she, too, hates to miss the evening and "waste the tickets." She sees disappointment in his eyes and wants to respond to that. There is no probability calculus that will solve this problem for her. After analysis and argument, and perhaps a period of watchfulness to see if the child's anxiety eases, she has to decide. When she decides, if she cares, she decides not by formula, nor by a process of strict "rational decision making." There is, as we have noted before, a turning point. She turns away from the abstract formulation of the problem and looks again at the persons for whom she cares. Perhaps her child is still anxious and irritable; she receives his pain clearly. Perhaps her husband is merely annoyed, not hurt; perhaps, at some deeper level, he too wants only support for his best self. If she sees this, having received both persons, she decides to stay with the child. If the child is sound asleep one-half hour after the decision—and we all know how likely this is—her decision is not thereby proved wrong, for this is not the sort of decision that can properly be labeled "right" or "wrong" according to the outcome. It is right or wrong according to how faithfully it was rooted in caring—that is, in a genuine response to the perceived needs of the others.

Another sort of conflict arises when the cared-for wants something that we cannot, in good faith, give him or help him to attain. Conflicts of this sort range from situations involving a child's desire for a strawberry sundae just before dinner to suggestions or commands that we find deeply wrong. Again, as thoughtful persons committed to rational deliberation, we talk to ourselves. We examine the implicit rules by which we usually operate. We ask ourselves whether the rule is a guideline, a useful and dependable aid to generally acceptable behavior, or whether it is an imperative never to be violated by us.

Again, after analysis—sometimes brief, sometimes long and agonizing —we turn back to the persons and the concrete situations. In the case of the child who is begging for a sundae, we may properly refuse him under many circumstances. But, then, there are times when the situation (as well as the child) just begs for an infraction of the rule. Perhaps the child needs to know that he is more important than the rule. We do not have to say this to him. We might just say, "Well, I wasn't planning much of a dinner anyway—let's do it!" When we care, the humor, the harmless desires, the tendency toward playfulness of the cared-for enter us. We see the desired sundae with our own eyes and with the child's. If our own view reveals nothing very important and even seems a bit stuffy, we turn to the child with eyes brightened and refreshed with delight. Interestingly, when we interact in this way with a child, he is not likely to become spoiled. Rather, when we have to say no, he is likely to believe that our reasons are worth his attention. We shall discuss situations of this sort more fully when we consider the cared-for and his role in caring.

But suppose the situation is more serious. Suppose the cared-for wants us to participate in some activity we regard as wrong. Clearly, if an open-minded analysis leaves our evaluation unchanged, we cannot participate. What sort of thinking does the one-caring do in such a situation? Must she turn away from persons and toward some principle?

Let's consider an example. Professor A receives a research proposal from graduate student B. B proposes to do research that requires deceiving the subjects involved in the research. A would not, herself, propose such research. She is prepared to care for these subjects and fears possible bad effects on them. But she knows B and cares for him. She can feel the anxiety with which B approaches her: the pride in a well-written proposal, the fear that months will have been wasted, the eagerness to get on with the job. Proximity, as we have seen, is powerful in caring. A is in direct contact with B, but she is not in direct contact with the still-to-be-chosen subjects. She cannot be sure that they would be hurt by the experiment. Perhaps it is harmless. Perhaps there is no other way to answer the question B has raised. What should A do?

There are several approaches to problems of this sort. A might put her feelings about the research aside and concentrate on the possible outcomes. What adverse effects might occur? How likely are they? How significant is the question that guides the experiment? This is a rational approach that leads A to consider "average subjects," probabilities, and utilities. Thinking of this sort can be valuable, because some great utility may be discovered and, if it is, its consideration may induce a change in A's attitudes. But we see that, while this sounds plausible, if great utility were embedded in the question, A probably would have seen it at the outset. This approach, unless it is moderated by frequent "turnings," might easily lead A beyond rational thinking to mere rationalization. If, however, A takes the view of one-caring, she will attempt to visualize concrete subjects. Instead of "average subjects" she will consider real persons about whom she cares. And she will look at the situation from two perspectives: How might C, a known and loved other, react to the proposed deception? How do I feel about C's being thus deceived? This kind of thinking keeps A in contact with the particular, the concrete, the personal. It can be decisive, but we note that A's thinking did not proceed from a principle nor will it, of necessity, lead to one, although it might. The dangers that A perceives during her reflection may be so great, and her own revulsion so strong, that she will be led to propose guidelines for the control of all research that requires deception. But this need not be the case. The one-caring is wary of rules and principles. She formulates and holds them loosely, tentatively, as economies of a sort, but she insists upon holding closely to the concrete. She wants to maintain and to exercise her receptivity. Further, she sees the potential weakness in her own form of thinking: When she substitutes the concrete "C" for "subject" in B's research, she opens the channels to her own feeling. But to get an accurate picture of the effects on the cared-for, C must be a legitimate substitution (someone to whom this could actually happen), and A must evaluate C's reactions realistically. Clearly, there is danger in this concretization, also, and the one-caring is unwilling to formulate principles on the basis of her concrete experience.

We have been looking at the conflicts of caring, and we have seen that conflict may arise between the perceived need of one person and the desire of another; between what the cared-for wants and what we see as his best interest; between the wants of the cared-for and the welfare of persons yet unknown. We may even find ourselves in conflict between two persons for whom we care and whose interests and beliefs are incompatible. Sometimes, the conflict cannot be resolved and must simply be lived. A host of examples comes to mind. Consider parents during a civil war whose sons choose opposite sides; they are, themselves, neutral. Consider the woman who lives next door to a known Mafia mobster. She knows what the man is in the larger world, what effects his activities have on unknown, potential cared-fors. But she has also seen his tenderness to his own children, his respectability in neighborhood matters, his kindness as a neighbor. And then someone comes to the door and asks for information that she can give. What should she do? The answer is by no means clear to me. Many of us would, in great relief, turn to a principle, but I am not going to suggest that. I am not suggesting, either, that we embrace a code of family or tribe to which we adhere rigidly; such a move would, clearly, be even less consonant with caring than an adherence to principle in a larger world. Nor am I suggesting that crimes not be reported when they involve persons we know and care for. I am suggesting, rather, that rules cannot guide us infallibly in situations of conflict, and I am suggesting strongly that we have no ethical responsibility to cooperate with law or government when it attempts to involve us in unethical procedures. Spying, infiltration, entrapment, betrayal are all anathema to one-caring, and she cannot justify them on the basis of principle. The suggestion that she should participate in such activities is met by a firm, "This I will not do," delivered not in obedience to a principle but in faithfulness to the fundamental relatedness that induces caring.

Is the one-caring, then, a capricious and unprincipled character who is swayed this way and that by intensity, proximity, and the conditions of the moment? As our picture unfolds more completely, we shall see that moral life based on caring is coherent, although it may defy description in terms of systematic consistency. It is swayed, but not determined, by intensity, proximity, and temporal conditions. The one-caring is dependable, not capricious. Her principles are guides to behavior, and she sees clearly that their function is largely to simplify situations, to prevent hundreds of similar questions from arising. She sees, also, that they may be of little use if a serious question actually arises.

This is enormously tricky, and perhaps we should consider another example. Suppose the one-caring has decided that she will not steal. She has come to this general rule or principle after more deliberation than I can record here, and the decision is firm. Once she has made the decision, temptation does not arise. Stealing is beneath her; it does not befit the picture she has formed of her ethical self. But, while the decision is firm and clear—and simplifies life greatly—it is not ultimate, not absolute, and the one-caring knows this. The chances are excellent that the one-caring, in the kinds of situations those of us participating in this dialogue are likely to face, will never steal. But, related as she is by the basic bonds of life, she will not place principle where it cannot possibly hold. It is too fragile to stay her hand in the presence of, say, a hungry child, a hungry friend, a hungry stranger. Thus, while the one-caring may lead a life described by others as "highly principled," she is herself peculiarly wary of principles. She will not easily be distracted from the dynamic and complex events of concrete life by promises of abstract simplicity and permanence. Indeed, as we shall see, she might prefer to explain her abstinence from stealing without reference to a principle at all.

The example we just considered is one that may easily win virtually universal assent. Decisions of the sort may be reached not only by one-caring but by the sophisticated moral thinker using principles deductively. Perhaps another example should be considered. Suppose that I give my son permission to stay home from school in order to do something both of us consider worthwhile. I must write a note explaining his absence. If I do not say that he was ill, he will be punished with detention. The school has such a rule because it is dependent on state funds, and those funds are withheld for absences other than those due to illness or death. The school thus prefers to hear that my son was ill. I prefer to say that he was because not saying it will cause my son to be punished. So I may choose to lie regularly in order to meet my son as one-caring rather than as one conforming to principle. I do not attempt to justify my behavior on the grounds that the absence rule is foolish and unfair, because my behavior is not primarily constrained by rules. I do not need that excuse. One who does argue thus is obliged, I think, to fight the rule —to get it changed—or to live in some deceit. I do not have this problem. I can brush off the whole debate as foolishness and remain faithful to the ideal of one-caring.

I shall leave this result in its stark, and perhaps shocking, form. My male colleague may insist that I must justify my actions—in particular, that I must justify telling a lie. But need I do this, and what will I be admitting if I engage in such an attempt? If I attempt to justify every disobedience or rejection of principle, I tacitly acknowledge that principles are paramount in ethical life. He will have won his main case. So I shall be content with the observation that there has been no violation of caring. Indeed, if he pushes me, I shall turn the argument about and ask how he might justify hurting his son by telling the truth. I know the form his argument will take. It will put principle over person, and we shall be at loggerheads.

The form of moral decision making that I have suggested is, perhaps, more powerfully illustrated in a story told of Pablo Casals's younger brother, Enrique. When he was young and faced with the prospect of fighting in the Spanish army, he confessed to his mother that he did not want to kill or to risk being killed. "Then run away," advised his mother. Now, one might also arrive at this decision through a chain of reasoning on principles but, clearly, in reasoning on principles one might just as plausibly arrive at the opposite decision. The one-caring, in the absence of imminent danger to loved ones, can make only one decision. In arguing from principles, one often suppresses the basic feeling or longing that prompts the justification. One is led to suppose that reason produces the decision. This is the ultimate and tragic dishonesty, and it is the one that we shall try to avoid by insisting upon a clear-eyed inspection of our feelings, longings, fears, hopes, dreams.

Now, this entire book is about caring and so, in an important sense, about the one-caring. In this chapter, I have concentrated on the inner dynamics of caring: on the constitutive engrossment and receptivity, on the consequent displacement of motivational energy, on the circles and chains that reflect and sustain the caring, and on the conflicts of caring. We have discussed what it means to care genuinely about self and how caring for the ethical self sustains us through periods of lapsed caring, and we have hinted at the role caring plays in ethical behavior.

But caring is a relationship that contains another, the cared-for, and we have already suggested that the one-caring and the cared-for are reciprocally dependent. We shall not leave the one-caring but shall look at the relationship next through the eyes of the cared-for.

3

THE CARED-FOR

THE ONE-CARING'S ATTITUDE AND ITS EFFECTS

THE ONE-CARING comes across to the cared-for in an attitude. Whatever she does, she conveys to the cared-for that she cares. If she is in conversation with a colleague, she listens, and her eyes reflect the seriousness, humor, or excitement of the message being spoken. If she tends the sick, her hands are gentle with the anticipation of pain and discomfort. If she comforts the night-terrored child, her embrace shields from both terror and ridicule. She feels the excitement, pain, terror, or embarrassment of the other and commits herself to act accordingly. She is present to the cared-for. Her attitude is one of receptivity. But there is a receptivity required of the cared-for also.

Suppose that a child of, say, eight years comes home from school angry. He storms into the kitchen and throws his books on the floor. His mother, startled, says, "What happened, honey?" (She resists the temptation to say something to the effect that "in this house we do not throw things.") The child says that his teacher is "impossible," "completely unfair," "mean," "stupid," and so on. His mother sympathizes and probes gently for what happened. Gradually, under the quiet influence of a receptive listener, the child calms down. As his mother sympathizes, he may even relax enough to say, "Well, it wasn't that bad," in answer to his mother's sympathetic outrage. Then the two may smile at each other and explore rational solutions; they can speculate about faults, mistakes, and intentions. They can plot a course of action for the future. The child, accepted and supported, can begin to examine his own role in the incident and, perhaps, even suggest how he might have behaved differently.

The receptivity of the one-caring need not lead to permissiveness nor to an abdication of responsibility for conduct and achievement. Rather, it maintains and enhances the relatedness that is fundamental to human reality and, in education, it sets the stage for the teacher's effort in maintaining and increasing the child's receptive capacity. As the teacher receives the child and works with him on cooperatively designed projects, as she resists the temptation—or the mandate—to manipulate the child, to squeeze him into some mold, she establishes a climate of receptivity. The one-caring reflects reality as she sees it to the child. She accepts him as she hopes he will accept himself—seeing what is there, considering what might be changed, speculating on what might be. But the commitment, the decision to embrace a particular possibility, must be the child's. Her commitment is to him. While she expresses herself honestly when his vision of himself is unlovely and enthusiastically when it is beautiful, she never reflects a reality that pictures him detached, alone, abandoned. If her standards seem mysterious at times to outsiders, they are not so to the cared-for who has participated in their construction.

We shall return again and again to a discussion of receptivity. It is in the relaxation of detached and objective self, in this engrossment, that the one-caring assumes her full individuality in relatedness. The child who retains his receptivity can lose himself not only in others for whom he becomes one-caring, but also in ideas and objects. The teacher who encourages receptivity wants the child to look, to listen, to touch and, perhaps, to receive a vision of reality. When we speak of receiving reality, we do not deny that each human consciousness participates in the construction of reality, but we give proper emphasis to the relatedness that must be perceived and accepted before any coherent picture can be constructed. The other is received, his reality is apprehended as possibility for oneself. The object is received; its reality stands out against the background of its possibilities in the one receiving.

One learns to participate in cycles. At one stage, things are allowed to enter with little restriction; a reservoir of images and energy is stored up. Then a focusing takes place; the energies are made dense, brought sharply to focus on a point of interest. Then a diffusion may occur. The energy is converted to light and scattered over the entire field of interest illuminating elements and ground. The field is now characterized by coherence and grace. Both initial and final stages may be characterized as receptive. In the first we receive what is there; in the last, we receive what-is-there in relation to what-is-here. We see how we are related to this object to which we are related. We shall return to these matters in some detail when we discuss *caring for ideas*.

The cared-for responds to the presence of the one-caring. He feels the

difference between being received and being held off or ignored. Whatever the one-caring actually does is enhanced or diminished, made meaningful or meaningless, in the attitude conveyed to the cared-for. This attitude is not something thought by either the one-caring or the cared-for
although, of course, either one may think about it. It is a total convey-
ance of self to other, a continual transformation of individual to duality
to new individual to new duality. Neither the engrossment of the one-
caring nor the perception of attitude by the cared-for is rational; that is,
neither is reasoned. While much of what goes on in caring is rational and
carefully thought out, the basic relationship is not, and neither is the
required awareness of relatedness. The essentially nonrational nature of
caring is recognized by, for example, Urie Bronfenbrenner when he
claims: "In order to develop, a child needs the enduring, irrational
involvement of one or more adults in care and joint activity with the
child."[1] In answer to what he means by "irrational," he explains:
"Somebody has got to be crazy about that kid!"[2]

The child about whom no one is "crazy" presents a special problem
for teachers. Obviously, the teacher cannot be "crazy about" every
child; the notion loses its force spread so thin. But the teacher can try to
provide an environment in which affection and support are enhanced, in
which children not passionately loved will at least receive attention and,
perhaps, learn to respond to and encourage those who genuinely address
them. Such a child may herself someday be "crazy about" some other
child even though she herself was never the recipient of such affection.

Now, of course, philosophers are certain to point out that being
"crazy" about a child is not necessarily irrational. But Bronfrenbren-
ner's way of talking nevertheless makes an essential point about the caring relationship in which a child thrives. It is at bottom not rational; that
is, it is fundamentally nonrational. However rational the decision making processes, however rational the investigation of means-ends relations, the commitment that elicits the rational activity precedes it and
gives it personal meaning. We do not usually, as caring parents, select
activities to share with our children on the basis of some "learning
plan"; we do not, for example, take our children to the zoo so that they
will be able to name and describe ten animals native to Africa. Rather,
we decide more or less spontaneously to spend an afternoon at the zoo,
because we remember our own childish pleasure in such occasions and
anticipate delight in sharing the experience with our children. That our
children learn things through visits to zoos, museums, national monu-

ments, and the like is something we all take for granted but, for most of us, the potential learning is not what motivates the visits. We often find ourselves in teaching-learning situations with our children, but these arise naturally in the companionable relationship established through caring. We commit ourselves to our children.

Bronfenbrenner suggests, further, that children embraced in such non-rational relationships gain competence; that is, they become able to master situations of greater and greater complexity through their cooperative participation with adults. When parent and child work together on various projects over a period of time, the child gradually becomes competent in more and more tasks constituting the project. The parent who cares, who receives the child, allows him to take hold of what he can do. She does not keep him in a subservient position but welcomes his growing competence and independence.

We hear the word "competence" often these days. We hear it in the context of competency based education (CBE) and in reference to competence tests for high school graduation. But "competence" in these contexts refers more accurately to performance, to a demonstrated mastery of prespecified and discrete tasks. "Competence" as I am using it points to a global mastery of conditions in one's personal or professional environment and, indirectly, to the desire for such mastery. The psychologist Robert White suggests that the desire for competence is innate; that is, human beings naturally experience what may be termed "effectance motivation." He notes that activity thus engaged produces a feeling of efficacy:

> . . . it is maintained that competence cannot be fully acquired simply through behavior instigated by drives. It receives substantial contributions from activities which, though playful and exploratory in character, at the same time show direction, selectivity, and persistence in interacting with the environment. Such activities in the ultimate service of competence must therefore be conceived to be motivated in their own right.[3]

Small children practice going up and down stairs, turning lights and faucets on and off, dropping things and retrieving them. All of these activities, which seem to adults repetitiously boring and even annoying, are engaged in for the sake of mastering the environment. The competent individual enjoys a sense of control over the objects and events with which he regularly comes in contact.

If this is right, we can see the importance of arranging the environment appropriately for growing children. To call forth a natural effectance motivation, the challenge must be within the optimal range. If the challenge is too great, the child may become frustrated and look for a way to avoid it entirely or to meet it—however unsatisfactorily—for the mere purpose of terminating it. Failing just to "get it over with" is not an unusual strategy in schools. If, on the other hand, the challenge is too slight, the child may become bored and, again, his approach may deteriorate—this time to perfunctory performance.

The one-caring receives the child and views his world through both sets of eyes. Martin Buber calls this relational process "inclusion."[4] The one-caring assumes a dual perspective and can see things from both her own pole and that of the cared-for. If this were not so, arranging an educational environment for the child would be very difficult. One would have to resort to descriptions of the child as abstraction and, indeed, many educators do exactly this. They say such things as "Children are interested in their own surroundings," and use this pronouncement as a reason for including a study of the neighborhood in beginning social studies and for excluding studies of foreign lands and ancient times. The result is often deadening. The one-caring, on the other hand, watches for incipient interest in the child—the particular, concrete child—and arranges the educational environment accordingly. Possibly no insight of John Dewey's was greater than that which reveals the vital importance of building educational strategy on the purposes of the child. The principle of the leading out of experience does not imply letting the child learn what he pleases; it suggests that, inescapably, the child will learn what he pleases. That means that the educator must arrange the effective world so that the child will be challenged to master significant tasks in significant situations. The initial judgment of significance is the teacher's task.

But there is another, vital aspect to "learning what one pleases." "Because it pleases me" is rarely our basic reason for acting. We might better think here of what we choose to do and consider the kinds of reasons we might give for our choices. A child—or anyone—can be forced to learn what he initially finds uninteresting or even repugnant. Indeed, we saw in the last chapter how we may be forced to deny our principles and betray our loved ones if sufficiently terrible tactics are employed against us. How, then, can we support a position that insists that the child will learn what he chooses? The answer lies in recognizing that we sometimes choose against ourselves. We give way for reasons that do not make us proud of ourselves. We rationalize. We concoct reasons that are far removed from our normal pattern of motivation or, in the most dreadful situations, we act directly and unreflectively to preserve what we can of our physical or public selves. We deteriorate, and our ethical ideals are diminished. But we still choose, and recognition of the choice induces a new agony. I am in the sleazy motive, the panicked betrayal, the reluctant obedience.

The educator or parent, then, is not powerless. On the contrary, her power is awesome. Somehow the child must be led to choose for himself and not against himself, and this means that he will choose not only for his physical self but, more importantly, for his ethical self.

The child, as one cared-for, will often respond with interest to challenges proffered by the one-caring, if the one-caring is loved and trusted by the child. As an initial impulse to engage particular subject matter, love for the adult and the desire to imitate her are powerful inducements. Further, working together on tasks makes it possible for the child to accept greater challenges and to maintain a high level of effectance motivation. What is conveyed to the child is that there is something delightful about the companionship that continues through every stage of developing competence. At the earliest stages, a young child is not much help in, say, preparing meals. But he can do some things: he can hand me a spoon, poke the Jello to see if it has set, pat the hamburgers flat. He can share with me the sights, smells, sounds, tastes, and textures encountered in working with foods. As he watches me and helps me, he is learning the names of things, acquiring a sense of orderliness, learning to recognize phenomena such as boiling, thickening, and the like. After a while he can pour milk, crack eggs without squashing them, sift flour, and take turns stirring the batter. Eventually, he can prepare individual dishes and take responsibility for whole meals. Through all of these stages, there is mutual pleasure not only in the child's growing competence, but also in the shared activities and their products.

It would be easy to spend several chapters talking about what children can learn through working with their parents in food preparation, but our main interest here is the attitude of the one-caring and how it affects the cared-for. The child is encouraged to try by the acceptance of the parent, and he is made to feel a partner in the enterprise. As we shall see later, the parent's attitude goes beyond acceptance to what Buber calls "confirmation." The one-caring sees the best self in the cared-for and works with him to actualize that self. The child is affected not only by his parent's attitude toward him, but also by her attitudes toward a multitude of objects and events. She may treat meals as celebrations or as duties. She may show an appreciation for the beauty of fresh fruits and vegetables or she may be indifferent to them. Cooking may be work or play or both. The kitchen may be clean or dirty, attractive or dreary. More important than anything else, however, is whether the child is welcome, whether he is seen as a contributing person.

APPREHENSION OF CARING NECESSARY TO THE CARING RELATIONSHIP; UNEQUAL MEETINGS

This attitude of warm acceptance and trust is important in all caring relationships. We are primarily interested in parent-child and teacher-student relationships, but it is clear that caring is completed in all relationships through the apprehension of caring by the cared-for. When this attitude is missed, the one who is the object of caretaking feels like an object. He is being treated, handled by formula. When it is present and recognized, the natural effectance motivation is enhanced.

A mother recounts the story of an upsetting experience with school counselors and administrators. She and her husband requested that their very bright daughter be skipped a grade. The child had suffered two serious illnesses and, during her long bed stay, had read, studied, and written well beyond her grade placement. On returning to school, she was bored with both the studies and the childishness of her classmates. The parents, quite naturally, feared that their child would lose interest in school entirely, and so they requested a special hearing. The school team received them in a physically cordial manner that quickly revealed a total lack of presence. They spoke patronizingly of how "all professional parents want to push their children," of how doting parents tend to "overestimate their children's abilities," of how the practice of skipping children "damages their social competence." The parents, of course, became more and more frustrated. The harder they tried to explain, the more quickly came smiling responses: "We understand." "Of course." "You think your child is exceptional." Finally, in utter frustration, the couple suggested that the matter be left to an evaluation of the school psychologist. Fortunately (things could have turned out differently), the school psychologist recommended that the child be advanced. Three reasons supported the recommendation: The child was large for her age, she was socially and emotionally advanced, and she exhibited a tested I.Q. over

160. These parents have never since been comfortable with school officials and school rulings, and they have assumed primary responsibility for the education of their children.

To be talked at by people for whom we do not exist, as Marcel points out, throws us back upon ourselves. To be treated as "types" instead of individuals, to have strategies exercised on us, objectifies us. We become "cases" instead of persons. Those of us who are able to escape such situations do so with alacrity, but escape is not always possible, and for some of us it is rarely possible. The fact is that many of us have been reduced to cases by the very machinery that has been instituted to care for us.

It is not easy for one entrusted with a helping function to care. A difference of status and the authorization to help prevent an equal meeting between helper and the one helped. In a dialogue with Carl Rogers, Martin Buber emphasizes this point:

> ...A man coming to you for help.... The essential difference between your role in this situation and his is obvious. He comes for help to you. You don't come for help to him. And not only this, but you are *able,* more or less, to help him. He can do different things to you, but not to help you. And not this alone. You *see* him, *really.* I don't mean that you cannot be mistaken, but you *see* him,...he cannot, by far, cannot *see you.*[5]

In this discussion, Buber was, of course, acknowledging the legitimacy and—more importantly—the sensitivity of Rogers's therapy. Not every helper sees the patient or client. Indeed, we just reviewed a case in which the counselors were totally absent to the struggling clients. But even if the therapist is sensitive and receptive, Buber points out that the fact of his or her authorization to help gets in the way of an equal meeting. Social worker and client, physician and patient, counselor and student in their formal roles necessarily meet each other unequally. Insofar as the client, patient, and student are part of their work load, professionals may even find it desirable "to forget" them at the end of the workday. To think of them, to be engrossed in them, would be to take their "work" home. But to think this way is to misunderstand the nature of engrossment in caring. It misses the potentiality and latency that characterize caring.

It is not only the authorization to help or to instruct that makes unequal meetings in therapy or teaching inevitable. It is also the nature of the cared-for's situation. The patient needs help; the student needs instruction or information or interpretation. The teacher as one-caring needs to see from both her own perspective and that of the student in order to teach—in order to meet the needs of the student. Achieving inclusion is part of teaching successfully, and one who cannot practice inclusion fails as a teacher. The student, however, achieves his ends without inclusion. He is freed by the teacher's engrossment in him and his projects to pursue those projects without considering their significance for the personal development of the teacher. I think Buber is right when he says that mutual inclusion moves a relationship away from that of teacher-student toward friendship. Occasional equal meetings may occur between teacher and student, of course, but the meetings between teacher as teacher and student as student are necessarily and generously unequal.

It is only through inclusion that the parent or teacher can practice confirmation. I must see the cared-for as he is and as he might be—as he envisions his best self—in order to confirm him. The attitude that is perceived by the cared-for as caring is generated by efforts of the one-caring at inclusion and confirmation. It is an attitude that both accepts and confirms. It does not "accept" and shrug off. It accepts, embraces, and leads upward. It questions, it responds, it sympathizes, it challenges, it delights.

So far, we have been discussing an attitude on the part of the one-caring which conveys the caring to the cared-for. We have spoken of acceptance and confirmation, of receiving, of inclusion, and of "unequal meetings," and we have considered some examples in the area of parent-child relationships and helper-client relationships. I have been proceeding in an informal phenomenological way, exploring situations and how the participants within them feel and see things. But it is important to keep sight of the logic of our concept of caring as it is being developed, and it is important, also, to recognize that there is empirical evidence for much of what has been claimed.

I have claimed that the cared-for "grows" and "glows" under the perceived attitude of the one-caring. Support for such claims can be found in many sources. It is especially impressive in the negative; that is, the evidence is clear that the rejection characteristic of non-caring has observable effects in the "cared-for." Although the evidence from any one case cannot be conclusive, it is overwhelming in its collective form. Many researchers—among them, Sanger,[6] Montagu,[7] and Wengraf[8]—present evidence that even the fetus is affected by the attitude of acceptance or rejection in its mother. A review of the undesirable effects that may be induced in children, both prenatal and postnatal, by maternal attitudes of rejection can be found in Edward Pohlman's discussion on birth planning.[9] Further, the attitude itself seems to be causal. Zilboorg says that it "has its rather mysterious ways of conveying itself to the child and provoking a considerable number of undesirable and at time directly pathological reactions."[10]

By "mysterious ways," Zilboorg and other researchers mean that it is an attitude that itself seems to do the mischief. Sears, for example, found few significant differences in child rearing practices between accepting and rejecting parents,[11] and a similar conclusion was reached by Schaefer and Bell.[12] But behavioral differences were found in the children. Hence a claim that attitude is crucial to an analysis of caring, that feeling is somehow conveyed directly, is partially supported empirically.

In addition to providing empirical support for what we see reflectively in a phenomenological view, I want to provide a logical analysis of the caring relation. I have claimed that the perception by the cared-for of an attitude of caring on the part of the one-caring is partially constitutive of caring. It and its successful impact on the cared-for are necessary to caring. Does this mean that I cannot be said to care for X if X does not recognize my caring? In the fullest sense, I think we have to accept this result. By looking closely at caring from the view of the one-caring, from the position of the cared-for, and from the perspective of a third-person observer, we see pictures of caring that are potentially conflicting and yet, at bottom, complementary. The third-person aspect will be important for us when we consider institutional problems of caring, but it does not enter or alter the essential description of caring. Caring involves two parties: the one-caring and the cared-for. It is complete when it is fulfilled in both. We are tempted to say that the caring attitude is characteristic of caring, that when one cares, she characteristically exhibits an attitude. But, then, it could be missed by the cared-for. Suppose I claim to care for X, but X does not believe that I care for him. If I meet the first-person requirements of caring for X, I am tempted to insist that I do care—that there is something wrong with X that he does not appreciate my caring. But if you are looking at this relationship, you would have to report, however reluctantly, that something is missing. X does not feel that I care. Therefore, sadly, I must admit that, while I feel that I care, X does not perceive that I care and, hence, the relationship cannot be characterized as one of caring. This result does not necessarily signify a negligence on my part. There are limits in caring. X may be paranoid or otherwise pathological. There may be no way for my caring to reach him. But, then, caring has been only partly actualized.

It may seem paradoxical to some that my caring should be in any way dependent on the other. A similar difficulty arises in the analysis of teaching. Some analysts find it unacceptable to pronounce teaching conceptually dependent on learning. Still, this position is clearly not a nonsensical one. Aristotle noted long ago that one process may find its actualization in another. So, that teaching is completed in learning and that caring is completed in reception by the cared-for should be neither incredible nor incomprehensible. We may still say, "I care," when we are prepared to care, and not every failure of caring is one to which blame attaches. But in recognizing that my use of "I care" in the incomplete relation is an ellipsis of sorts, I acknowledge that I am not alone—not solely to be credited or blamed—in the caring relation.

Logically, we have the following situation: (W, X) is a caring relation if and only if
   i) W cares for X (as described in the one-caring) and
   ii) X recognizes that W cares for X.
When we say that "X recognizes that W cares for X," we mean that X receives the caring honestly. He receives it: he does not hide from it or deny it. Hence, its reception becomes part of what the one-caring feels when she receives the cared-for. We do not need to add a third condition and a fourth, as in, "W is aware that X recognizes," "X is aware that W is aware that . . . ," and so on.

Caring requires the typical engrossment and motivational displacement in W and, also, the recognition of caring by X. Now, of course, the relationship can be mutually (or doubly) caring if we can interchange W and X and retain true expressions. This seems the correct logical analysis of caring, and it has the merit that it accounts for the ambivalence that may arise in such a situation. By that, I mean that it allows me to say "I care for X," even if I must admit that (I, X) is not a fully caring relationship.

RECIPROCITY ·

We must turn now to a problem that will draw our attention repeatedly—that of reciprocity. Later, we shall be concerned with it in connection with caring for ideas, creativity, and intuition. Right now we are concerned with reciprocity in terms of the contribution of the human cared-for. We have already noted that the cared-for must "receive" the caring. But what is the nature of this reception?

What part does the cared-for play in caring? Clearly, in equal meetings, there may be mutual caring and, when this happens, we need not, in a practical sense, try to distinguish the roles of the one-caring and cared-for. But we are interested in the logic of caring; further, in parent-child and teacher-student relations the meetings often are not equal. The child may like, even love, the parent or teacher, but he is incapable of the motivational displacement of caring and, usually, incapable of perceiving or understanding what the parent or teacher wants for herself. Now, obviously, this inequity is neither permanent nor invariant. Even a small child may have occasional equal meetings with an adult. But, by and large, it is the parent or teacher who is capable of inclusion; it is she who sees with two pairs of eyes.

We readily accept the inequality of meetings between adult and child, but we may wonder about the teacher-student relationship when both are adults. Are unequal meetings still likely? Is the inequality perhaps necessary to the relation? The teacher, because she is a teacher, must see things through the eyes of her student in order to teach him. She looks at and speaks about subject matter, of course, but she looks at it and speaks about it from two poles. She must interpret what she sees from one pole in the language that she hears at the other. Further, it is not only the subject matter that she must view dually. She must also grasp the effectance motivation of the student. What does he want to accomplish? Of what use may the proposed subject matter be to him in his striving for competence? What interests has he that may help her to persuade him to look at the subject matter? The teacher, I shall argue, is necessarily one-caring if she is to be a teacher and not simply a textbooklike source from which the student may or may not learn. Hence, when we look at "pedagogical caring" we shall begin not with pedagogy but with caring. Then we shall see what *form* caring takes in the teaching function.

Let us look at the student. Is it not true that he also sees things through his teacher's eyes as well as his own? We talk this way at times, but we can readily see that what we say so easily in metaphor is not possible. The student sees not what the teacher at her own pole sees but what the teacher presents by way of interpretation. This represents a kind of "seeing through the teacher's eyes," but it is a reflection that brightens the student's own vision.

The work of the teacher is facilitated by her dual vision. If, however, the student were to attempt inclusion with respect to the teacher, to discern her motives, to concentrate on what she was trying to accomplish, he would be distracted from his own learning task. Indeed, we often see this sort of thing happen in schools. Instead of concentrating on the objective elements of the problematic situation in, say, mathematics, the student focuses on what the teacher wants. The result is a catalog of non-mathematical heuristics that the student compiles in order to cope with the demands of schooling. John Holt, in *How Children Fail,* records many such incidents. Observing another teacher in a lesson using Cuisenaire rods, he observes:

> It was Barbara who really made the dent on me, because she is usually such a thoughtful and capable student. You held up the black (7) and the blue (9), and reversing your previous procedure, said, "What is the blue of the black?" She said, "seven-ninths." You hesitated. Her face got red, she stared at you, not at the rods, for a second and then said, "nine-sevenths." Nothing in her face, voice or manner gave me the feeling that she had the slightest idea why the first answer was wrong and the second right.[13]

The student may, then, to his ultimate disadvantage, make what seems to be an effort at inclusion. The inclusion is necessarily incomplete, however, because it is induced by the student's needs and not by engrossment in the teacher-as-subject. In the event that inclusion becomes actual, the relation is converted, as we have noted, from that of teacher-student to one of friendship. This may, of course, happen, but even if it does, when the teacher assumes her function as teacher, the relation becomes again, temporarily, unequal. Two friends, may, indeed, assume the functions of teacher and student interchangeably.

We are trying to establish the role of the cared-for in caring. I have claimed that the recognition of caring by the cared-for is necessary to the caring relation. It is clear, however, that the cared-for need not be one-caring in order to constitute the relation. He does not have to receive the one-caring as she receives him. Yet he must respond to her somehow. There is, necessarily, a form of reciprocity in caring. How shall we describe this reciprocity?

A mother describes her two babies and the difference in responsiveness to her. As she holds one on her knee, the child looks right at her, responding to her smiles, frowns, and funny-faces. The other child, held in the same playful attitude, looks across the room. Both children are very bright and pleasant, but the mother confesses that she enjoys her responsive baby more. He is fun to be with. She is a bit baffled by the other.

Another mother describes typical differences in the behavior of two of her children. Let's say one of the children, about junior high age, comes home late to dinner. The mother, anxious, meets him at the door. This child spots the worry immediately and says, "Gee, I'm sorry to be so late but, Mother, I had the best time! Wait till you hear." And he spills over with a recitation of what he has been doing. The other child, in a similar situation, comes in, notes the times and says, "I'm sorry about being late. We didn't realize what time it was. There was a lot of traffic on the way home." He gives an explanation, sometimes a detailed one, but he neither responds to the worry and relief in his mother's eyes nor shares his experiences with her. The mother does not push the second child to share his life more fully with her, but she cannot help being drawn more to the first child. Now, of course, some mothers do demand that children share their lives with them. Some even profess to "live for" (and we might say through) their children. But that is not the case with the mother in our story. She sees and describes the difference with some surprise and with some chagrin because she realizes that she, in turn, feels differently toward the children.

The first child contributes to the caring relation in two ways. First, he acknowledges and responds to the particular form of his mother's present engrossment—worry and relief. Second, he shares his aspirations, appraisals, and accomplishments with her. This sharing enables her to care more easily. With a fuller knowledge of what he is striving for, of what pleases and delights him, she can readily contribute her support to his efforts. The motivational displacement of caring occurs naturally, supported by the buoyant responsiveness of the cared-for. The one-caring for a fully participating cared-for is sustained and invigorated, and her caring is unlikely to deteriorate to "cares and burdens."

To accept the gift of responsiveness from the cared-for is natural for the one-caring. It is consistent with caring. To demand such responsiveness is both futile and inconsistent with caring. The one-caring is motivated in the direction of the cared-for and she must, therefore, respect his freedom. She meets him as subject—not as an object to be manipulated nor as a data source. Indeed, this recognition of the freedom-as-subject of the cared-for is a fundamental result of her genuine receiving of the cared-for. The responsive cared-for, in the fullness of the caring relation, feels the recognition of freedom and grows under its expansive support. The child genuinely cared for is free to respond as himself, to create, to follow his interests without unnecessary fear and anxiety. We are interested at this stage in developing a coherent account of the part played by the cared-for in caring, but it is worth noting, once again, that there is empirical support for what emerges in the logical component of our conceptual framework. In studies of the backgrounds of creative architects, Donald MacKinnon found that parental respect for the child's freedom seemed to support the creative impulse:

> What appears most often to have characterized the parents of these future creative architects was an extraordinary respect for the child and confidence in his ability to do what was appropriate. Thus they did not hesitate to grant him rather unusual freedom in exploring his universe and in making decisions for himself—and this early as well as late. The expectation of the parent that the child would act independently but reasonably and responsibly appears to have contributed immensely to the latter's sense of personal autonomy which was to develop to such a marked degree.[14]

The cared-for is free to be more fully himself in the caring relation. Indeed, this being himself, this willing and unselfconscious revealing of self, is his major contribution to the relation. This is his tribute to the one-caring, but it is not delivered up as tribute. A mother is more drawn to the child who reveals himself spontaneously than to the one who presents formal explanations in response to what he takes to be her assessment of the problematic situation. A teacher is captivated by the student who thinks aloud and uses what his teacher has presented in his own way and for his own purposes. Obviously, when I say "a mother" and "a teacher" here I mean to point to a mother or a teacher as one-caring.

I shall return to the question of what the cared-for contributes to the caring relation when we discuss teaching and learning. As a foreshadowing of that discussion, we might mention one factor contributing to teacher burnout: Demands that the teacher constrain the student to behave in specified ways as a result of her instruction might well lead to a diminution of the free response that represents a major intrinsic reward of teaching.

It is hard to overestimate the importance of what we are discussing now. The cared-for plays a vital role in the caring relation. Buber underscores the role of the one-caring, that is, of the one-caring as the I in I-Thou relations, insisting: "The relation can obtain even if the human being to whom I say Thou does not hear it in his experience. For Thou is more than It knows. Thou does more, and more happens to it, than It knows. No deception reaches this far: here is the cradle of actual life."[15] But in other places, Buber emphasizes the reciprocity of relation: "One should not try to dilute the meaning of the relation: relation is reciprocity."[16]

The problem that is raised here is precisely the one we must solve, for saying Thou—being engrossed—is a necessary condition for the one-caring to be in a relation of caring. The engrossment of caring is not necessarily typical of that of the lover, and I am not proposing a form of agapism or obligatory love. When one cares, there are active moments of caring in which the engrossment must be present. In those moments the cared-for is not an object. In Buber's words: "He is no longer He or She, limited by other Hes and Shes, a dot in the world grid of space and time, nor a condition that can be experienced and described, a loose bundle of named qualities. Neighborless and seamless, he is Thou and fills the firmament."[17]

The one-caring is engrossed; the cared-for "fills the firmament." Does it make no difference how the cared-for responds to the one-caring? On the one hand, Buber insists that "relation is reciprocity"; on the other, that the relation may obtain even though the cared-for does not hear the Thou "in his experience." There must, then, be reciprocity, but what form does it take? Obviously reciprocity does not imply an identity of gifts given and received. Something, not necessarily identical to my engrossment as one-caring, is required of my Thou, the cared-for. The key lies in Buber's peculiar use of "experience." For him, "experience" points to the object-world of It. When we "experience" something, we have already made that which we experience into an object or thing. Thus the cared-for need not hear my Thou in his experience; that is, he need not acknowledge it propositionally. But he must respond to it. "Thou is more than It knows." The freedom, creativity, and spontaneous disclosure of the cared-for that manifest themselves under the nurture of the one-caring complete the relation. My Thou must be *in* the relation for the relation to obtain, but he need not acknowledge my Thou-saying in words so that others may discuss it. What the cared-for gives to the relation either in direct response to the one-caring or in personal delight or in happy growth before her eyes is genuine reciprocity. It contributes to the maintenance of the relation and serves to prevent the caring from turning back on the one-caring in the form of anguish and concern for self.

THE ETHICS OF BEING CARED-FOR

Is there a way in which we can move from the natural responsiveness of being cared-for in a genuine relation of caring to an ethical responsibility for behaving as cared-for in a situation where natural affection and receptivity break down? This is a question similar to that which occupied us briefly in our discussion of the one-caring and will occupy us at length in our discussion of ethics. We saw that caring arises naturally in the inner circles of human intercourse and that it must be summoned by a concern for the ethical self in situations where it does not arise naturally. Because I have come to care for my ethical self and not just my physical self, I behave as one-caring toward one for whom I feel no natural affection. Our question now is this: Is there a comparable ethical aspect for the cared-for to consider?

Suppose X and Y are in a relation that might be supposed on some formal criterion—X is Y's mother, let us say—to be a caring relation. Suppose, further, that X professes to care or, at least, does not deny that she cares. Y does not feel that X cares; the necessary attitude is not perceived by Y. Should Y respond as one cared-for?

So long as contact between X and Y must be maintained, our answer to this question must be, yes. Let us see how we may defend this answer. First, there is an argument from self-interest. In traditional wisdom, the one-to-be-cared-for in a standard caretaking situation—such as parent/child, physician/patient, teacher/student—acknowledges both the wisdom and motivational displacement of the one-supposed-caring. Parents, doctors, and teachers do things for us and to us for our own good. In the Biblical commandment we are told to honor our fathers and mothers so that our days may be long upon the earth. Thus we are called upon to respond to the one-supposed-caring with respect and obedience. But obedience and respect may or may not be the sort of free, creative, and joyous response we expect of our genuinely cared-for. Indeed, they may be signs that we have abdicated our subjectivity and taken our indicated place in the It-World of the one-supposed-caring. If we have done this, we are not genuine cared-fors and cannot contribute to a caring relation.

To behave ethically in the potential caring relation, the cared-for must turn freely toward his own projects, pursue them vigorously, and share his accounts of them spontaneously. This is what the one-genuinely-caring wants but never demands. The one-supposed-caring, however, may not want freedom for the cared-for and may yet demand "spontaneous" accounts. The situation is very difficult for the cared-for. He must never feel guilt for the failed projects of the one-caring but only for his own failed projects. His contribution to the relation is not the same as that of the one-caring. But the one-supposed-caring may demand that he behave as cared-for when she really wants herself to be cared-for. This is the intolerable position the child is put into when the parent "lives for" her child. The child is not free to become more fully the self he aspires to be but must nevertheless behave as though he is.

It is easy to see that, in dependent relations, the greater responsibility belongs to the one-caring. As soon as the cared-for must consider the needs and motives of the one-caring, he becomes one-caring himself or he falls into a life of inauthenticity or he becomes an ethical hero—one who behaves as though cared-for without the sustenance of caring. I think this last is possible for a particular Y in relation to a particular X; that is, I think it is possible for Y to behave as though cared-for by X even though the caring is not felt and perhaps not present. But I shall argue that it is not possible if *no* one comes through to Y as caring.

What we are exploring here is the possibility that one-to-be-cared-for may contribute genuinely as cared-for in a relation of caring even though the necessary reception of caring attitude is missing. Clearly, the relation in such cases is deficient and cannot properly be called caring, and the one-to-be-cared-for is not actually cared-for, but I am arguing that he may behave as cared-for. Why should he do this?

One possibility, as we have seen, is that he might behave as cared-for out of self-interest. Second, he may behave freely and spontaneously as cared-for because he has a vision of self and ethical self and, if this is the case, he may strain to receive that which should come through in a caring relation. He feels the lack but maintains an intellectual doubt concerning it. He may consciously reach beyond the emptiness at the heart of the relation to fill it with induced caring. Every move of the one-supposed-caring is interpreted in its best light, and each response is to that which should be meant.

It seems to me that there are two ways in which a potential cared-for might achieve such a state of magnanimous receptivity. First, he might have a long and rich history of being genuinely cared-for. As a result, he is already strong, receptive, expecting to be cared-for. He meets others with the expectation of genuine encounter. He is ingenuous—a loving innocent of sorts. This may happen even within a relation. X may, for example, have been in a genuine relation of caring to Y during infancy and early childhood and then, for whatever reason, she may lapse into caring and worrying for herself in such a way that the relation is filled with double messages, disavowed demands, and subtle pressures on Y to do what X wishes she might have done. The early love may, however, have contributed to Y's ability to see the relation as possibly-caring. It may also have made him strong enough to seek caring elsewhere and so contribute from a position of strength to the X-Y relation as cared-for.

One behaving as cared-for may, of course, be doing so simply because he is enormously self-centered. He expects others to be engrossed in him, shares spontaneously to promote his own ego, and grows in his nonethical dimensions without even considering the relation. His show of cared-for behavior is not ethical but, interestingly, he may contribute just enough of what the genuine cared-for usually gives to maintain relations that either look like caring relations or are actually half-caring relations. It is possible, that is, for the one-caring in such a relation to be genuinely one-caring and for the one-to-be-cared-for to behave very like a genuine cared-for even though there is no recognition of the caring. In cases like this, the one-caring may eventually realize her irrelevance and withdraw. We see, then, that one may behave as cared-for in a relation where the necessary feeling is absent more or less accidentally and egocentrically.

But there is a second way in which one may ethically behave as cared-for when the necessary attitude is not detected, and I think this second way is more commonly taken than the first. The one-to-be-cared-for turns about and responds to the needs of the one-caring. In doing this, he consciously gives up his status as cared-for and, out of concern for the one-supposed-caring, behaves as cared-for. Clearly, once again, the relation is not one of genuine caring (there is as yet no cared-for), but the external features of caring may be retained and, should the one-supposed-caring recognize the reversal of functions and respond to it, the relation may become fully caring with X and Y positionally exchanged. Our second way of behaving ethically as cared-for is, thus, not authentic. It puts such a burden on the one-to-be-cared-for turned one-caring that it may ultimately be very difficult for both parties. The fundamental deception, however generously initiated, warps the relation. In this case, one behaves ethically in a strict, narrow sense but diminishes the ethical ideal.

The first way is the way of hope and beauty. It gently turns toward the motives of the one-caring to satisfy them and, at the same time, to reflect them transformed to what they should have been. It generously assumes that the one-caring is caring, that the lack of feeling is (or may be) a lack in the cared-for or a result of accident or a product of too much effort— or anything that preserves the one-caring as one-caring. The cared-for lives as cared-for without the sustaining attitude and with persistent doubt strongly managed by his own commitment. This is a position of ethical heroism.

Our logic may be summarized. A caring relation requires the engrossment and motivational displacement of the one-caring, and it requires the recognition and spontaneous response of the cared-for. When caring is not felt in the cared-for, but its absence is felt, the cared-for may still, by an act of ethical heroism, respond and thus contribute to the caring relation. This possibility, as we shall see, gives weight to our hope that one can learn to care and learn to be cared for.

4

AN ETHIC OF CARING

FROM NATURAL TO ETHICAL CARING

DAVID HUME LONG ago contended that morality is founded upon and rooted in feeling—that the "final sentence" on matters of morality, "that which renders morality an active virtue"—"...this final sentence depends on some internal sense or feeling, which nature has made universal in the whole species. For what else can have an influence of this nature?"[1]

What is the nature of this feeling that is "universal in the whole species"? I want to suggest that morality as an "active virtue" requires two feelings and not just one. The first is the sentiment of natural caring. There can be no ethical sentiment without the initial, enabling sentiment. In situations where we act on behalf of the other because we want to do so, we are acting in accord with natural caring. A mother's caretaking efforts in behalf of her child are not usually considered ethical but natural. Even maternal animals take care of their offspring, and we do not credit them with ethical behavior.

The second sentiment occurs in response to a remembrance of the first. Nietzsche speaks of love and memory in the context of Christian love and Eros, but what he says may safely be taken out of context to illustrate the point I wish to make here:

> There is something so ambiguous and suggestive about the word love, something that speaks to memory and to hope, that even the lowest intelligence and the coldest heart still feel something of the glimmer of this word. The cleverest woman and the most vulgar man recall the relatively least selfish moments of their whole life, even if Eros has taken only a low flight with them.[2]

This memory of our own best moments of caring and being cared for sweeps over us as a feeling—as an "I must"—in response to the plight of the other and our conflicting desire to serve our own interests. There is a transfer of feeling analogous to transfer of learning. In the intellectual domain, when I read a certain kind of mathematical puzzle, I may react by thinking, "That is like the sailors, monkey, and coconuts problem," and then, "Diophantine equations" or "modulo arithmetic" or "congruences." Similarly, when I encounter an other and feel the natural pang conflicted with my own desires—"I must—I do not want to"—I recognize the feeling and remember what has followed it in my own best moments. I have a picture of those moments in which I was cared for and in which I cared, and I may reach toward this memory and guide my conduct by it if I wish to do so.

Recognizing that ethical caring requires an effort that is not needed in natural caring does not commit us to a position that elevates ethical caring over natural caring. Kant has identified the ethical with that which is done out of duty and not out of love, and that distinction in itself seems right. But an ethic built on caring strives to maintain the caring attitude and is thus dependent upon, and not superior to, natural caring. The source of ethical behavior is, then, in twin sentiments—one that feels directly for the other and one that feels for and with that best self, who may accept and sustain the initial feeling rather than reject it.

We shall discuss the ethical ideal, that vision of best self, in some depth. When we commit ourselves to obey the "I must" even at its weakest and most fleeting, we are under the guidance of this ideal. It is not just any picture. Rather, it is our best picture of ourselves caring and being cared for. It may even be colored by acquaintance with one superior to us in caring, but, as I shall describe it, it is both constrained and attainable. It is limited by what we have already done and by what we are capable of, and it does not idealize the impossible so that we may escape into ideal abstraction.

Now, clearly, in pointing to Hume's "active virtue" and to an ethical ideal as the source of ethical behavior, I seem to be advocating an ethic of virtue. This is certainly true in part. Many philosophers recognize the need for a discussion of virtue as the energizing factor in moral behavior, even when they have given their best intellectual effort to a careful explication of their positions on obligation and justification.[3] When we discuss the ethical ideal, we shall be talking about "virtue," but we shall not let "virtue" dissipate into "the virtues" described in abstract categories. The holy man living abstemiously on top of the mountain, praying thrice daily, and denying himself human intercourse may display "virtues," but they are not the virtues of one-caring. The virtue described by the ethical ideal of one-caring is built up in relation. It reaches out to the other and grows in response to the other.

Since our discussion of virtue will be embedded in an exploration of moral activity we might do well to start by asking whether or under what circumstances we are obliged to respond to the initial "I must." Does it make sense to say that I am obliged to heed that which comes to me as obligation?

OBLIGATION

There are moments for all of us when we care quite naturally. We just do care; no ethical effort is required. "Want" and "ought" are indistinguishable in such cases. I want to do what I or others might judge I ought to do. But can there be a "demand" to care? There can be, surely, no demand for the initial impulse that arises as a feeling, an inner voice saying "I must do something," in response to the need of the cared-for. This impulse arises naturally, at least occasionally, in the absence of pathology. We cannot demand that one have this impulse, but we shrink from one who never has it. One who never feels the pain of another, who never confesses the internal "I must" that is so familiar to most of us, is beyond our normal pattern of understanding. Her case is pathological, and we avoid her.

But even if I feel the initial "I must," I may reject it. I may reject it instantaneously by shifting from "I must do something" to "Something must be done," and removing myself from the set of possible agents through whom the action should be accomplished. I may reject it because I feel that there is nothing I can do. If I do either of these things without reflection upon what I might do in behalf of the cared-for, then I do not care. Caring requires me to respond to the initial impulse with an act of commitment: I commit myself either to overt action on behalf of the cared-for (I pick up my crying infant) or I commit myself to thinking about what I might do. In the latter case, as we have seen, I may or may not act overtly in behalf of the cared-for. I may abstain from action if I believe that anything I might do would tend to work against the best interests of the cared-for. But the test of my caring is not wholly in how things turn out; the primary test lies in an examination of what I considered, how fully I received the other, and whether the free pursuit of his projects is partly a result of the completion of my caring in him.

But am I obliged to embrace the "I must"? In this form, the question is a bit odd, for the "I must" carries obligation with it. It comes to us as obligation. But accepting and affirming the "I must" are different from feeling it, and these responses are what I am pointing to when I ask whether I am obliged to embrace the "I must." The question nags at us; it is a question that has been asked, in a variety of forms, over and over by moralists and moral theorists. Usually, the question arises as part of the broader question of justification. We ask something of the sort: Why must I (or should I) do what suggests itself to reason as "right" or as needing to be done for the sake of some other? We might prefer to supplement "reason" with "and/or feeling." This question is, of course, not the only thorny question in moral theory, but it is one that has plagued theorists who see clearly that there is no way to derive an "I ought" statement from a chain of facts. I may agree readily that "things would be better"—that is, that a certain state of affairs commonly agreed to be desirable might be attained—if a certain chain of events were to take place. But there is still nothing in this intellectual chain that can produce the "I ought." I may choose to remain an observer on the scene.

Now I am suggesting that the "I must" arises directly and prior to consideration of what it is that I might do. The initial feeling is the "I must." When it comes to me indistinguishable from the "I want," I proceed easily as one-caring. But often it comes to me conflicted. It may be barely perceptible, and it may be followed almost simultaneously by resistance. When someone asks me to get something for him or merely asks for my attention, the "I must" may be lost in a clamor of resistance. Now a second sentiment is required if I am to behave as one-caring. I care about myself as one-caring and, although I do not care naturally for the person who has asked something of me—at least not at this moment—I feel the genuine moral sentiment, the "I ought," that sensibility to which I have committed myself.

Let me try to make plausible my contention that the moral imperative arises directly.[4] And, of course, I must try to explain how caring and what I am calling the "moral imperative" are related. When my infant cries in the night, I not only feel that I must do something but I want to do something. Because I love this child, because I am bonded to him, I want to remove his pain as I would want to remove my own. The "I must" is not a dutiful imperative but one that accompanies the "I want." If I were tied to a chair, for example, and wanted desperately to get free, I might say as I struggled, "I must do something; I must get out of these bonds." But this "must" is not yet the moral or ethical "ought." It is a "must" born of desire.

The most intimate situations of caring are, thus, natural. I do not feel that taking care of my own child is "moral" but, rather, natural. A woman who allows her own child to die of neglect is often considered sick rather than immoral; that is, we feel that either she or the situation into which she has been thrust must be pathological. Otherwise, the impulse to respond, to nurture the living infant, is overwhelming. We share the impulse with other creatures in the animal kingdom. Whether we want to consider this response as "instinctive" is problematic, because certain patterns of response may be implied by the term and because suspension of reflective consciousness seems also to be implied (and I am not suggesting that we have no choice), but I have no difficulty in considering it as innate. Indeed, I am claiming that the impulse to act in behalf of the present other is itself innate. It lies latent in each of us, awaiting gradual development in a succession of caring relations. I am suggesting that our inclination toward and interest in morality derives from caring. In caring, we accept the natural impulse to act on behalf of the present other. We are engrossed in the other. We have received him and feel his pain or happiness, but we are not compelled by this impulse. We have a choice; we may accept what we feel, or we may reject it. If we have a strong desire to be moral, we will not reject it, and this strong desire to be moral is derived, reflectively, from the more fundamental and natural desire to be and to remain related. To reject the feeling when it arises is either to be in an internal state of imbalance or to contribute willfully to the diminution of the ethical ideal.

But suppose in a particular case that the "I must" does not arise, or that it whispers faintly and disappears, leaving distrust, repugnance, or hate. Why, then, should I behave morally toward the object of my dislike? Why should I not accept feelings other than those characteristic of caring and, thus, achieve an internal state of balance through hate, anger, or malice?

The answer to this is, I think, that the genuine moral sentiment (our second sentiment) arises from an evaluation of the caring relation as good, as better than, superior to, other forms of relatedness. I feel the moral "I must" when I recognize that my response will either enhance or diminish my ethical ideal. It will serve either to increase or decrease the likelihood of genuine caring. My response affects me as one-caring. In a given situation with someone I am not fond of, I may be able to find all sorts of reasons why I should not respond to his need. I may be too busy. He may be undiscerning. The matter may be, on objective analysis, unimportant. But, before I decide, I must turn away from this analytic chain of thought and back to the concrete situation. Here is this person with this perceived need to which is attached this importance. I must put justification aside temporarily. Shall I respond? How do I feel as a duality about the "I" who will not respond?

I am obliged, then, to accept the initial "I must" when it occurs and even to fetch it out of recalcitrant slumber when it fails to awake spontaneously.[5] The source of my obligation is the value I place on the relatedness of caring. This value itself arises as a product of actual caring and being cared-for and my reflection on the goodness of these concrete caring situations.

Now, what sort of "goodness" is it that attaches to the caring relation? It cannot be a fully moral goodness, for we have already described forms of caring that are natural and require no moral effort. But it cannot be a fully nonmoral goodness either, for it would then join a class of goods many of which are widely separated from the moral good. It is, perhaps, properly described as a "premoral good," one that lies in a region with the moral good and shades over into it. We cannot always decide with certainty whether our caring response is natural or ethical. Indeed, the decision to respond ethically as one-caring may cause the lowering of barriers that previously prevented reception of the other, and natural caring may follow.

I have identified the source of our obligation and have said that we are obligated to accept, and even to call forth, the feeling "I must." But what exactly must I do? Can my obligation be set forth in a list or hierarchy of principles? So far, it seems that I am obligated to maintain an attitude and, thus, to meet the other as one-caring and, at the same time, to increase my own virtue as one-caring. If I am advocating an ethic of virtue, do not all the usual dangers lie in wait: hypocrisy, self-righteousness, withdrawal from the public domain? We shall discuss these dangers as the idea of an ethical ideal is developed more fully.

Let me say here, however, why it seems preferable to place an ethical ideal above principle as a guide to moral action. It has been traditional in moral philosophy to insist that moral principles must be, by their very nature as moral principles, universifiable. If I am obligated to do X under certain conditions, then under sufficiently similar conditions you also are obligated to do X. But the principle of universifiability seems to depend, as Nietzsche pointed out, on a concept of "sameness."[6] In order to accept the principle, we should have to establish that human predicaments exhibit sufficient sameness, and this we cannot do without abstracting away from concrete situations those qualities that seem to reveal the sameness. In doing this, we often lose the very qualities or factors that gave rise to the moral question in the situation. That condition which makes the situation different and thereby induces genuine moral puzzlement cannot be satisfied by the application of principles developed in situations of sameness.

This does not mean that we cannot receive any guidance from an attempt to discover principles that seem to be universifiable. We can, under this sort of plan, arrive at the doctrine of "prima facie duty" described by W. D. Ross.[7] Ross himself, however, admits that this doctrine yields no real guidance for moral conduct in concrete situations. It guides us in abstract moral thinking; it tells us, theoretically, what to do, "all other things being equal." But other things are rarely if ever equal. A and B, struggling with a moral decision, are two different persons with different factual histories, different projects and aspirations, and different ideals. It may indeed be right, morally right, for A to do X and B to do not-X. We may, that is, connect "right" and "wrong" to faithfulness to the ethical ideal. This does not cast us into relativism, because the ideal contains at its heart a component that is universal: Maintenance of the caring relation.

Before turning to a discussion of "right" and "wrong" and their usefulness in an ethic of caring, we might try to clear up the problem earlier mentioned as a danger in any ethic of virtue: the temptation to withdraw from the public domain. It is a real danger. Even though we rejected the sort of virtue exhibited by the hermit-monk on the mountaintop, that rejection may have been one of personal choice. It still remains possible that an ethic of caring is compatible with the monk's choice, and that such an ethic even induces withdrawal. We are not going to be able to divide cases clearly. The monk who withdraws only to serve God is clearly under the guidance of an ethic that differs fundamentally from the ethic of caring. The source of his ethic is not the source of ours, and he might deny that any form of human relatedness could be a source for moral behavior. But if, when another intrudes upon his privacy, he receives the other as one-caring, we cannot charge him with violating our ethic. Further, as we saw in our discussion of the one-caring, there is a legitimate dread of the proximate stranger—of that person who may ask more than we feel able to give. We saw there that we cannot care for everyone. Caring itself is reduced to mere talk about caring when we attempt to do so. We must acknowledge, then, that an ethic of caring implies a limit on our obligation.

Our obligation is limited and delimited by relation. We are never free, in the human domain, to abandon our preparedness to care; but, practically, if we are meeting those in our inner circles adequately as ones-caring and receiving those linked to our inner circles by formal chains of relation, we shall limit the calls upon our obligation quite naturally. We are not obliged to summon the "I must" if there is no possibility of completion in the other. I am not obliged to care for starving children in Africa, because there is no way for this caring to be completed in the other unless I abandon the caring to which I am obligated. I may still choose to do something in the direction of caring, but I am not obliged to do so. When we discuss our obligation to animals, we shall see that this is even more sharply limited by relation. We cannot refuse obligation in human affairs by merely refusing to enter relation; we are, by virtue of our mutual humanity, already and perpetually in potential relation. Instead, we limit our obligation by examining the possibility of completion. In connection with animals, however, we may find it possible to refuse relation itself on the grounds of a species-specific impossibility of any form of reciprocity in caring.

Now, this is very important, and we should try to say clearly what governs our obligation. On the basis of what has been developed so far, there seem to be two criteria: the existence of or potential for present relation, and the dynamic potential for growth in relation, including the potential for increased reciprocity and, perhaps, mutuality. The first criterion establishes an absolute obligation and the second serves to put our obligations into an order of priority.

If the other toward whom we shall act is capable of responding as cared-for and there are no objective conditions that prevent our receiving this response—if, that is, our caring can be completed in the other—then we must meet that other as one-caring. If we do not care naturally, we must call upon our capacity for ethical caring. When we are in relation or when the other has addressed us, we must respond as one-caring. The imperative in relation is categorical. When relation has not yet been established, or when it may properly be refused (when no formal chain or natural circle is present), the imperative is more like that of the hypothetical: I must if I wish to (or am able to) move into relation.

The second criterion asks us to look at the nature of potential relation and, especially, at the capacity of the cared-for to respond. The potential for response in animals, for example, is nearly static; they cannot respond in mutuality, nor can the nature of their response change substantially. But a child's potential for increased response is enormous. If the possibility of relation is dynamic—if the relation may clearly grow with respect to reciprocity—then the possibility and degree of my obligation also grows. If response is imminent, so also is my obligation. This criterion will help us to distinguish between our obligation to members of the nonhuman animal world and, say, the human fetus. We must keep in mind, however, that the second criterion binds us in proportion to the probability of increased response and to the imminence of that response. Relation itself is fundamental in obligation.

I shall give an example of thinking guided by these criteria, but let us pause for a moment and ask what it is we are trying to accomplish. I am working deliberately toward criteria that will preserve our deepest and most tender human feelings. The caring of mother for child, of human adult for human infant, elicits the tenderest feelings in most of us. Indeed, for many women, this feeling of nurturance lies at the very heart of what we assess as good. A philosophical position that has difficulty distinguishing between our obligation to human infants and, say, pigs is in some difficulty straight off. It violates our most deeply cherished feeling about human goodness. This violation does not, of course, make the position logically wrong, but it suggests that especially strong grounds will be needed to support it. In the absence of such strong grounds—and I shall argue in a later chapter that they are absent—we might prefer to establish a position that captures rather than denies our basic feelings. We might observe that man (in contrast to woman) has continually turned away from his inner self and feeling in pursuit of both science and ethics. With respect to strict science, this turning outward may be defensible; with respect to ethics, it has been disastrous.

Now, let's consider an example: the problem of abortion. Operating under the guidance of an ethic of caring, we are not likely to find abortion in general either right or wrong. We shall have to inquire into individual cases. An incipient embryo is an information speck—a set of controlling instructions for a future human being. Many of these specks are created and flushed away without their creators' awareness. From the view developed here, the information speck is an information speck; it has no given sanctity. There should be no concern over the waste of "human tissue," since nature herself is wildly prolific, even profligate.[8] The one-caring is concerned not with human tissue but with human consciousness—with pain, delight, hope, fear, entreaty, and response.

But suppose the information speck is mine, and I am aware of it. This child-to-be is the product of love between a man deeply cared-for and me. Will the child have his eyes or mine? His stature or mine? Our joint love of mathematics or his love of mechanics or my love of language? This is not just an information speck; it is endowed with prior love and current knowledge. It is sacred, but I—humbly, not presumptuously—confer sacredness upon it. I cannot, will not destroy it. It is joined to loved others through formal chains of caring. It is linked to the inner circle in a clearly defined way. I might wish that I were not pregnant, but I cannot destroy this known and potentially loved person-to-be. There is already relation albeit indirect and formal. My decision is an ethical one born of natural caring.

But suppose, now, that my beloved child has grown up; it is she who is pregnant and considering abortion. She is not sure of the love between herself and the man. She is miserably worried about her economic and emotional future. I might like to convey sanctity on this information speck; but I am not God—only mother to this suffering cared-for. It is she who is conscious and in pain, and I as one-caring move to relieve the pain. This information speck is an information speck and that is all. There is no formal relation, given the breakdown between husband and wife, and with the embryo, there is no present relation; the possibility of future relation—while not absent, surely—is uncertain. But what of this possibility for growing response? Must we not consider it? We must indeed. As the embryo becomes a fetus and, growing daily, becomes more nearly capable of response as cared-for, our obligation grows from a nagging uncertainty—an "I must if I wish"—to an utter conviction that we must meet this small other as one-caring.

If we try to formalize what has been expressed in the concrete situations described so far, we arrive at a legal approach to abortion very like that of the Supreme Court: abortions should be freely available in the first trimester, subject to medical determination in the second trimester, and banned in the third, when the fetus is viable. A woman under the guidance of our ethic would be likely to recognize the growing possibility of relation; the potential is clearly dynamic. Further, many women recognize the relation as established when the fetus begins to move about. It is not a question of when life begins but of when relation begins.

But what if relation is never established? Suppose the child is born and the mother admits no sense of relatedness. May she commit infanticide? One who asks such questions misinterprets the concept of relatedness that I have been struggling to describe. Since the infant, even the near-natal fetus, is capable of relation—of the sweetest and most unselfcon-scious reciprocity—one who encounters the infant is obligated to meet it as one-caring. Both parts of this claim are essential; it is not only the child's capability to respond but also the encounter that induces obliga-tion. There must exist the possibility for our caring to be completed in the other. If the mother does not care naturally, then she must summon ethi-cal caring to support her as one-caring. She may not ethically ignore the child's cry to live.

The one-caring, in considering abortion as in all other matters, cares first for the one in immediate pain or peril. She might suggest a brief and direct form of counseling in which a young expectant mother could come to grips with her feelings. If the incipient child has been sanctified by its mother, every effort must be made to help the two to achieve a stable and hopeful life together; if it has not, it should be removed swiftly and mer-cifully with all loving attention to the woman, the conscious patient. Between these two clear reactions is a possible confused one: the young woman is not sure how she feels. The one-caring probes gently to see what has been considered, raising questions and retreating when the questions obviously have been considered and are now causing great pain. Is such a view "unprincipled"? If it is, it is boldly so; it is at least connected with the world as it is, at its best and at its worst, and it re-quires that we—in espousing a "best"—stand ready to actualize that pre-ferred condition. The decision for or against abortion must be made by those directly involved in the concrete situation, but it need not be made alone. The one-caring cannot require everyone to behave as she would in a particular situation. Rather, when she dares to say, "I think you should do X," she adds, also, "Can I help you?" The one under her gaze is under her support and not her judgment.

One under the guidance of an ethic of caring is tempted to retreat to a manageable world. Her public life is limited by her insistence upon meet-ing the other as one-caring. So long as this is possible, she may reach out-ward and enlarge her circles of caring. When this reaching out destroys or drastically reduces her actual caring, she retreats and renews her con-tact with those who address her. If the retreat becomes a flight, an avoid-ance of the call to care, her ethical ideal is diminished. Similarly, if the

retreat is away from human beings and toward other objects of caring—
ideas, animals, humanity-at-large, God—her ethical ideal is virtually
shattered. This is not a judgment, for we can understand and sympathize
with one who makes such a choice. It is more in the nature of a perception: we see clearly what has been lost in the choice.

Our ethic of caring—which we might have called a "feminine ethic"—
begins to look a bit mean in contrast to the masculine ethics of universal
love or universal justice. But universal love is illusion. Under the illusion,
some young people retreat to the church to worship that which they cannot actualize; some write lovely poetry extolling universal love; and
some, in terrible disillusion, kill to establish the very principles which
should have entreated them not to kill. Thus are lost both principles and
persons.

RIGHT AND WRONG

How are we to make judgments of right and wrong under this ethic?
First, it is important to understand that we are not primarily interested in
judging but, rather, in heightening moral perception and sensitivity. But
"right" and "wrong" can be useful.

Suppose a mother observes her young child pulling the kitten's tail or
picking it up by the ears. She may exclaim, "Oh, no, it is not nice to hurt
the kitty," or, "You must not hurt the kitty." Or she may simply say,
"Stop. See—you are hurting the kitty," and she may then take the kitten
in her own hands and show the child how to handle it. She holds the kitten gently, stroking it, and saying, "See? Ah, ah, kitty, nice kitty...."
What the mother is supposing in this interaction is that the realization
that his act is hurting the kitten, supplemented by the knowledge of how
to avoid inflicting hurt, will suffice to change the child's behavior. If she
believes this, she has no need for the statement, "It is wrong to hurt the
kitty." She is not threatening sanctions but drawing dual attention to a
matter of fact (the hurting) and her own commitment (I will not hurt).
Beyond this, she is supposing that her child, well-cared-for himself, does
not want to inflict pain.

Now, I am not claiming through use of this illustration that moral
statements are mere expressions of approval or disapproval, although
they do serve an expressive function. A. J. Ayer, who did make a claim
of this sort before modifying his position somewhat, uses an illustration

very like the one just given to support an emotivist position.⁹ But even if
it were possible to take a purely analytic stance with respect to moral
theory, as Ayer suggests he has done, that is certainly not what I intend
to do. One who labels moral statements as expressions of approval or disapproval, and takes the matter to be finished with that, misses the very
heart of morality. He misses the commitment to behave in a fashion compatible with caring. Thus he misses both feeling and content. I may, after
all, express my approval or disapproval on matters that are not moral.
Thus it is clear that when I make a moral judgment I am doing more than
simply expressing approval or disapproval. I am both expressing my own
commitment to behave in a way compatible with caring and appealing to
the hearer to consider what he is doing. I may say first to a child, "Oh!
Don't hurt the kitty!" And I may then add, "It is wrong to hurt the
kitty." The word is not necessary, strictly speaking, but I may find it
useful.

What do I mean by this? I certainly mean to express my own commitment, and I show this best by daily example. But I may mean to say more
than this. I may explain to the child that not only do I feel this way but
that our family does, that our community does, that our culture does.
Here I must be very careful. Our community may say one thing and do
quite another. Such contradiction is even more likely at the level of "our
culture." But I express myself doubly in words and in acts, and I may
search out examples in the larger culture to convince the child that significant others do feel this way. The one-caring is careful to distinguish
between acts that violate caring, acts that she herself holds wrong, and
those acts that "some people" hold to be wrong. She need not be con-
descending in this instruction. She is herself so reluctant to universalize
beyond the demands of caring that she cannot say, "It is wrong," to
everything that is illegal, church-forbidden, or contrary to a prevailing
etiquette. But she can raise the question, attempt to justify the alien view,
express her own objections, and support the child in his own exploration.

Emotivists are partly right, I think, when they suggest that we might
effectively substitute a statement describing the fact or event that triggers
our feeling or attitude for statements such as "It is wrong to do X."
When I say to my child, "It is wrong to hurt the kitty," I mean (if I am
not threatening sanctions) to inform him that he is hurting the kitten and,
further, that I believe that if he perceives he is doing so, he will stop. I am
counting on his gradually developing ability to feel pain in the other to
induce a decision to stop. To say, "It is wrong to cause pain needlessly,"

contributes nothing by way of knowledge and can hardly be thought likely to change the attitude or behavior of one who might ask, "Why is it wrong?" If I say to someone, "You are hurting the cat," and he replies, "I know it—so what? I like hurting cats," I feel "zero at the bone." Saying to him, "It is wrong to hurt cats," adds little unless I intend to threaten sanctions. If I mean to equate "It is wrong to hurt cats" with "There will be a sure and specific punishment for hurting cats," then it would be more honest to say this. One either feels a sort of pain in response to the pain of others, or one does not feel it. If he does feel it, he does not need to be told that causing pain is wrong. If he does not feel it in a particular case, he may remember the feeling—as one remembers the sweetness of love on hearing a certain piece of music— and allow himself to be moved by this remembrance of feeling. For one who feels nothing, directly or by remembrance, we must prescribe re-education or exile. Thus, at the foundation of moral behavior—as we have already pointed out—is feeling or sentiment. But, further, there is commitment to remain open to that feeling, to remember it, and to put one's thinking in its service. It is the particular commitment underlying genuine expressions of moral judgment—as well as the special content— that the emotivist misses.

The one-caring, clearly, applies "right" and "wrong" most confidently to her own decisions. This does not, as we have insisted before, make her a relativist. The caring attitude that lies at the heart of all ethical behavior is universal. As the mother in chapter two, who had to decide whether or not to leave her sick child, decided on the basis of a caring evaluation of the conditions and feelings of those involved, so in general the one-caring evaluates her own acts with respect to how faithfully they conform to what is known and felt through the receptivity of caring. But she also uses "right" and "wrong" instructively and respectfully to refer to the judgments of significant others. If she agrees because the matter at hand can be assessed in light of caring, she adds her personal commitment and example; if she has doubts—because the rule appealed to seems irrelevant or ambiguous in the light of caring—she still acknowledges the judgment but adds her own dissent or demurrer. Her eye is on the ethical development of the cared-for and, as she herself withholds judgment until she has heard the "whole story," she wants the cared-for to encounter others, receive them, and reflect on what he has received. Principles and rules are among the beliefs he will receive, and she wants him to consider these in the light of caring.

But is this all we can say about right and wrong? Is there not a firm foundation in morality for our legal judgments? Surely, we must be allowed to say, for example, that stealing is wrong and is, therefore, properly forbidden by law. Because it is so often wrong—and so easily demonstrated to be wrong—under an ethic of caring, we may accede that such a law has its roots *partly* in morality. We may legally punish one who has stolen, but we may not pass moral judgment on him until we know why he stole. An ethic of caring is likely to be stricter in its judgment, but more supportive and corrective in following up its judgment, than ethics otherwise grounded. For the one-caring, stealing is almost always wrong:

Ms. A talks with her young son. *But, Mother,* the boy pleads, *suppose I want to make you happy and I steal something you want from a big chain store. I haven't hurt anyone, have I? Yes, you have,* responds his mother, and she points to the predicament of the store managers who may be accused of poor stewardship and to the higher prices suffered by their neighbors. *Well, suppose I steal from a rich, rich person? He can replace what I take easily, and... Wait,* says Ms. A. *Is someone suffering? Are you stealing to relieve that suffering, and will you make certain that what you steal is used to relieve it?... But can't I steal to make someone happy?* her son persists. Slowly, patiently, Ms. A explains the position of one-caring. *Each one* who comes under our gaze must be met as one-caring. When I want to please X and I turn toward Y as a means for satisfying my desire to please X, I must now meet Y as one-caring. I do not judge him for being rich—for treasuring what I, perhaps, regard with indifference. I may not cause him pain by taking or destroying what he possesses. *But what if I steal from a bad guy—someone who stole to get what he has?* Ms. A smiles at her young son, struggling to avoid his ethical responsibility: *Unless he is an immediate threat to you or someone else, you must meet him, too, as one-caring.*

The lessons in "right" and "wrong" are hard lessons—not swiftly accomplished by setting up as an objective the learning of some principle. We do not say: It is wrong to steal. Rather, we consider why it was wrong or may be wrong in this case to steal. We do not say: It is wrong to kill. By setting up such a principle, we also imply its exceptions, and then we may too easily act on authorized exceptions. The one-caring wants to consider, and wants her child to consider, the act itself in full context. She will send him into the world skeptical, vulnerable, courageous, disobedient, and tenderly receptive. The "world" may not depend upon him to obey its rules or fulfill its wishes, but you, the individual he encounters, may depend upon him to meet you as one-caring.

THE PROBLEM OF JUSTIFICATION

Since I have chided the emotivist for not digging beneath the expressive layer of moral sentiment to the nature of the feeling itself and the commitment to act in accord with the feeling, one might ask whether I should not dig beneath the commitment. Why should I be committed to not causing pain? Now, clearly, in one sense, I cannot answer this better than we already have. When the "Why?" refers to motivation, we have seen that the one-caring receives the other and acts in the other's behalf as she would for herself; that is, she acts with a similar motive energy. Further, I have claimed that, when natural caring fails, the motive energy in behalf of the other can be summoned out of caring for the ethical self. We have discussed both natural caring and ethical caring. Ethical caring, as I have described it, depends not upon rule or principle but upon the development of an ideal self. It does not depend upon just any ideal of self, but the ideal developed in congruence with one's best remembrance of caring and being cared-for.

So far, in recommending the ethical ideal as a guide to ethical conduct, I have suggested that traditional approaches to the problem of justification are mistaken. When the ethical theorist asks, "Why should I behave thus-and-so?" his question is likely to be aimed at justification rather than motivation and at a logic that resides outside the person. He is asking for reasons of the sort we expect to find in logical demonstration. He may expect us to claim that moral judgments can be tested as claims to facts can be tested, or that moral judgments are derived from divine commandment, or that moral truths are intuitively apprehended. Once started on this line of discussion, we may find ourselves arguing abstractly about the status of relativism and absolutism, egoism and altruism, and a host of other positions that, I shall claim, are largely irrelevant to moral conduct. They are matters of considerable intellectual interest, but they are distractions if our primary interest is in ethical conduct.

Moral statements cannot be justified in the way that statements of fact can be justified. They are not truths. They are derived not from facts or principles but from the caring attitude. Indeed, we might say that moral statements come out of the moral view or attitude, which, as I have described it, is the rational attitude built upon natural caring. When we put it this way, we see that there can be no justification for taking the moral viewpoint—that in truth, the moral viewpoint is prior to any notion of justification.

But there is another difficulty in answering the request for justification. Consideration of problems of justification requires us to concentrate on moral judgments, on moral statements. Hence we are led to an exploration of the language and reasoning used to discuss moral conduct and away from an assessment of the concrete events in which we must choose whether and how to behave morally. Indeed, we are often led far beyond what we feel and intuitively judge to be right in a search for some simple and absolute guide to moral goodness.

For an ethic of caring, the problem of justification is not concentrated upon justified action in general. We are not "justified"—we are *obligated*—to do what is required to maintain and enhance caring. We must "justify" not-caring; that is, we must explain why, in the interest of caring for ourselves as ethical selves or in the interest of others for whom we care, we may behave as ones-not-caring toward this particular other. In a related problem, we must justify doing what this other would not have us do to him as part of our genuine effort to care for him. But even in these cases, an ethic of caring does not emphasize justification. As one-caring, I am not seeking justification for my action; I am not standing alone before some tribunal. What I seek is completion in the other—the sense of being cared-for and, I hope, the renewed commitment of the cared-for to turn about and act as one-caring in the circles and chains within which he is defined. Thus, I am not justified but somehow fulfilled and completed in my own life and in the lives of those I have thus influenced.

It sounds all very nice, says my male colleague, but can you claim to be doing "ethics"? After all, ethics is the study of justified action.... Ah, yes. But, after "after-all," I am a woman, and I was not party to that definition. Shall we say then that I am talking about "how to meet the other morally"? Is this part of ethics? Is ethics part of this?

WOMEN AND MORALITY: VIRTUE

Many of us in education are keenly aware of the distortion that results from undue emphasis on moral judgments and justification. Lawrence Kohlberg's theory, for example, is widely held to be a model for moral education, but it is actually only a hierarchical description of moral reasoning.[10] It is well known, further, that the description may not be accurate. In particular, the fact that women seem often to be "stuck" at stage three might call the accuracy of the description into question. But perhaps the description is accurate within the domain of morality conceived as moral justification. If it is, we might well explore the possibility that feminine nonconformity to the Kohlberg model counts against the justification/judgment paradigm and not against women as moral thinkers.

Women, perhaps the majority of women, prefer to discuss moral problems in terms of concrete situations. They approach moral problems not as intellectual problems to be solved by abstract reasoning but as concrete human problems to be lived and to be solved in living. Their approach is founded in caring. Carol Gilligan describes the approach:

> ...women not only define themselves in a context of human relationship but also judge themselves in terms of their ability to care. Woman's place in man's life cycle has been that of nurturer, caretaker, and helpmate, the weaver of those networks of relationships on which she in turn relies.[11]

Faced with a hypothetical moral dilemma, women often ask for more information. It is not the case, certainly, that women cannot arrange principles hierarchically and derive conclusions logically. It is more likely that they see this process as peripheral to or even irrelevant to moral conduct. They want more information, I think, in order to form a picture. Ideally, they need to talk to the participants, to see their eyes and facial expressions, to size up the whole situation. Moral decisions are, after all, made in situations; they are qualitatively different from the solution of geometry problems. Women, like act-deontologists in general, give reasons for their acts, but the reasons point to feelings, needs, situational conditions, and their sense of personal ideal rather than universal principles and their application.

As we have seen, caring is not in itself a virtue. The genuine ethical commitment to maintain oneself as caring gives rise to the development and exercise of virtues, but these must be assessed in the context of caring situations. It is not, for example, patience itself that is a virtue but patience with respect to some infirmity of a particular cared-for or patience in instructing a concrete cared-for that is virtuous. We must not reify virtues and turn our caring toward them. If we do this, our ethic turns inward and is even less useful than an ethic of principles, which at least remains indirectly in contact with the acts we are assessing. The fulfillment of virtue is both in me and in the other.

A consideration of caring and an ethic built upon it give new meaning to what Kohlberg assesses as "stage three" morality. At this stage, persons behave morally in order to be thought of—or to think of themselves as—"good boys" or "good girls." Clearly, it makes a difference whether one chooses to be good or to be thought of as good. One who chooses to be good may not be "stuck," as Kohlberg suggests, in a stage of moral reasoning. Rather, she may have chosen an alternative route to moral conduct.

It should be clear that my description of an ethic of caring as a feminine ethic does not imply a claim to speak for all women nor to exclude men. As we shall see in the next chapter, there is reason to believe that women are somewhat better equipped for caring than men are. This is partly a result of the construction of psychological deep structures in the mother-child relationship. A girl can identify with the one caring for her and thus maintain relation while establishing identity. A boy must, however, find his identity with the absent one—the father—and thus disengage himself from the intimate relation of caring.[12]

There are many women who will deplore my insistence on locating the source of caring in human relations. The longing for something beyond is lovely—alluring—and it persists. It seems to me quite natural that men, many of whom are separated from the intimacy of caring, should create gods and seek security and love in worship. But what ethical need have women for God? I do not mean to suggest that women can brush aside an actually existing God but, if there is such a God, the human role in Its maintenance must be trivial. We can only contemplate the universe in awe and wonder, study it conscientiously, and live in it conservatively. Women, it seems to me, can accept the God of Spinoza and Einstein. What I mean to suggest is that women have no need of a conceptualized God, one wrought in the image of man. All the love and goodness commanded by such a God can be generated from the love and goodness found in the warmest and best human relations.

Let me say a little more here, because I know the position is a hard one for many—even for many I love. In our earlier discussion of Abraham, we saw a fundamental and deeply cut chasm between male and female views. We see this difference illustrated again in the New Testament. In Luke 16, we hear the story of a rich man who ignored the suffering of

Lazarus, a beggar. After death, Lazarus finds peace and glory, but the rich man finds eternal torment. He cries to Abraham for mercy:

> Father Abraham, have mercy on me, and send Lazarus, that he may dip the tip of his finger in water, and cool my tongue; for I am tormented in this flame.
>
> But Abraham said, Son, remember that thou in thy lifetime receivedst thy good things, and likewise Lazarus evil things: but now he is comforted and thou art tormented.
>
> And beside all this, between us and you there is a great gulf fixed: so that they which would pass from hence to you cannot; neither can they pass to us, that would come from thence.[13]

But what prevents their passage? The judgmental love of the harsh father establishes the chasm. This is not the love of the mother, for even in despair she would cast herself across the chasm to relieve the suffering of her child. If he calls her, she will respond. Even the wickedest, if he calls, she must meet as one-caring. Now, I ask again, what ethical need has woman for God?

In the stories of Abraham, we hear the tragedy induced by the traditional, masculine approach to ethics. When Kierkegaard defends him in an agonized and obsessive search for "something beyond" to which he can repeatedly declare his devotion, he reveals the emptiness at the heart of his own concrete existence. If Abraham is lost, he, Kierkegaard, is lost. He observes: "So either there is a paradox, that the individual as the individual stands in an absolute relation to the absolute/or Abraham is lost."[14]

Woman, as one-caring, pities and fears both Abraham and Kierkegaard. Not only are they lost, but they would take all of us with them into the lonely wilderness of abstraction.

THE TOUGHNESS OF CARING

An ethic built on caring is thought by some to be tenderminded. It does involve construction of an ideal from the fact and memory of tenderness. The ethical sentiment itself requires a prior natural sentiment of caring and a willingness to sustain tenderness. But there is no assumption of innate human goodness and, when we move to the construction of a philosophy of education, we shall find enormous differences between the view developed here and that of those who find the child innately good. I shall not claim that the child is "innately wise and good," or that the aim of life is happiness, or that all will be well with the child if we resist interfering in its intellectual and moral life.[15] We have memories of caring, of tenderness, and these lead us to a vision of what is good—a state that is good-in-itself and a commitment to sustain and enhance that good (the desire and commitment to be moral). But we have other memories as well, and we have other desires. An ethic of caring takes into account these other tendencies and desires; it is precisely because the tendency to treat each other well is so fragile that we must strive so consistently to care.

Far from being romantic, an ethic of caring is practical, made for this earth. Its toughness is disclosed in a variety of features, the most important of which I shall try to describe briefly here.

First, since caring is a relation, an ethic built on it is naturally other-regarding. Since I am defined in relation, I do not sacrifice myself when I move toward the other as one-caring. Caring is, thus, both self-serving and other-serving. Willard Gaylin describes it as necessary to the survival of the species: "If one's frame of reference focuses on the individual, caring seems self-sacrificing. But if the focus is on the group, on the species, it is the ultimate self-serving device—the sine qua non of survival."[16]

Clearly, this is so. But while I am drawn to the other, while I am instinctively called to nurture and protect, I am also the initiator and chooser of my acts. I may act in accordance with that which is good in my deepest nature, or I may seek to avoid it—either by forsaking relation or by trying to transform that which is feeling and action into that which is all propositional talk and principle. If I suppose, for example, that I am somehow alone and totally responsible for either the apprehension or creation of moral principles, I may find myself in some difficulty when it comes to caring for myself. If moral principles govern my conduct with respect to others, if I must always regard the other in order to be moral, how can I properly meet my own needs and desires? How can I, morally, care for myself?

An ethic of caring is a tough ethic. It does not separate self and other in caring, although, of course, it identifies the special contribution of the one-caring and the cared-for in caring. In contrast to some forms of agapism, for example, it has no problem in advocating a deep and steady caring for self. In a discussion of other-regarding forms of agapism, Gene Outka considers the case of a woman tied to a demanding parent.

He explores the possibility of her finding justification for leaving in an assessment of the greatest good for all concerned, and he properly recommends that her own interests be included. In discussing the insistence of some agapists on entirely other-regarding justification, he explores the possibility of her breaking away "to become a medical doctor," thereby satisfying the need for multilateral other-interests.[17] The one-caring throws up her hands at such casting about for reasons. She needs no special justification to care for herself for, if she is not supported and cared-for, she may be entirely lost as one-caring. If caring is to be maintained, clearly, the one-caring must be maintained. She must be strong, courageous, and capable of joy.

When we looked at the one-caring in conflict (e.g., Mr. Jones and his mother), we saw that he or she can be overwhelmed by cares and burdens. The ethical responsibility of the one-caring is to look clear-eyed on what is happening to her ideal and how well she is meeting it. She sees herself, perhaps, as caring lovingly for her parent. But perhaps he is cantankerous, ungrateful, rude, and even dirty. She sees herself becoming impatient, grouchy, tired, and filled with self-pity. She can stay and live by an honestly diminished ideal—"I am a tired, grouchy, pitiful caretaker of my old father"—or she can free herself to whatever degree she must to remain minimally but actually caring. The ethical self does not live partitioned off from the rest of the person. Thinking guided by caring does not seek to justify a way out by means of a litany of predicted "goods," but it seeks a way to remain one-caring and, if at all possible, to enhance the ethical ideal. In such a quest, there is no way to disregard the self, or to remain impartial, or to adopt the stance of a disinterested observer. Pursuit of the ethical ideal demands impassioned and realistic commitment.

We see still another reason for accepting constraints on our ethical ideals. When we accept honestly our loves, our innate ferocity, our capacity for hate, we may use all this as information in building the safeguards and alarms that must be part of the ideal. We know better what we must work toward, what we must prevent, and the conditions under which we are lost as ones-caring. Instead of hiding from our natural impulses and pretending that we can achieve goodness through lofty abstractions, we accept what is there—all of it—and use what we have already assessed as good to control that which is not-good.

Caring preserves both the group and the individual and, as we have already seen, it limits our obligation so that it may realistically be met. It will not allow us to be distracted by visions of universal love, perfect justice, or a world unified under principle. It does not say, "Thou shalt not kill," and then seek other principles under which killing is, after all, justified. If the other is a clear and immediate danger to me or to my cared-fors, I must stop him, and I might need to kill him. But I cannot kill in the name of principle or justice. I must meet this other—even this evil other—as one-caring so long as caring itself is not endangered by my doing so. I must, for example, oppose capital punishment. I do not begin by saying, "Capital punishment is wrong." Thus I do not fall into the trap of having to supply reasons for its wrongness that will be endlessly disputed at a logical level. I do not say, "Life is sacred," for I cannot name a source of sacredness. I may point to the irrevocability of the decision, but this is not in itself decisive, even for me, because in many cases the decision would be just and I could not regret the demise of the condemned. (I have, after all, confessed my own ferocity; in the heat of emotion, I might have torn him to shreds if I had caught him molesting my child.)

My concern is for the ethical ideal, for my own ethical ideal and for whatever part of it others in my community may share. Ideally, another human being should be able to request, with expectation of positive response, my help and comfort. If I am not blinded by fear, or rage, or hatred, I should reach out as one-caring to the proximate stranger who entreats my help. This is the ideal one-caring creates. I should be able to respond to the condemned man's entreaty, "Help me." We must ask, then, after the effects of capital punishment on jurors, on judges, on jailers, on wardens, on newspersons "covering" the execution, on ministers visiting the condemned, on citizens affirming the sentence, on doctors certifying first that the condemned is well enough to be executed and second that he is dead. What effects have capital punishment on the ethical ideals of the participants? For me, if I had to participate, the ethical ideal would be diminished. Diminished. The ideal itself would be diminished. My act would either be wrong or barely right—right in a depleted sense. I might, indeed, participate ethically—rightly—in an execution but only at the cost of revising my ethical ideal downward. If I do not revise it and still participate, then my act is wrong, and I am a hypocrite and unethical. It is the difference between "I don't believe in killing, but..." and "I did not believe in killing cold-bloodedly, but now I see that I must and for these reasons." In the latter case, I may retain my ethicality, but at considerable cost. My ideal must forever carry with it not only what I would be but what I am and have been. There is no unbridgeable chasm between what I am and what I will be. I build the bridge to my future self, and this is why I oppose capital punishment. I do not want to kill if other options are open to me, and I do not want to ask others in the community to do what may diminish their own ethical ideals.

While I must not kill in obedience to law or principle, I may not, either, refuse to kill in obedience to principle. To remain one-caring, I might have to kill. Consider the case of a woman who kills her sleeping husband. Under most circumstances, the one-caring would judge such an act wrong. It violates the very possibility of caring for the husband. But as she hears how the husband abused his wife and children, about the fear with which the woman lived, about the past efforts to solve the problem legally, the one-caring revises her judgment. The jury finds the woman not guilty by reason of an extenuated self-defense. The one-caring finds her ethical, but under the guidance of a sadly diminished ethical ideal. The woman has behaved in the only way she found open to protect herself and her children and, thus, she has behaved in accord with the current vision of herself as one-caring. But what a horrible vision! She is now one-who-has-killed once and who would not kill again, and never again simply one who would not kill. The test of ultimate blame or blamelessness, under an ethic of caring, lies in how the ethical ideal was diminished. Did the agent choose the degraded vision out of greed, cruelty, or personal interest? Or was she driven to it by unscrupulous others who made caring impossible to sustain?

We see that our own ethicality is not entirely "up to us." Like Winston in *Nineteen Eighty-Four,* we are fragile; we depend upon each other even for our own goodness. This recognition casts some doubt on Immanuel Kant's position:

> It is contradictory to say that I make another person's *perfection* my end and consider myself obliged to promote this. For the *perfection* of another man, as a person, consists precisely of *his own* power to adopt his end in accordance with his own concept of duty; and it is self-contradictory to demand that I do (make it my duty to do) what only the other person himself can do.[18]

In one sense, we agree fully with Kant. We cannot define another's perfection; we, as ones-caring, will not even define the principles by which he should live, nor can we prescribe the particular acts he should perform to meet that perfection. But we must be exquisitely sensitive to that ideal of perfection and, in the absence of a repugnance overwhelming to one-caring, we must as ones-caring act to promote that ideal. As parents and educators, we have perhaps no single greater or higher duty than this.

The duty to enhance the ethical ideal, the commitment to caring, invokes a duty to promote skepticism and noninstitutional affiliation. In a deep sense, no institution or nation can be ethical. It cannot meet the other as one-caring or as one trying to care. It can only capture in general terms what particular ones-caring would like to have done in well-described situations. Laws, manifestos, and proclamations are not, on this account, either empty or useless; but they are limited, and they may support immoral as well as moral actions. Only the individual can be truly called to ethical behavior, and the individual can never give way to encapsulated moral guides, although she may safely accept them in ordinary, untroubled times.

Everything depends, then, upon the will to be good, to remain in caring relation to the other. How may we help ourselves and each other to sustain this will?

5

CONSTRUCTION OF
THE IDEAL

THE NATURE OF THE IDEAL

T HE ETHICAL IDEAL as I have described it springs from two sentiments: the natural sympathy human beings feel for each other and
the longing to maintain, recapture, or enhance our most caring
and tender moments. Both sentiments may be denied, and so commitment is required to establish the ethical ideal. We must recognize our
longing for relatedness and accept it, and we must commit ourselves to
the openness that permits us to receive the other. The effort required to
summon ethical caring is greatly reduced by renewed commitment to the
sentiment from which it springs. For if we commit ourselves to receptivity, natural caring occurs more frequently, and conflicts may thereby be
reduced.

The twin sentiments, commitment and construction of the ideal, fur-
nish a logical framework for the discussion of ethicality. All but the most
deprived (and, perhaps, depraved) of human beings feel the pain and joy
of others, and each of us has access through memory to our own caring
and being cared-for. But I am not claiming that every person who behaves ethically refers to her ethical ideal as the motivation for her acts.
Clearly, there are those who are out of touch with their feelings; the "I
must" has faded to a whisper and finally been stilled. There are those
who locate the source of their ethicality in God, and others who find
theirs in reason, and still others who find theirs in self-interest. I am certainly not denying the existence of these positions nor their power to
motivate some individuals, but I am suggesting that they do not ring true
to many of us and that they seem off the mark or unnecessarily cumber-
some in their search for justification. Indeed, as we have seen, the search

for justification often carries us farther and farther from the heart of morality.

An ethic of caring strives to maintain the caring attitude. That means that the one-caring must be maintained, for she is the immediate source of caring. The one-caring, then, properly pays heed to her own condition. She does not need to hatch out elaborate excuses to give herself rest, or to seek congenial companionship, or to find joy in personal work. Everything depends on the strength and beauty of her ideal, and it is an integral part of her. To go on sacrificing bitterly, grudgingly, is not to be one-caring and, when she finds this happening, she properly but considerately withdraws for repairs. When she is prevented by circumstances from doing this, she may still recognize what is occurring and make heroic efforts to sustain herself as one-caring. Some are stronger than others, but each has her breaking point.

Caring itself and the ethical ideal that strives to maintain and enhance it guide us in moral decisions and conduct. We have considered a host of examples in which the one-caring struggles with moral questions: Ms. Brown, who had to decide whether or not to leave her child for the symphony; the professor who felt both the disappointment of her student and the potential pain of his subjects under deception; the woman who was asked to inform on her Mafia neighbor; the mother refusing abortion for herself but accepting it as a solution for her daughter; even Ceres, struggling in deep despair to go on caring. But perhaps a "standard" example will be useful.

The following problem is posed. You are the leader of a team of ten explorers, and you are all captured by a fierce tribe that places the highest value on ruthless decision making. The chief announces that you will all be killed unless you, the leader, can prove by your ruthlessness that your tribe is worthy to be spared. He requires that you demonstrate your worthiness by picking one of your group and killing him. As usual in such problems, you must accept as given that there is no escape, no possibility of persuasion, etc. Kill one or all will die. What should you do?

Faced with this moral dilemma, many of us would like to begin by attacking the dilemma itself. This is exactly the sort of moral play-thinking to which we object. Our real moral problems do not appear clearly constrained and decked out like so many textbook problems in algebra—problems in which, also, we are deliberately set free from actual conditions. Having registered our objection, however, let us agree, somewhat reluctantly, to play the game. Does everyone understand that it is a game? The perpetual confusion of games with real life tempts us to give up games entirely. But let us see.

Surely, looking into the future, it would be better to find nine explorers alive and returning home than to record all dead. If I simply seize one of my party and kill him swiftly, mercifully (and sorrowfully—will that help?), I can save the rest. Should I not do this? How shall I choose? The oldest? weakest? one with no family? Hmm. My eye falls on A. He is sick and probably will not live through the arduous trip home. He is unmarried. He will not struggle. Perhaps I can avoid his eyes. But as I reach toward him, I feel the life, and fear, and trust, and hope, and whatever else is emanating from him. My long practice in receiving holds me back. What am I doing? What irrationality is upon me? I have actually considered proving, or attempting to prove, that I am precisely the opposite of what I have always posed for myself as an ideal. I have considered demonstrating that I am ruthless, whereas my ethical ideal insists that this is the one thing that I must not be. So to prove to this savage chieftain that I am worthy, I must demonstrate conclusively to myself that I am not. This cannot be the solution.

But is it not ruthless to prefer the maintenance of my ethical ideal over the lives of eight others (and my own)? "Look who is talking about ruthlessness," scoffs one of the players. "You would let all ten die, whereas I would kill only one!" But there it is, I protest: a question of letting die, because I am helpless to prevent the one proposing evil from committing it, or killing, and thereby cooperating with the evil itself. As one-caring, I can only look with contempt upon the choice I have been given. I must argue with this chieftain—show him our vision of worthiness. We must all be willing to die rather than do his bidding. It is the solution of Damon and Pythias, but we are not allowed to anticipate the happy ending of that story. The possibility of persuasion is constrained out of the problematic situation.

So we all die. There are, after all, worse things than death. To see this, all we need to do is add further hypothetical horrors to our initial conditions. Suppose each of the nine had to participate in skinning the tenth alive or drinking his blood Dracula-style or—substitute your own horror. Would the picture of nine returning home after completing their demonstration still be so much more attractive than ten decently dead? We could go on with this grisly game. We could imagine threats that all would die in this horrible fashion unless we performed our atrocity on one. What then? The same, the same. Now we are at the slimy bottom of the human soul. Some of us, overwhelmed with terror and revulsion, will slip in the slime and sink into it. Our only hope is that someone will care, will receive, will extend a hand to help. Without this caring, every depravity conceived and yet to be conceived is a real possibility.

We may note, finally, that a possible solution from the view of Christian love is wrong also. As the leader of the group, I may not sacrifice myself (that is constrained out, also), but one of my party might volunteer to die in order to save the others. This might be an acceptable solution if he could deliver himself straight into the hands of the conceivers of evil, but I still stand between. Standing between, I am not absolved of guilt nor relieved of responsibility. We have been inclined, in the past, to concentrate our moral judgment on the conceiver of evil and to treat his executor more leniently. But in the stander-in-between we have either positive complicity in acquiescence or deterioration under pressure. We forgive one in the latter circumstance, but he may find it hard to forgive himself and he is, ever after, one who did X once and who would not do X again. The commission of X is a permanent constraint upon his ethical ideal.

We see, then, that an ethic of caring is not merely formal, although it presents an initial form. It refers the moral agent to her own memory of caring and her commitment to act in accordance with it—as one might refer to conscience for moral guidance. But to receive guidance from consideration of either caring or conscience there must be content in that caring or conscience.[1] Neither can tell us as a mere form what to do but only how to conduct our deliberation. That is why so much space has been given to the description of caring—to fill it out with concrete examples, because it must be filled out, and it cannot be completely constructed by rule or definition. An ethic of caring, then, seeks something: it seeks to maintain caring itself.

In sustaining and enhancing caring, an ethic of caring conserves many traditional values but not each one for its own sake. Rather, it conserves them as a requirement of caring. The one-caring, generally, finds it wrong to kill, but if the cared-for is objectively hopeless in his misery, her caring may find it better to kill than to abstain from killing. She cannot say to him, "I would like to help you, but I cannot kill," because that would be to put principle above person. Similarly, she can grieve with and understand the Belgian mother who fed her thalidomide-damaged baby a poison formula as she rocked it to a lethal sleep. Was this act *right* or *wrong*? The one-caring does not know, but she can identify which internal conditions in the mother might make it right and which might make it wrong. While traditional values are often conserved, then, the ultimate locus of right and wrong is shifted to an internal examination of predecision considerations and acts. We can often make judgments from the outside, but there are disturbing and crucial situations in which we cannot. We must be willing to say: I do not know whether that was right or wrong—tell me more, give me a more complete picture.

An ethic of caring has its source in natural human caring, and it seeks the maintenance and enhancement of that caring. Its conservation of traditional values is a sign that it is the wellspring of moral values and that moral deliberation may safely be referred to it. But it is not a life-denying ethic. Even though its source and focus are the other, it is not a dour, dutiful, or cowardly ethic. It finds joy as well as obligation in its relation to the other. Unlike Nietzsche's ethic, it does not despise pity; it is not contemptuous. In its high-spiritedness—but not in what it seeks—it is, however, rather like Nietzsche's "noble type": "In the foreground there is the feeling of fullness, of power that seeks to overflow, the happiness of high tension, the consciousness of wealth that would give and bestow."[2] In its enactment, in its application, it is energetic, resilient, proud—many options are easily rejected as beneath its vision and demands. But it returns to humility in its recognition of dependence, for if it is energetic, it is also energized by the reciprocal gifts of the cared-for; if things are beneath it and remain beneath it, conditions have helped to maintain its lofty position. It is a proud ethic with a humble and wary heart.

CONSTRAINTS AND ATTAINABILITY

Now we want to ask why the ethical ideal must drag about—like Marley's ghost with its chain of coin boxes and keys—all of the past deeds of its moral agent. It must do this to avoid self-deception and to remain in contact with what is. Since the locus of ultimate decisions concerning true-false and right-wrong is in the internal dialogue of the one-caring, self-deception has the potential to destroy the ethical ideal. The one-caring, then, must look clearly and receptively on what is there-in-herself. This does not mean that she must spend a great deal of time self-indulgently "getting to know" herself before reaching out to others. Rather, she reflects on what is inside as she relates to others. Reflection sometimes produces a revelation. The one-caring sees herself as having been jealous, or small-minded, or greedy. She sees this; she does not approve it, but she accepts it. So this dwells in me also, she acknowledges. She does not flagellate herself with these failings and clutch them to her bosom in some ecstasy of guilt, but she notes them with raised eyebrow and heightened wariness. This is here-in-me, and I must keep an eye on it as on a predisposition to backache or heart disease.

Construction and acceptance of the constrained ideal keep the one-caring close to the concrete. As she is tempted to soar into clouds of abstraction—where everything but gross contradiction can be set right— she is reminded by the weight of her Marley's chain of who is speaking. It is she, this real creature with flawed ideal. How lovely she would be without the flaws! But this is nonsensical yearning. The flaws are earned and permanent. The task now is to confine them and stem their increase. Acceptance of the constrained ideal is one element in the requirement to connect the descriptive and prescriptive parts of the ethic. One must not push the moral agent into artificial solutions contrived in a parallel world of abstraction.

Like Nietzsche's new philosopher, we are of "yesterday and tomorrow." From our yesterdays we accept the earned constraints upon our ideal. Toward our tomorrows we fashion what may be attained. The requirement of attainability is as important as that of constraint. Indeed, it is a forward-looking set of constraints. It is not necessary that I, a concrete moral agent, actually attain my ideal—surely, I shall fail repeatedly—but the ideal itself must be attainable in the actual world. It must be possible for a finite human being to attain it, and we should be able to describe the attainment. The attainment must be actually possible; that is, if I am faithful and energetic and fortunate, I should be able to attain it in my actual relations with actual persons. I should not be diverted into abstraction and the endless solution of hypothetical problems.

Ms. A recounts an experience she had as a graduate student. The time was the late sixties, a time of antiwar sentiment and strong feeling for civil rights at home. A problem concerning the rights and education of blacks arose, and the only black student in class spoke eloquently of the prevailing injustice and inhumanity against blacks, of his growing despair. He spoke of "going to the barricade." Ms. A was nearly moved to tears. He was clearly right in condemning the treatment of his people and in demanding something better. But the barricade, guns, violence—

must it come to this? Perhaps. But if it does, what then: what would I do? Ms. A asked. She saw clearly what she would do, would really do. I could not, she said, ever—not ever—oppose my bigoted old father or my hysterical Aunt Phoebe with physical violence. I do not agree with either. Aunt Phoebe! Imagine a person in this day who would actually say (and demonstrate her statement by fainting at the thought) "Ah would just die if a niggah touched me!" Oh, she is wrong, and my father is wrong. But there are years of personal kindness. They must count for something, must they not? My father and the delight in his eyes as he shared *my* delight with a new bicycle; Aunt Phoebe staying up half the night to re-fashion a prom dress for me; the chocolate cakes for parties; the cold cloths and baking soda pastes for measles. Would I shoot them? Ever? No. You see, if it came to the barricades, and I had to be on this side or that, I would stand beside my dad and Aunt Phoebe. Oh, I would curse them, and try to undo it, and try to bring peace, but I would fight to pro-tect them. I know I could not fight—really fight on the other side. And what now of the black man, Jim, who is, after all, "right"? If my sights picked him out, says Ms. A, I would note that it was Jim and pass on to some other target.

Is this thinking "deplorable"? Does it ring untrue? Or is it part of Ms. A's inexorable insistence on the filling out of situations, part of her insistence on inserting herself—her real, finite, flawed self—in the moral situation? Everything must be done, then, to prevent "going to the barri-cades," for if that occurs, diminution of the ideal is inevitable. Tragedy is induced by clinging to the unattainable, by believing it with our heads while knowing otherwise in our hearts.

But, a philosopher may argue: diminution has already occurred, and dramatically! Ms. A acknowledges that she would discard principle in favor of two bigoted persons. Is this not diminution par excellence? To the one-caring, this is not diminution but agonized fulfillment. Her atten-tion to what is colors all her hopes for what might be. It does not decide such matters; one can surmount anything, but it is unlikely. It colors everything. It guides her toward deliberation, compromise, solicitation, even retreat. But always, always she warns the other: *Touch not these who are my beloved.* This is reality, and an ethic of caring faces it clear-eyed. The one-caring sees where diminution occurs; in this case, it occurs if she makes no effort at prevention, and it occurs, inevitably, if violence is demanded. She never claims to place principle above persons.

But, persists the philosopher, would you really call Ms. A's decison ethical? Suppose a loved one decides to establish an Auschwitz: Would Ms. A support him out of memory for past kindness? *Not if she is ethical as one-caring.* But how can we block this revolting possibility? What if the cared-for turns rotten—must be judged evil—in light of the ethic of caring? Let us consider. It is likely that, in Ms. A's description of Jim, her father, and Aunt Phoebe, she anticipated a typical chain of events: the gradual deterioration of relations, the estrangement of Jim, mistakes and atrocities on both sides. And recall that the decision to move "to the barricade" was Jim's. She grieves at all this and must work toward its prevention, but she will neither initiate violence nor leave her inner circle unprotected.

But you have not answered the basic objection, insists the philosopher. Suppose members of her inner circle initiate the violence, and innocent others need protection. Will she act against these representatives of her inner circle? If they are very close to her—her own children, say—she may respond by saying: *They wouldn't do such a thing!* Is this another example of Ms. A's hopeless inability to face the constraints of the problem and reason from principle to conclusion? I do not think so. I believe she is trying to tell us that sensitive, well-informed relations are established in her inner circle, and that having been part of a caring relation over years, it is unlikely that they would suddenly show themselves as violent and uncaring. So her answer is not frivolous.

But suppose they do initiate violence. Again, chances are that Ms. A would have seen this coming. She would be aware of the deterioration in her loved-ones. Striving to maintain caring, she would already be somewhat alienated from them. They might even have become once-cared-fors. She would protect Jim in whatever way would require the least physical harm to her once-cared-fors.

But suppose it was sudden and unexpected. The ones now loved and cared-for commit this unspeakable act of violence or intend to do it. All right, says Ms. A, you have pushed me far enough. I will not collaborate with evil wherever it occurs. I would defend Jim against this violation of caring, but I tell you again, my cared-fors would not do this.

Does this inversion of the circles mean that the one-caring does, after all, place principle above specific persons? I do not think that conclusion is justified. When the one-caring is in a conflict of caring because two of her cared-fors are warring, she must act to preserve and to protect both if she can. Her attention must, therefore, go first to the one threatened. The commitment to receive the other, to preserve the possibility of caring, is unshakable. Ms. A's commitment to caring is clear but, even more importantly, her answers reveal the fundamental strength of caring. It is not simply a matter of principle that compels us to defend one threatened or abused, to aid one who cries out to us for help, or to respond to one who addresses us. It is an attitude that pervades life and establishes the human bonds upon which we depend as upon a faith. Ms. A's insistence that her loved ones "would not do such a thing" is a manifestation of trust, and that trust is grounded in relation. It is not a blind trust, nor a tribal faith, nor an evaluation of the sort that produces, "My country right or wrong!" It is a grounded claim—one backed by the evidence of years lived in relation. Such a claim, evidentially made, requires that the claimant know those about whom she is speaking. It requires that caring has been maintained and completed in the others.

We cannot love everyone. We cannot even care for everyone, and we do not need to love in order to care for. I have brushed aside "caring about" and, I believe, properly so. It is too easy. I can "care about" the starving children of Cambodia, send five dollars to hunger relief, and feel somewhat satisfied. I do not even know if my money went for food, or guns, or a new Cadillac for some politician. This is a poor second-cousin to caring. "Caring about" always involves a certain benign neglect. One is attentive just so far. One assents with just so much enthusiasm. One acknowledges. One affirms. One contributes five dollars and goes on to other things.

I am not condemning "caring about." We—all of us—give here and there and hope that others who care for will be enabled by our caring about. One might say that we should, occasionally, care about, but we should not suppose that in doing so we are caring for. Caring requires engrossment, commitment, displacement of motivation. The requirement that an ideal be attainable is attentive to this difference. It counsels that we construct an attainable ideal so that we will plan ahead and focus our efforts on what can in fact be done. If by "I love everyone" I mean that I would not without just cause harm anyone, that is acceptable. It is not trivial, for there are those who would harm others for their own worldly gain. But it is wildly ambiguous. If that is all I mean when I say that I love my child, or my husband, or my student, then each of these has, I think, been cheated.

So the one-caring acknowledges her finitude with both sadness and relief. She cannot do everything. She must meet the proximate other as one-caring. What else must she do? Is there room for one great cause?

For more than one? Is one intellectual passion permitted? And, who is the proximate other?

The proximate other. Let's concentrate for now on him, for his treatment is integral to the attainable ideal. Who or what is he? He is the one who addresses me, under whose gaze I fall. He is the stray cat at the back door, Carl Tiflin's Mr. Gitano, the hired man in Frost's "The Death of the Hired Man," my student, my colleague, my stranger at the door selling his religion. He is also the one who must be brought into proximity if I would transform my caring about into caring for. If I care about students who are having difficulty with mathematics, I must do two things: I must make the problem my own, receive it intellectually, immerse myself in it; I must also bring the student having difficulty into proximity, receive such students personally. These two facets of my concentration will inform each other, but the second will impose special problems on me. For this second area of concentration is a person. I cannot bring him into proximity merely for the sake of the problem. He is, in that regard, a case study, but he is necessarily more than that. Brought into proximity, so that his gaze falls upon me, he is my proximate other and must be met as cared-for by me, one-caring.

If we look ahead to our discussion of teaching, we see that teaching involves a meeting of one-caring and cared-for. I can lecture to hundreds, and this is neither inconsequential nor unimportant, but this is not teaching. To teach involves a giving of self and a receiving of other. I can receive, as one-caring, just so many, and I cannot reveal myself adequately through verbal symbols. I must explain, question, doubt, explore, revise, discover, err, and correct, but I must also receive, reflect, and act. Further, and especially, as one-caring I have a special obligation to maintain and enhance the ethical ideal of the cared-for. To do this, I need to know what it is, and I need to share mine. We must together consider what is right-in-this-case. No constraint on the way teaching is can remove the constraint on me as one-caring.

DIMINISHED ETHICAL CAPACITY

We spoke in an earlier chapter about a woman who killed her abusive husband as he slept. I referred then to that act as "ethical" but under the guidance of a diminished ethical ideal. Since her husband was sleeping when he was killed, the woman could not claim self-defense as that claim is usually accepted (although the jury used a modified definition of "self-defense" in its acquittal). Further, the act was not committed impulsively, and it seems clear that she knew what she was doing; that is, she understood the legal status and implications of the act. Her act seems to be properly labeled murder. Can murder be ethical?

Under the guidance of an ethic of caring, ethicality is determined in part by the degree of receptivity one has effectively exercised. This means that one must make an effort to receive the others involved in a situation, of course, but it also means that we must reflect upon that reception. There are times when we know upon reflection that we failed to receive the other adequately. Martin Buber describes such an incident in his own life—a time when a young man came to him ostensibly to talk about other things but actually contemplating suicide.[3] The young man did commit suicide, and Buber faulted himself not for failing to prevent it—he might not have been able to do this in any case—but for a failure in receptivity. He did not receive what was plainly there. All of us have had experiences of this type in which, afterward, we know that we should have sensed what the other was feeling. The cared-for should have "filled the firmament" but did not. We were, perhaps, preoccupied or in an assimilative mode, hearing and sensing selectively.

Now in the case we are considering, the woman was receiving an increasing load of pain and fear from her children. Possibly she could see their ethical ideals diminishing under the continual abuse they suffered. There was apparently no way to reduce the husband's malice and cruelty through receiving him. (Only she can know what effort was made here. Let us suppose that nothing we can see contradicts her claim.) She was no match for him physically and could not, without increased risk to the physical safety of her children, engage him in a "fair fight" (whatever that is). She had tried repeatedly and unsuccessfully to enlist lawful relief of her suffering. These efforts, which were a matter of record, made it possible for the jury to acquit her legally. But, morally, only she can know how adequately she received and responded to the others in the situation. Assuming that her receptivity was adequate and that her motivational displacement was directed toward the needs of her children, she acted as one-caring but under a diminished ideal or capacity for ethical caring.

Feeling, thinking, and behaving as one-caring mark ethical behavior; but when caring must retreat to an inner circle, confine itself, and consciously exclude particular persons or groups, the ideal is diminished, that is, it is quantitatively reduced. When this must be done to maintain the quality of the ideal for remaining cared-fors, it is not without its effects on the one-caring. She has had to say to one whom she would have received as one-caring, "I don't care anymore!" What justifies her in doing this? The one no longer cared-for cannot simply be cut out in preference for others in the inner circle. As leader of the explorers, the one-caring could not simply choose one of her party at random and slay him to preserve the others. She must meet the other as one-caring until he is, intentionally, a positive threat to her physical or ethical self. Then, and only then, she must withdraw. First, she withdraws. Like Ceres, in great pain and baffled rejection, she ceases to be one-caring. If the one no longer cared-for violates her withdrawal, increases his threat, and persists in his malicious approach, she is justified in acting to prevent further abuse. Acting to prevent further abuse is, of course, guided by the ethic of caring. We are obviously not justified in shooting an obnoxiously persistent salesperson. The one-caring must preserve the possibility of future caring if she can. If she herself can no longer care for the proximate other, she must not interfere with his caring-for or being cared-for by others. If she is convinced that he is a real threat to all those-caring in the community, she must say so but in a way that preserves the possibility until that alternative is no longer available to her.

The perceived lack of alternative induces minimal ethical functioning under the diminished ideal. The ethical agent accepts responsibility; it is she who is, personally, committed to caring. Built on perceived autonomy cooperating with one form of natural feeling, her ethic treasures both the natural feeling that it seeks to preserve and the autonomy by which it is embraced. When the one-caring is driven to the point where she perceives only one solution, and that in opposition to the enhanced ideal, she is badly shaken and, in extreme cases, broken. For while she must still say, "It is I performing this act," it is clearly not the "I" she would have chosen. There can be no greater evil, then, than this: that the moral autonomy of the one-caring be so shattered that she acts against her own commitment to care.

But this evil is not An Evil sustained by cosmic forces and just waiting to trap the weak and unwary. It is created by individual human beings making conscious choices. When one intentionally rejects the impulse to care and deliberately turns her back on the ethical, she is evil, and this evil cannot be redeemed. Sartre also says that "evil cannot be redeemed," and I think he is pointing to the same thing—that evil is chosen by the evil one as good is chosen by the good. One cannot be rescued from evil as from a burning house; one must choose its opposite. Nor can evil be redeemed with compensation; it can only be terminated, rejected un-equivocally. Evil is not likely, either, to be weakened or reversed by the submission of its victim. Again we see that an ethic of caring is a proud ethic. It does not turn the other cheek in meek submission. It seeks to pre-vent a second blow. It does not seek to "heap coals of fire upon the head" of the transgressor nor to prove its own superiority in accepting evil while giving good. It seeks to preserve and enhance caring. As a con-sequence, the one caring considers always the possibility that the one-appearing-to-do-evil is actually in a deteriorated state, that he is acting under intolerable pressure or in error. She retains a responsibility, then, to relieve the pressure and to inform the error; indeed, she remains responsible for the actualization of the other's ethical ideal. How often are we lost because we do not know until too late that we are dealing with evil. This is an unavoidable danger of acting under the guidance of an ethic of caring.

But most of us are not evil, and many of us commit wrongs supposing we are doing right. Clearly, we can support each other or undermine each other in our ethical quest. Ridicule, scorn, sarcasm, and attribution of evil motives all tend to undermine the ethical ideal. The child who is told not to stuff himself with goodies because he will "get fat" may associate fatness with disobedience and general wickedness. He may, then, try out his hypothesized association by acting cruelly toward a fat child. If no one talks to him about his mistake and if others join and support him in his cruelty, he is led to diminish his own ethical ideal. We may, then, unwittingly contribute to the diminution of another's ethical ideal, and we must consider what we are inducing by way of ethical effects when we admonish children against fatness, pimples, tooth decay and other ailments.

Clearly, we may contribute as individuals to the diminution of an-other's ethical ideal. But institutions may also contribute to this diminu-tion. The military is an organization that seems on formal criteria to have the capacity to reduce the ethical ideal. The requirement of obedience can be understood as both necessary for military goals and even life-preserv-ing for individuals in battle situations, but it tends to reduce individual responsibility and the reflection necessary for one-caring to make her decisions. One is at the mercy of an "ethical" elite: if they are ethical, the one obeying is judged "ethical" by a sort of ethical transitivity. But this is not ethicality; it is merely obedience. To take another's life in direct defense of my own preserves me physically and as one-potentially-caring;

but to take another's life because we cannot leave informants behind, or because we must destroy a military target regardless of who may be haplessly near it, leaves me ethically destroyed. I become the instrument of some other, alien force that would have me destroy instead of reaching out receptively to the other. It may be that some wars must be fought, but none can be fought ethically. We are all, and necessarily, ethically diminished by war.

Unfortunately, many organizations tend to diminish the ethical ideal. As we noted earlier, organizations cannot be ethical. They demand loyalty, insist upon the affirmation of certain beliefs, and separate members from nonmembers on principle. Even religious organizations often tend to diminish the ethical ideal. They take a special responsibility for the moral education of their members and, especially, that of the young. Often they do effectively immunize the young against certain conventional immoralities (many of which are not immoral for one-caring), but they seem to be notoriously ineffective in preventing the great, fatal ills. Indeed, it must be acknowledged that they often contribute to these great ills. Cruelty and harsh judgment are not strangers to religion. Further, the frequent insistence on obedience to rules and adherence to ritual contributes to the erosion of genuine caring. One is led to seek self-preservation in the form of salvation. Even the precious other—he who defines me in human relation—becomes an instrument of my salvation. If the church wills it, I behave benevolently toward him and win stars in my crown; if the church wills it, I destroy him and, again, find my reward in paradise. Only if the church allows and promotes unlimited freedom of caring can it be an instrument of ethicality. Then it becomes a collection of persons who share an attitude and a commitment but not necessarily a set of beliefs.

Similar comments may be made about organizations such as unions, political parties, fraternities, and various societies. They provide a meeting place, a coming together, but they also establish the lines along which the ethical ideal may fade off asymptotically. Beyond this, they command, you will not go. But if I am to grow under the guidance of an ethic of caring, I must be free to proceed with the construction of the ideal. I cannot simply accept what must be added to it or deleted from it. I, defined in caring relations, am not alone in my ethical quest and I must remain open to guidance and correction, but I am and remain responsible. I cannot seek ethical shelter in the arms of an institution and its lofty principles.

Everyday life is replete with customs that may undermine or warp the ethical ideal. The notion of a "fair fight" is indicative of one such custom, and competitive games may well be another. There may even be distinctively masculine and feminine attitudes toward fair fights and competitive games.

Ms. A offers an anecdote: I like "Westerns." Most of all, I guess, I like the clear-cut distinction between good and bad that usually typifies such films. But I am always amazed by barroom brawls. There they are, both good guys and bad guys, tumbling about the floor pummeling one another. They knock one another through stair railings, swinging doors, and windows indiscriminately. They enjoy it. I always chuckle and say, "Well, it's those male hormones." If women are present, they stand aside aghast. In the rare cases where they become involved, it is even more rarely for fun and almost always to save some loved man from injury.

What Ms. A comments on is of some importance. Is it possible that women see their own ferocity so clearly that they cannot imagine encouraging it by simulation? After all, I would not fight unless I absolutely had to; I would meet the other as one-caring. But if I had to, the stakes would be so high that I could not possibly consider a "fair fight." The concept would be irrelevant. One worries about competitive games of all sorts. Are they harmless sublimations of aggressive instincts and even admirable training for competent performances of various kinds? Or are they simulations, supports for the wildly fantastic notion that life itself can be conducted as a "fair fight"? One recalls the saying about the playing fields of Eton.

Many women avoid competitive games. Is this a matter purely of socialization? Is it a matter of physical or mental infirmity? or submissiveness? Or is it, rather, that women see clearly the loss of playfulness in such games? What starts out as inventive, capricious, and fanciful often becomes rule-bound, skillful, and deadly serious. The seriousness concerns Ms. A most of all, for it underscores her fear that it is a simulation, that her male companion may see life this way, too. She tries. Ms. A plays football with her family, but she cheats. She hugs and tickles her opponents. She picks up dropped balls and makes touchdowns, and sometimes she runs from the field and claims that her side has won and that's that. If she plays at all, she insists on remaining playful.

Are women noncompetitive? What is it in us, or in me? Well, I am not sure. There are so many things other than human beings to compete with, to fight: There are snails in my garden, dust-kittens on the floor, concepts for my students to master, personal problems for my children to struggle with, tomatoes that will rot if I do not can them, ten pounds that I must be rid of, seedlings that must be defended against damping-off, birds to be saved from cats. There are, in short, so many tasks, so many natural opponents, that one finds no reason for creating opponents in the world of human beings. Still, I am not innocent. I enjoy the spectacle.

In the coming months and years, women will have to decide whether to demand entrance into the full world of competitive sports or to suggest a deemphasis of such activity. Most signs suggest that we will do the former. In an age concerned with equity and justice—and far less concerned with relatedness and cooperation—we shall almost surely find it easier to join men in their traditional ways than to induce them to join us. Further, we feel justified in seeking equity but, quite naturally, we are fearful and unsure when we dare to question the institutions and customs from which we have been excluded. Shall we insist that we can march, obey, and kill as well as our brothers and should, therefore, hold equal places in the military? Should we show that we care so little for our bodies that we, too, shall start knocking each other senseless in violent "sports"?

Similar decisions will have to be made as we consider penetrating other male institutions. Should we, for example, demand the right to don cere-monial robes and scatter ritual blessings on our peers, or should we gently and firmly insist that our brothers yield to the real and special blessings of human tenderness and caring? Should we maintain—by join-ing in full measure—institutions that separate the saved from the pagan, the believer from the infidel, the circumcised from the uncircumcised, man from woman, as though the first set were privileged of God and the second scorned? This seems the sort of madness we see again and again as the oppressed, in wide-eyed naivete, seeing only their oppression, join in energetically and loyally to become one with the oppressor. It may be nothing less than the ethical ideal of caring that is at stake in our deci-sions.

We have been looking at diminished ethical capacity, how it is freely chosen in evil, how it is resorted to under intolerable external pressure, and how it is induced by our institutions and customs. We do not con-demn those in concentration camps who steal from each other; we find them and their plight tragic. We do not find Orwell's Winston evil; we find him, too, pathetic—tragic. Mustering all our ethical compassion, we may even understand why Carl Tiflin could "not afford" to find Mr. Gitano. But where were the rest of us, real and fictional, while all this was happening? How did we "educate" each other for this? What did we contribute to the diminution? After all, if you become weary of caring for cantankerous old X, I may be able to help simply by caring more about you. The eternal question is: Will I?

NURTURING THE IDEAL

In our discussion of caring, we have put great emphasis on the role of the cared-for. Even the infant plays a part as he smiles and gurgles at his mother. We have not divided human beings into "persons" and those who have not yet achieved (or never will achieve) that status. Our regard for beings is not derived from a concept of "respect for persons"; rather, it furnishes the foundation for such views. There are, strictly speaking, no natural rights—only rights we confer upon each other out of natural inclination and commitment.

The child has a special capacity for love. Long before the capacity for sustained reasoning develops, there is the capability of tenderness, of feeling, and reciprocation. Some today even claim that the child is capable of altruism.[4] This might surprise us if we found something unnatural in altruism. But the child, I think, is responding to natural inclination, and that inclination is encouraged by the caring that nourishes him. The early years of a child's life are rather like the early chapters of this book, in that they establish the host of concrete situations, the memories, and the ground against which things are later thought through. So far as is possible, the words and acts of those caring must confirm that they do care, for when the message is ambiguous, the child has to entertain the thought that either he is not cared-for or it is permissible to hurt those we care for. So he looks for reasons and tries things out. Perhaps he even wonders whether others are hurt by the kinds of things that hurt him.

Our adult warnings to children are laced with unintended double messages: *You mustn't run about with scissors because you'll poke your eyes out.* When a child breaks something overreaching, *That wasn't very smart, was it? Quit stuffing yourself—you'll be fat as a pig! Lay off the candy—your teeth will rot! Be careful or you'll hurt yourself. Study or you'll fail your test.* Perhaps we do not spend enough time talking about undeserved ill fortune and naturally limited abilities. Our children may sometimes be cruel, then, because they are using faulty heuristics—positing cause and effect where these do not apply.

The danger of rules is twofold. Not only may the child draw faulty connections between observed consequences and posited faults but his ethical ideal may be constructed as though it were the rule book for some elaborate game. The one-caring wants her child to refer his ethical dilemmas to the ethical ideal of caring, and she must show him how to do this. She talks with him about feelings—his own, hers, and those of others. She invites his observations because she is concerned about his developing receptive capacities. Most important of all, she listens to him, and both her listening and her advice are perceptive and creative rather than judgmental. Listening, that supremely important form of receiving, is essential. One tuned to it, interested in it, committed to it, sees tragic examples of its failure everywhere. One respects both the candor and beauty of C. S. Lewis's account of his conversion to Christianity, but one cannot help but wonder whether it would have been the fulfillment of such intense longing if he had not lost his mother so early and if his father had been able to listen. Over and over he describes his father's inability: "His intense desire for my total confidence coexisted with an inability to listen (in any strict sense) to what I said. He could never empty, or silence, his own mind to make room for an alien thought."[5]

The one-caring is first and foremost committed to receiving. Her concern for the ethical ideal of the cared-for involves the elements we have discussed in concrete form. Stories about his own infancy and early childhood contribute to the memories of tenderness he will draw upon repeatedly. Discussions about what was done, what might have been done, and why we might choose to act differently in the future are engaged openly. Emphasis is always on the maintenance of caring, on how to be better—just some, realistically better—than we are.

The ones-caring for a child need not be perfect nor unfailingly patient and gentle. Indeed, it is assumed we cannot be. The child is resilient, and it is the dominant tone that counts most. If my child carelessly spills hot tea in my lap, I may shout, "You idiot!" or "Clumsy, stupid...." These are words that hurt, but I can explain myself if this happens. I can tell him that such outbursts are not assessments but cries of pain, anger, or frustration. They represent my special weakness under pressure. Treated this way, my child may admit that it is his special weakness to be clumsy and, thus, we each learn a little more about the challenging possibility of receiving the other.

What I have been emphasizing so far is the central importance of dialogue in nurturing the ethical ideal. Training for receptivity involves sharing and reflecting aloud. It involves the kind of close contact that makes personal history valuable, and this will be important when we explore the possibility of caring in schools. A relationship is required. One must be able to say, "Remember when...?" and elicit a response to that which does not need detailed explication.

Practice is also required. No part of the self-image is best constructed as pure fantasy. Imagining oneself as a good mathematics student may be a facilitative move if it is accompanied by the acquisition of real skills and time spent in their practice. Similarly, the child in the process of building an ethical ideal needs practice in caring. Simply talking about or writing about caring is a poor substitute for actual caring. Practice in caring is a form of apprenticeship. We mentioned in an earlier chapter Urie Bronfenbrenner's recommendation that the child be allowed to work toward increasing competence in a variety of tasks in cooperation with an interested adult. In this manner, the child has a competent model to follow, he engages in practice, and he is allowed to assume increasing responsibility. Responsibility is not simply a matter of accountability; that is, it involves much more than simply answering for a prescribed result. Consider, for example, the matter of pets. Many parents acquire pets for their children in the belief that "caring for" a pet will increase their children's sense of responsibility. By "responsibility," here, they mean that their children will learn to perform specific tasks on schedule, preferably "without being told." But if the parent sees the pet as a nuisance—something by which she makes a sacrifice for her child—the child is sure to feel this. How can the cared-for tenderly receive this being that is a nuisance and, perhaps, an increasingly onerous duty? The child is thus, once again, the receiver of a double message; he is not an apprentice in caring. If, however, the parent feels some affection for the pet, she willingly spends time with it, touches it gently, talks to it, plays with it. Even if she becomes exasperated at times by puddles on the floor, tattered draperies, and chewed slippers (and, also, by her child's forgetfulness in feeding the creature), the dominant tone is one of affection, of caring. In this environment, parent and child enjoy the pet, and, through it, each other. What is aimed at is not duty—not accountability—but the renewed possibility of taking pleasure in caring and in each other.

I have not used the term "practice" lightly. There is a dimension of competence in caring.[6] I have not dwelt on it in previous chapters, because it is, theoretically, derivative. My engrossment and motivational displacement push me to acquire skills in caretaking. But it is important to recognize that there *are* skills. Girls often quite naturally learn these skills by close and continuing apprenticeship to their mothers; boys often fail to learn them because they are diverted to more impersonal and abstract worlds.[7] Thus, although the pursuit and acquisition of skills in caring are theoretically derivative, they are instrumental to its actualization. One must have encounters, legitimate opportunities to care, in order to go on caring effectively.

Dialogue and practice are essential in nurturing the ethical ideal. Another crucial matter is the respect for and attribution of motive. The cared-for, when he is old enough to engage in sustained reasoning, has a special obligation to attribute caring motives to the one-supposed-caring. Understanding this, the one-caring is scrupulous in the way she models her attributions and assessments. She does not look for ulterior motives, although she knows they may upon occasion be present. Rather, she always approaches the other as though the other has a respectable motive. Indeed, the motive of the other has an a priori respectability that may be denied only with justification—if it is to be discredited at all. Always, the one-caring moves toward the other's needs and projects; she withdraws when her ethical ideal compels her to do so. She operates very much as the skillful teacher does. The skillful, generous teacher receives ordinary questions and, through her sensitive reception and faithful interpretation, confers special significance and dignity on them. Similarly, the one-caring interprets the words and acts of the cared-for in the best possible light. Often the cared-for responds in delight and wonder: That is what I mean! That is what I want. The shadowy, always threatening, world of the niggardly and mean falls away as belonging to someone else. It does not belong to him. Is it not evident? This other sees that his vision is far lovelier than that.

Nothing is more important in nurturing the ethical ideal than attribution and explication of the best possible motive. The one-caring holds out to the child a vision of this lovely self actualized or nearly actualized. Thus the child is led to explore his ethical self with wonder and appreciation. He does not have to reject and castigate himself, but he is encouraged to move toward an ideal that is, in an important sense, already real in the eyes of a significant other. It is vital that the one-caring not create a fantasy. She must see things—acts, words, consequences—as they are; she must not be a fool. But seeing all this, she reached out with the assurance that this—this-which-was-a-mistake—might still have occurred with a decent motive. *I can see what you were trying to do,* she says, or *what you were feeling,* or *how this could have happened.* Her function is always to raise the appraisal, never to lower it. Thus, she both accepts and confirms the child.

When the teacher confronts a child cheating, she may say, *I know you want to do well,* or *I know you want to help your friend,* but she then explains how difficult it is for her to work from a faulty diagnosis. She may, depending upon how she feels about competition in learning, talk also about fairness and caring for other classmates. But she does not attribute grubby motives to the child. She explains why he, who wants to do well and right, should not do this particular thing. She is not enforcing a rule but nurturing an ideal. There is always the possibility in this open and good-seeking dialogue that the one-caring will alter her own views and procedures. She is not by status or knowledge a priori right; she is just one-caring—who wants to do what is right and remains willing to explore the possibilities.

Dialogue, practice, attribution of the best possible motive: all these are essential in nurturing the ethical ideal. But the ethical ideal does not exist in isolation from the whole self and a larger self-image. It is sustained by others-caring, and by cared-fors, and by its own past success. It is also sustained by a reservoir of strength in the general self-image. It has recourse in time of trouble and abandonment.

MAINTAINING THE IDEAL

Now we wish to give attention to ways in which the moral agent can maintain her ethical ideal from within. This involves building a reservoir of sustenance from activity in the nonhuman world. (It involves, also, turning away from present and difficult cared-fors toward others who will act as ones-caring, but we have already discussed this possibility.)

Sustenance may come from a variety of sources, of course, but let us consider some of the obvious and, perhaps on that account, most neglected. An appreciation and affirmation of repetition seem likely candidates. Affirmation of life entails affirmation of repetition. The repetition to which I refer is not Nietzsche's eternal cosmic recurrence nor Kierkegaard's endless, repetitive affirmation of faith. It is just the repetition of feelings and events in ordinary life. The body becomes repeatedly hungry; it requires food. The sexual appetite persists and recurs; it requires satisfaction. Hair and fingernails grow; they must be trimmed.

Dust accumulates; it must be displaced. The seasons change predictably; to each special functions are assigned. There are sleeping, walking, breathing, and heartbeat. For women there is the regularity of the lunar cycle—repetition and promise, over and over. Daily we have meals and dishes; cleaning and soiling; growing and cutting; making and using and making again; sallying forth and returning home. Each of these may be decried or celebrated.

The one-caring chooses to celebrate. Just as the Jew, or Christian, or Moslem chooses to celebrate that which is integral to his religion—that which represents its source—so the one-caring chooses to celebrate the ordinary, human-animal life that is the source of her ethicality and joy. She may find delight in her garden. As I write this, a hummingbird has come to work the geraniums and hibiscus outside my window. He is not an object of knowledge for me, although he might be. He has an iridescent purple-black band around his neck, and I could identify him if I wished. But I am content with delighting in him and knowing what pleases him. The red blossoms are especially for him. Similarly, the backyard contains borage, sage, thyme, lemon balm, and other mints planted especially for the bees. As I work among them, they hum and I hum. I know that it is probably a matter of good fortune, but I have never been stung, and I—if not they—experience a sort of comradeship. Here, too, there are cycles: western rains accompanied by weeds and wildflowers, followed by the dry season that brings neatness and the special effort of artificial watering. Always there is something emerging, something maturing, something fading, and something passing away.

One may celebrate meals and food. It can be a sort of ceremony to start the water boiling before picking the corn, to offer homemade chicken soup to an ailing family member, to make chocolates at Christmas in one's own garage (coolness is needed), to sit down together day after day to share both food and thoughts. This most repetitious of all communal events—eating—may be either a festival or a matter of survival. Always, alongside and leading upward from repetition, there is something new: how to cook cardoons, what acidulated water is, how and what a rose geranium leaf contributes to a white cake. Thus repetition is not mere repetition, leading to boredom and disgust, but it represents opportunities to learn, to share, and to celebrate.

"Doing a Descartes" in the morning is another delightful bit of repetition. You may recall that Descartes was rather sickly as a child and was allowed to remain abed mornings by a wise headmaster. Here, Descartes said, he did much of his best and freshest thinking. So we, too, may awaken early and feel cheated of sleep or prop ourselves up in delight to enjoy thinking on things. Over and over the sleeplessness may occur; over and over, frustration, or resignation, or delight in a new day may direct one's thoughts. Bathing may be a routine or a luxury. The quiet, the hot steaminess, the relaxation of grateful limbs. The blessed privacy. One may daydream or talk to oneself; or read until one's fingers wrinkle, or sing "The Toreador Song," or whatever one pleases. There is renewal. One can read favorite books and poems repeatedly, or go to see old films again and again. There is the joy of familiarity, of anticipation of lines and the amazement of discovery: Here is something newly discovered that was always there!

The one-caring, then, is not bored with ordinary life. As the Christian-Catholic finds new truth and strength in repeated celebrations of the mass, so the one-caring finds new delight in breakfast, in welcoming home her wanderers, in feeding the cat who purrs against her ankle, in noticing the twilight. She does not ask, "Is this all there is?," but wishes in hearty affirmation that what-is might go on and on.

Now one may ask just how the celebration of everyday life contributes to the maintenance of the ethical ideal. First, of course, as we have seen, such celebration turns the one-caring in wonder and appreciation to the source of her ethicality. It is for the most part in ordinary situations that we meet the others for whom we shall care and who care for us. Second, celebration of ordinary life requires and is likely to enhance receptivity. The magic of daily life may be missed by one who constantly seeks adventure and "something new." Celebration of daily experience provides opportunities for engrossment, for complete involvement in living. Third, it provides practice in caretaking skills; one becomes more and more competent in matters of daily life. Finally, it induces joy, a deep, serene, receptive joy, and I shall say more about that in the next chapter.

Clearly, however, not all repetitions are worthy of celebration. Assembly line repetition does not provide opportunities for receptive and creative encounters with either living others or ideas. It represents, rather, a suspension of real life. What-is-there is always the same, and what one must do is always the same. Oddly, many women look at domesticity as unrelieved sameness, also. Are they simply lacking in imagination and appreciation, or is something else operating here? If domestic life is filled with opportunities for receptive and creative encounters, why do so many of us devote only part-time to it and that often with a feeling of being overworked and underpaid?

When there is a sharp separation between public and private life, as there is in our society, and when men assume public roles and women private ones, very little public value is attached to domestic work. It is public, salary-making work that is valued. So much has been written on this problem already that I shall not dwell on it here. But many women in our society simply must participate in the larger world of work; they need the public recognition that is granted for this work in order to sustain themselves as persons and, I shall claim, as ones-caring. The ethical ideal is, after all, constructed by a whole person and embedded in a larger self-image. If a woman does not feel that her abilities are being either exercised or acknowledged, she is likely to turn in upon herself. While she may even then go on caretaking, her actual caring may all but disappear. She may seek credit and recognition for her caretaking, and this focus on self impairs caring. Philip Wylie's *Generation of Vipers,* if it existed at all, was created by such in-turning and desperate need for recognition.[8]

It seems to me that if men and women participate more fully and equally in these two great worlds, both may reap unexpectedly large rewards. Women, with stronger self-images to sustain them, may care more joyfully in private life and may insist upon caring in public life as well. Men, participating in the responsibilities of domestic life, may learn its real joys and potential for self-renewal. They, too, may begin to celebrate the ordinary events of life more frequently. Mutual appreciation may enhance the perceived responsiveness of both human and nonhuman objects. Let me try to explain what I mean by this. Suppose a woman enjoys growing things. She finds seeds, and cuttings, and plants responsive to her engrossment and motivational displacement. But her husband and children find her activity "cute"—a "playing with plants." Her relationship with the plants is then clouded by the projected notion that what she is doing with them is not very important or interesting. If, on the other hand, family members find her work interesting and important, she may set to it more freely. Her capacity to be engrossed in these particular others is enhanced in freedom. Now, of course, I am repeating in a new context what has already been said about the effects of the one-caring's attitude on the cared-for. The problem that I am highlighting here is that women are too often cast as the one-caring; they are the ones who engage in psychological caring.[9] Even though they are, psychologically, the ones-caring, however, they are often thought of as being taken care of by the men who provide salaries. Our society often seems to put a higher value on what I have called "caretaking" than it does on genuine caring. You may recall our earlier discussion of Mr. Jones, who claimed that he "cared" when he paid the bills for his mother and that he had "sisters who could provide company." My contention, then, is that men need to learn how to care, and women must learn how to maintain themselves as ones-caring through a general strengthening of self-image.

I have not, in all this talk of everyday life and professional life, mentioned mothering, but, clearly, mothering and caring are deeply related. Several contemporary writers have raised a question that seems odd at first glance: Why is it that women in our society do the mothering? In asking this question they are certainly not asking why it is that women, rather than men, bear children. Biology has the final word in that task. They are asking why it is that women in virtually all societies are the caretakers of children. The biological view holds that women, having given birth and entered lactation, are naturally nurturant toward their infants. The socialization view denies arguments for natural instinct and natural nurturance and insists that mothering is a role—something learned. Finally, the psychological view suggested by Nancy Chodorow holds that the tendency for girls to want to mother, and to actually engage in mothering, is the result of deep psychological processes established in close and special relationships with their own mothers.

The socialization view, as an explanatory theory, seems nonsense. We are not nearly so successful at socializing people into roles as we are at reproducing mothering in women. Mothering is not a role but a relationship. The psychological view, however, seems very strong, and it is compatible, as Chodorow has described it, with what we have discussed on caring. One difficulty is that those endorsing psychological views have felt the need to set aside or minimize biological arguments. It is true that a woman's natural inclination to mother a newborn does not explain why she continues to mother a child into adolescence or why she mothers other people's half-grown children. But it may well be that a completely adequate theory will have to embrace both biological and psychological factors—and, perhaps, even socialization factors—if we are going to consider competence in mothering.

If the psychological view is correct, we might reproduce mothering in men by establishing a relation between father and son like that already established between mother and daughter. The continual encouragement that a girl receives to turn toward her richest and tenderest caring moments, the constant companionship of a feminine caring model, and the practice that she engages in as an apprentice are very powerful in producing the woman as one-caring and, hence, in reproducing mothering in women. Will the same sort of structural relation reproduce mothering in men? Clearly, many men are psychological parents ("mothers") to their children, and many more might be. But if the biological imperatives are stronger than many believe, we might find it much more difficult to reproduce mothering in boys than in girls.

A concern arises, then, that our educational/psychological efforts might induce a deep sense of inferiority in young men who are not able to mother. Is this a foolish concern? Let me argue for a bit by analogy. Some writers hold that young women feel inferior in the world of paid work, that they are noncompetitive and "afraid of success."[10] The same writers generally attribute this noncompetitiveness and lack of interest in power to socialization processes. The clear implication is that women can be (should be?) socialized as men are to competitive public life. Other writers argue that women are naturally (biologically and/or psychologically) more interested in caring, supporting, and cooperating than they are in competing.[11] The clear implication on this view is that women should retain their natural orientation and find ways to make it work for them, and perhaps for others as well, in public life.[12] I, of course, find the latter view much more persuasive. It requires, we see, that a woman remain in touch with her deep feminine psychological structure and bring its great strength into the public world of work.

Similarly, rather than argue that men should adopt the characteristic relational patterns of women in parenting, I would like to suggest that men bring their best human and masculine qualities to the experience of parenting. It seems reasonable to suppose that men can be warmer, closer, less detached and rule-bound fathers than they have characteristically been in the past without being mothers. If we recall earlier examples in which the attitudes of particular fathers and mothers were dramatically contrasted, we can imagine ways in which the fathers might have contributed more directly to parenting simply by understanding, appreciating, and feeling with their wives. Their ways of parenting might have remained different but more deeply and appreciatively complementary.

All this needs to be carefully tied to the theme of this section, which is maintenance of the ethical ideal. In earlier sections, we emphasized the commitment to caring and the openness and receptivity that make natural caring more likely. We discussed, also, the critical role of the cared-for in sustaining the one-caring. But beyond the activities and commitment of actual caring, there is clearly the need to sustain the whole person who would be one-caring. I have suggested that women have been especially fortunate in their opportunities to celebrate the repetitions of ordinary life and thus achieve a balance between being and doing. Their responsibility for the functions of everyday living may even induce an increased and heightened receptivity. All this is at great risk, however, in a society that does not care enough about these projects to set people proudly free to engage them wholeheartedly. There is a resulting diminution in general self-image which may damage the ethical ideal.

Both men and women may, then, draw upon strengths in general self-image to maintain themselves as ones-caring. But for many women, caring is central to their self-image. They must care in order to live in internal truth and serenity. Is this true also for men, or might it be if relational structures were changed? Or might it be that being cared-for is central to the self-image of men? One thinks of Wittgenstein, who admitted that he needed love but was unable to give it. These are important questions to keep in mind when we move on to a discussion of caring in schools and education for caring.

I am aware that acknowledgment of the possibility of strong biological factors weakens my central claim that ethicality is rooted in and built upon natural caring. But the claim is thus only weakened, not destroyed. While rejecting universalizability of personal rules and moral judgments, I have relied on our universal accessibility to caring and memories of caring. If it is the case that females have easier and more direct access to caring through biologically facilitative factors, this does not imply that males have no access, but it might help to explain why men intellectualize, abstract, and institutionalize that which women treat directly and concretely. It might also explain why organized religions are so often created by and dominated by men. The longing for that which is not quite within reach is deep and constant.

For many women, motherhood is the single greatest source of strength for the maintenance of the ethical ideal. The young woman who has just given birth to a child may, if she has a religious faith, turn in wonder and gratitude toward the God she thanks for the safe delivery of her child. But she may equally well lie awake all night thinking on this strange God. Already she feels the likelihood of eternal love and tenderness toward her child; she cannot imagine visiting long or cruel punishment on him. What, then, of God or gods? Why, she wonders, would an all-knowing and all-good God create a world in which his creatures must eat each other to survive? Why, oh why, would he withhold his physical presence from them? Why would he demand that they—much the needier and weaker—love Him? When he-who-has-not-lost-his-faith answers her by saying, "We must not question," she turns, finally, reluctantly, decisively away. This, also, she would not say to her child: You must not question.

Thus she turns to this earth and to these concrete others for her strength.

6

ENHANCING THE IDEAL: JOY

OUR BASIC REALITY AND AFFECT

IN THE PRECEDING chapter, I suggested that joy often accompanies a realization of our relatedness. It is the special affect that arises out of the receptivity of caring, and it represents a major reward for the one-caring. Feeling joy in relatedness—whether in relation to persons, other living things, or ideas—encourages growth in the ethical ideal. Our joy enhances both the ideal and our commitment to it. We want to remain in direct contact with that which brings us joy and, somehow, with that joy itself.

What is joy? Is it an emotion, or should we more properly regard it as an affect or feeling? How does its occurrence support our fundamental claim about the basic nature of our reality—that is, that our basic reality is found in relatedness?

When I suggest that joy might be considered an "affect" or "feeling" rather than an emotion, I have in mind a distinction between reflective and nonreflective modes of consciousness. If we consider "affect" as the conscious subjective aspect of experience, we see that it may accompany both our activity in the instrumental world and our meetings in the relational world. Further, this description of affect allows for the possibility of our looking at ourselves feeling—that is, of our being aware of ourselves feeling. There may be a direct object involved in our feeling, but our relatedness to this object—perhaps even the relation itself—is the underlying or true object. It is the relation, or our recognition of the relation, that induces the affect we call joy.

Now, as we shall see, this is not an entirely new or bizarre distinction. Existentialist philosophers often speak of "anguish" as a basic affect of

132

the sort I am describing. Those, like Sartre, whose ontology posits a lonely emptiness trying to actualize itself, a consciousness forever subject to some object, see anguish as the inevitable accompaniment of our realization of our aloneness—of our essential freedom to choose ourselves and our world. A view of basic reality as relatedness invites the postulation of a basic affect that accompanies our recognition of relatedness. Our view does not deny the reality of anguish, but it suggests other reasons for its occurrence, among them the realization or recognition of obligation that we mentioned earlier. From this view, both joy and anguish may be considered as aspects of reflective modes of consciousness. In contrast, emotion is usually regarded as nonreflective—a mode in which we meet objects directly and unaware of ourselves as conscious beings.

Joy is regarded by most writers as an emotion, but we shall see that there are difficulties in so categorizing it. It often seems to sweep over us without being directed at an object. It is triggered by something; but the joy itself seems to arise from something beyond the immediate object. Further, it seems often to accompany a reflective mode of consciousness and, as I have already noted, we generally regard the emotional mode as nonreflective.

Perhaps joy is two things and not just one. There is precedent for thinking this way. Sartre, for example, separates joy into "joy-feeling which represents a balance, an adapted state, and joy-emotion"[1] which represents a degradation of consciousness—that is, a movement from reflective to nonreflective consciousness. But even within joy-emotion, there are two forms in Sartre's framework: there is the joy we project upon the world as we leave the realm of instrumentalities and enter a "magical" world, and there is the joy we receive as a real quality of the lived world. Sartre gives little attention to receptive joy and yet, I believe, it is the form that reveals most about our basic reality. Indeed, a major reason for us to examine joy is precisely the possibility of revealing something deeper about our fundamental reality. As Sartre himself puts it, one who would study emotion should

interrogate emotion about *consciousness* or *about man*. He will ask it not only what it is but what it has to teach us about a being, one of whose characteristics is exactly that he is capable of being moved. And inversely, he will interrogate consciousness, human reality, about emotion; what must a consciousness be for emotion to be possible, perhaps even necessary?[2]

We should like to know what emotionality signifies in human beings and, especially, what it tells us about women. More importantly, we should like to know what joy, as affect or as emotion, signifies for us. Before we look at joy as emotion, however, we should consider another possibility. If joy really does occur occasionally without an object, then either there are forms of joy that are not emotion or there is at least one objectless emotion. Joseph Fell, for example, discusses one objectless emotion, anguish, in the thinking of Sartre.[3] This may, however, be unfair, for Sartre does not call anguish an emotion. Anguish for Sartre, as we have seen, has a fundamental ontological status; it is unavoidable for a being with reflective consciousness. As we look at our situation and recognize our freedom to choose, we suffer anguish and anxiety. Now, if we reject Sartre's terrible aloneness as the fundamental characteristic of human existence (and Sartre himself seems to have done so in his last months), we might identify another objectless emotion (or affect) that points to an alternative ontological base. If relatedness rather than aloneness is our fundamental reality and not just a hopelessly longed-for state, then recognition or fulfillment of that relatedness might well induce joy. Recognition of our obligation in relation arouses anguish but recognition of the actual or possible caring in relation induces joy. Joy then—at least one form of joy—must be reflective; that is, it necessarily involves consciousness looking at itself.

In answer to writers, for example, Hazel Barnes,[4] who find an appreciation of relatedness or sense of oneness somewhat mystical, we must respond that the feeling or sense of appreciation is directly related to ethicality. Barnes asks what use we have for such a sense. Our reply is that the feeling itself tends or may tend to sustain the commitment to caring. Not only do I want to attain my ethical ideal, but also I want to feel this special joy. Further, when joy arises out of the nonhuman world, it may tend to sustain me as one-learning or one-investigating, and this will be important to us as we explore caring for animals, plants, things, and ideas.

We have ample reason, then, for considering the status of joy as emotion. My purpose is to show that some forms of joy are significantly different from other emotions, and that joy as affect reveals the fundamental nature of our reality—or, perhaps, I might better say that the occurrence of joy reveals the part of our fundamental reality that may be identified with the feminine as it is experienced by both men and women.

HOW SHOULD WE DESCRIBE EMOTION?

Philosophers have tried in a variety of ways to describe emotions both comprehensively and concisely. Each attempt to bring all of the emotions under one powerful set of descriptors has raised objections, and I shall not spend a great deal of time on these comprehensive theories, but we must look at a few to set the stage for discussion. From ancient times it has been recognized that there are connections among perception, emotion, and bodily change. A long-accepted ordering is described in the following:

(1) perception ——→ emotion ——→ bodily change[5]

This commonsense notion suggests that we perceive something that arouses a mental affect or emotion, and the emotion causes, or is followed by, some bodily change. If I see some frightful monster coming at me, for example, I feel fear, and my body responds with racing heart, sweating palms, and constricting blood vessels.

Now, clearly, not every emotion or affect is accompanied by obvious, distinctive bodily changes but, even in the case of emotions that are so accompanied, the commonsense ordering has been challenged. William James suggested, for example, that the proper ordering should be:

(2) perception ——→ bodily change ——→ consciousness of change[6]

(emotion)

James's "state of consciousness" theory directed a considerable body of physiological thinking and research on the emotions. It was followed, of course, by criticism from both philosophers and empirical researchers.[7] It seems now that James was correct in stating that the viscera are necessarily involved in emotion, but he seems to have been incorrect in naming visceral changes as *sufficient cause* of emotion. This view is, obviously, at odds with the nonreflective view of emotion, and we shall see that it is counterintuitive as well. When I am angry, for example, my consciousness does not seem to be turned on some internal state but outward to the object of anger. Indeed, that object seems to fill the world, blotting out all else and even myself as conscious being.

Following James there were refinements of physiological theories of emotion, but other theorists turned to an examination of behavior as a more fruitful way to describe emotion. Such behaviors as the tightening of facial muscles or clenched fists might characterize anger; trembling hands and shaky knees, fear; tears and abject droopiness, grief, and so on. Other theorists pointed out that the behavioral approach, promising as it seemed, could not account for silent anger, suppressed fear, or grief borne with a stiff upper lip. There remained a need to look at the inner (conscious) working of emotion. Physiological reactions, behavior, and cognition all seem to be importantly involved in emotion. Carroll Izard, for example, says that a "complete definition" of emotion must account for:

a) the experience or conscious feeling of emotion,

b) the processes that occur in the brain and nervous system, and

c) the observable expressive patterns of emotion, particularly those on the face. [8]

We shall be concerned here primarily with the first set of factors; that is, with the conscious or cognitive aspects of emotion. But, beyond the defining characteristics of manifest emotion, we would like to know, also, what induces emotion—what kinds of external factors combined with what sorts of internal factors lead to emotional states. As we consider these questions, we shall be most interested, of course, in how they might be answered with respect to joy.

PERCEPTION AND EMOTION: THE OBJECT OF EMOTION AND ITS APPRAISAL

How is perception involved in emotion? In common experience there is, as R. S. Peters points out, usually an object of emotion. [9] I am not just angry, but I am angry with someone or something. If I am grief-stricken, there is some event from which my grief has arisen and toward which it is directed. If I am afraid, I am afraid of something. Clearly, if I am afraid, I must perceive the object of my fear as something that threatens me. In this, I can be mistaken. If my son leaps out upon me unexpectedly and I jump or shriek in reaction, one might say that I made an instantaneous and incorrect appraisal of the event. I saw myself threatened, but in fact I was merely the victim of playful behavior. But it seems to me that my jumping or shrieking is not at all the product of appraisal; it is simply a bodily reaction. Similarly, when Sartre speaks of feeling "invaded by terror" at the sight of a grinning face at the window, [10] I think he is right to separate the initial reaction of being startled from the terror that follows consideration of what the face at the window means. This does not mean that the assessment must be objectively correct in order for genuine emotion to be present, but there must be some evaluation of this grinning face. What I undergo as I experience emotion is the result of perceiving something that matters to me. On this widely accepted view, then, we have both perception and appraisal involved in emotion, or we might, of course, prefer to insist that perception itself involves appraisal of some sort.

In Magda Arnold's view, the inner feeling of emotion is the "felt tendency toward or away from an object," and this tendency is induced by an appraisal of the object.[11] Similarly, in Asch's view, emotion is a direct consequence of the understanding of our situation.[12] In these "cognitive" perspectives, belief is centrally involved in emotion. I am invaded by terror at the sight of a grinning face if I believe either that it represents a direct threat to me or that it represents that which is horrible in itself and to be avoided. (In the latter case, of course, that which is horrible must be an indirect threat.)

If we agree that belief and appraisal are involved in emotion, we still have not explained why our reaction should be an emotional one and not simply one of rational decision making. But let us put that problem aside for a moment. I want to ask whether belief and appraisal are centrally involved in joy. In one sort of joy, the kind labeled "active," they do seem to be involved. I believe that certain things are "good" for me personally, and I assess the situation I am in as likely to produce those goods. Or I actually attain the desired good, perceive this attainment, and experience joy as a result. In this kind of joy there is an object of joy, and both belief and appraisal are involved.

But there are other forms of joy. There is the joy that unaccountably floods over me as I walk into the house and see my daughter asleep on the sofa. She is exhausted from basketball playing, and her hair lies curled on a damp forehead. The joy I feel is immediate. It is similar in this respect to Sartre's immediate perception of the horrible in the grinning face. Can it be simply a bodily reaction of which I am aware? This seems unlikely. My daughter seems to be the object of my consciousness; certainly it is not my own physiological condition of which I am aware. But my consciousness seems to be grasping its immediate object in a special relation. There is a feeling of connectedness in my joy, but no awareness of a particular belief and, certainly, no conscious assessment. Perhaps what I perceive as I look at my daughter is something that lies beyond her-as-object, just as the horrible-in-general lies beyond that grinning face at the window. It seems wrong to claim that my daughter is not the object of my joy, but it seems strangely and misleadingly incomplete to claim that she is. This joy arises out of an awareness of the caring relation. It is not something in this moment that brings the joy, even though my daughter is the direct object of my consciousness. Rather, it is something beyond the moment—a recognition of fulfillment of relatedness— that induces this joy.

Must there be an object of joy? Suppose I am working in my garden or lying on the beach under a starry sky. A seedling uncovered beneath the mulch may trigger joy (as my daughter did), or a shooting star may induce the feeling; but, then again, there may be no particular object of my joy. There is a sense of well-being, but more than that. I am not focusing consciousness on myself, but am aware peripherally of myself-perceiving. There is joy experienced as a real quality of the world—not as a state resulting from an appraisal of my situation in the world.

Now one might argue that there is, indeed, an appraisal in such situations. The appraisal is not explicit, but, as James described it, there is cortical awareness of bodily relaxation and well-being. I must concede that this is possible. But joy as a seemingly real quality of this lived world can invade us even in pain and periods of deep grief. It does not seem to be the case that joy and grief can occur simultaneously, but they can occur alternately; that is, the pervasive emotion may be grief, and yet joy can slip in momentarily. So it may happen that even in the deepest grief, filled with guilt and sorrow and regret and despair, I may still see and feel joy there-in-the-world, trembling at my fingertips. Turning from a graveside or leaving the hospital after holding a dying hand, joy may burst through like a rainbow over tears. Grief is not thereby lessened; indeed, it is often intensified. The pain-in-here contrasts sharply with the joy-out-there. Are such experiences to be dismissed as "mystical"? Or must they, too, be accounted for in adequate theories of emotion?

One difficulty here is that it seems nonsense to speak of an emotion or feeling detached from the feeling subject, and I am not suggesting that joy can be located entirely out-there. It is connected to me and to the object that triggers it, but it is focused somewhere beyond both, in the relation or in a recognition of relatedness. In the cases described earlier, it does not seem correct to name either the seedling or the shooting star as the object of my joy. Just as the human other can invade me in receptivity, so can the world in all its affective possibilities come in if I let it.

If we conclude that joy is different from anger, fear, and shame in its frequent appearance without an object, we might decide that it is not a basic emotion. Izard, for example, counts enjoyment as basic.[13] Or we might, of course, conclude that joy is sometimes a basic emotion and sometimes—perhaps one form should be renamed—a basic affect or feeling.

Besides pointing to an object of emotion, cognitive theorists frequently speak of emotion in the context of goal orientation or purpose. Taking a position very similar to Sartre's in this respect, Karl Pribram says that the organism tries to extend its repertoire to meet the conditions of the situation within which it strives toward a goal: "Whenever this attempt fails, is non-reinforced, frustrated, or interrupted, the organism becomes of necessity emotional, i.e., he must resort to mechanisms of self-regulation, self-control."[14]

In Sartre's view this switch from the externally oriented control of rational, instrumental thinking represents a "degradation of consciousness." If I cannot achieve my goal in the instrumental world, I create a magical world to replace that of instrumentalities. This is, in part, an answer to our earlier question, why consciousness should assume an emotional mode instead of a decision-theoretic mode. We might profitably look again at our chapter two example, in which I tried to open a window that was stuck. Very reasonably, I checked the lock and the sash cords or whatever mechanical parts the window contained. I tried this and that. I hypothesized. I even studied a neighboring window to find out how windows work when they are functioning properly. But the thing was stuck; it would not yield. My face flushed; I beat and cursed the window. I was no longer rational, but the window was still the object of my consciousness. My mode of consciousness had changed. I had transformed the world into one in which windows are treated like willful creatures.

This magical transformation, for which we remain responsible in Sartre's view, may be explained in Pribram's physiological view as an extreme state of redundancy enhancement. The object fills consciousness to a degree that peripheral but essential elements may be unperceived. Hence, in great anger, we "see red" and in love we are "blind."

Now, at first glance it is difficult to see how the "better" emotions could possibly arise as "degradations." But I think they can and do. Sartre discusses the possibility in terms of anticipation: "Joy is the magical behavior which tends by incantation to realize the possession of the desired object as instantaneous totality. This behavior is accompanied by certainty that the possession will be realized sooner or later, but it seeks to anticipate this possession."[15]

Suppose, for example, that I am working on a particularly difficult problem of some sort. I am totally engaged, struggling. I am rational, cool, objective, and the problem begins to yield. As the analysis unfolds, I feel a growing pleasure, a real excitement. The energy available is no longer necessary for the situation at hand. I may not shout "Eureka!," but then again, I may. I sing, or dance with the dog, or I close my eyes and grin. I have entered a world which Sartre describes as "magical," but I have projected the magic onto the world. It is the way I meet the world at this moment. (It is worth noting here that, in Pribram's terms, emotion might also result from extreme redundancy reduction. In so-called peak experiences, objects melt into one another, and everything assumes a unity. The world rushes in.)

While the exploration of emotion in terms of the connection between perception and action or in terms of the instrumental versus magical worlds is powerful, it cannot account for a second way in which consciousness assumes the affective mode we call joy. It does not seem at all proper to label the joy I felt with respect to my daughter, or the seedling, or the shooting star a "degradation" of consciousness since that joy seemed to be reflective. It went well beyond its immediate object to the perception of my relatedness to that object. Receptive joy, we may suggest, belongs not to a magical world but to the world of relation.

Now I do not control this receptive joy. It comes to me. I cannot say, with any reasonable expectation of success. "I shall go sit on the front steps and be filled with joy," but I can increase the likelihood that joy will come to me. I can quit thinking and manipulating. I can be quiet, emptying consciousness of its thought-objects and, then, a receptive mood may take over. Now, of course, I cannot "empty consciousness" of anything in Sartre's framework, for consciousness is a process and not a receptacle. But even in Sartre's framework, consciousness may play lightly over its objects, refusing to fix itself on any one. It may allow itself to be spoken to or appeared to even if, in doing so, it risks its autonomy as subject. It is precisely in the experience of what Sartre calls "joy-feeling" that his supremely alone and constantly intentional consciousness shows its weakness. In "joy-feeling," we are receptive, spoken to, supplied with intention. It is a fundamental, creative experience, and one over which we feel a peculiar lack of control. The great fear of many creative workers is that they will "run dry," that the source of inspiration will disappear, that the "muse will desert." The fear, here, seems to be that the other will not respond, that the relation will not be filled out in the other.

It is possible that the experience of joy as a real quality of the world can be explained by Sartre's "second way" in which consciousness may assume an emotional mode of being. In this second way, consciousness is invaded by the world, and the world's real magical qualities may be revealed. Just as the resulting emotions may be either "good" or "bad" in the first way, so too, in this way, I may experience joy or fear or revulsion. As Sartre puts it: "Thus, there are two forms of emotion, according to whether it is we who constitute the magic of the world to replace a deterministic activity which cannot be realized, or whether it is the world itself which abruptly reveals itself as being magical."[16]

In such pronouncements Sartre manages to avoid the extremes of both realism and idealism, but he fails to explore the second option fully. What does this capacity to receive, to be affected, signify? Must we intend or give assent to such affection? How far and to what extent do we determine it? Are we moved by something outside us, or do we choose to be moved?

Sartre's insistence on the intentionality of emotion leaves us unable to explain the joy that overcomes us unbidden in situations where no goal is either blocked or anticipated. Fell cites the ideas of Dewey and Freud as superior in this respect, since both allow the possibility "that emotion may signify a teleological response without itself being an intentional act."[17] It may come, then, in reaction to fulfillment of a goal. But this is still unsatisfactory. The joy I feel on seeing my daughter or watching the shooting star is not connected to a goal at all. It signals to me that I am not only a purposive creature but also a receptive one—one who may be acted upon as well as one who acts.

Now, clearly, Sartre cannot allow our being acted upon; that is, he cannot allow us to be caused to do or to feel such-and-such. To allow reactivity of that kind would be to open the doors to Clarence Darrow's world, in which, ultimately, even the basest fiend cannot be held responsible for his behavior. The emotional mode that reveals the world as magical is, as described by Sartre, spontaneous and passive. Although we do not choose it initially—it invades us—we sometimes choose to sustain it. The world of other subjectivities (both persons and objects) threatens to objectify us, and consciousness resists this threat.

But in our framework, consciousness does not resist the call to duality. It *seeks* relatedness; it is not reduced or degraded by the other's subjectness. We cannot escape responsibility, but that responsibility is always shared. Consciousness may, then, take on an explicit attitude of openness; that is, consciousness may make a commitment to give over the control that is always in its power to other forms of subjectivity. What follows is well described in Martin Buber's account of the I-Thou relation:

> Whoever says Thou does not have something for his object. For wherever there is something there is also another something; every It borders on other Its; It is only by virtue of bordering on others. But where Thou is said there is no something. Thou has no borders. Whoever says Thou does not have something; he has nothing. But he stands in relation.[18]

This is the commitment made by the one-caring. I do not think this is a mystical formulation, but, clearly, the ideas are very difficult to express in our available language. Consciousness is free and it is intentional; but its freedom arises in reciprocity and may be exercised in receiving, in placing itself in vulnerable reciprocity. It is this basic freedom that we feel when we experience joy of the second kind.

We have seen that receptive joy is different from other emotions in that it seems to arise without a direct object and with an element of reflection. We are aware of ourselves in relation. Does joy differ from the emotions in other respects?

EMOTIONS AS REASONS

R. S. Peters describes one use of emotion words, in the active sense of emotion, as motives or reasons for actions.[19] We say, "I hit him because I was angry," or, "I ran because I was afraid," or, "I lied because I was jealous." It is informative to note that joy is not often used in this way. We do not say, "I did X because I was joyful," although we might explain a lack of caution or discretion on "feeling good" or being elated. Similarly, we might speak of ourselves as "dancing for joy" but, again, this use seems to point to Sartre's anticipatory "joy-emotion" and not to the deep and quiet joy that invades unexpectedly and seems unconnected to either an immediate object or any particular goal.

Peters seems to be right when he points out that there are both emotions as motives and emotions as reactions.[20] I am suggesting, further, that there is joy that is receptive and reflective—aware of itself and complete without action.

When we consider emotion in connection with motivation and the achievement of goals, it is natural to ask whether emotion is facilitative or nonfacilitative in accomplishing our purposes. For Sartre, emotion represents a transformation of the world—an abandonment of the world of instrumentalities and the substitution of a "magical world." In this magical world we sometimes substitute new goals for those we cannot achieve in the instrumental world. When we cannot succeed in obtaining grapes that are out of our reach, we succeed at becoming critics and declare the grapes to be sour. Or we retain the old goals but find some magical way of satisfying ourselves that we have attained them. We grasp the object of our joy in anticipation, for example, when we dance, clap our hands, or run aimlessly about in delight.

Fell points out, however (and so does Peters), that we are not always less effective when we are emotional. Sometimes, indeed, emotion supplies us with the special motive power we need: increased physical strength, cunning, or patience. This seems obviously right, but it does not hurt Sartre's argument in any central way. We do not choose the increase in physical strength or the cunning that results from fear; instead, we choose to transform the world. What occurs, then, is less under our control. While we are still responsible, according to Sartre, we may protest that we are not. If things do not go well, we claim "diminished capacity." In general, then, it is acknowledged that emotion may be facilitative in a nonreflective way, and it is also recognized that the expression of emotion may be useful in restoring the organism to a stable and less stressful state. But neither of these effects lifts emotion to an exalted state. The emotional is still a degradation, a necessary evil in a world too difficult for constant rationality.

For our purposes, the important point here is that joy seems out of place when considered with other emotions. We do not offer joy as a reason for particular acts, although we may, of course, renew our commitment to caring as we are sustained by joy.

JOY AS EXALTED

We are not without exalted descriptions of emotion. Joy, in particular, is often described as a state not only desirable but superior to neutral states. In discussing the stoical concept of joy, Paul Tillich notes:

The affirmation of one's essential being in spite of desires and anxieties creates joy. Lucillus is exhorted by Seneca to make it his business "to learn how to feel joy." It is not the joy of fulfilled desires to which he refers, for real joy is a "severe matter"; it is the happiness of a soul which is "lifted above every circumstance." Joy accompanies the self-affirmation of our essential being in spite of the inhibitions coming from the accidental elements in us. Joy is the emotional expression of the courageous yes to one's own true being.[21]

Joy, in this sense, is an emotion expressed by an elite few. The same complaint, if it is a complaint, may be leveled at joy-as-oneness as described in Eastern philosophies. There is a learned and practiced tendency to move away from and above the world of everyday experience, and it is this moving away which prompts Hazel Barnes to ask about its usefulness in the realm of ethics. If we move beyond passion, no matter how beautiful the vision or state we attain, what can we be except negativity to our fellow human beings? Clearly, we may refrain from doing evil, but what impels us toward the positive good? I could argue that joy —as ordinarily experienced, and not as experienced at the level of religious ecstasy—is empirically linked with altruism,[22] and that it tends to increase appreciation and social responsiveness.[23] There are, it seems, significant answers to questions concerning the ethical connotations of joy. But our chief answer is that it tends to sustain the one-caring.

I am not, however, going to claim that joy is linked by necessity to ethical good. Indeed, it seems possible that an individual might experience "unholy joy" on having achieved a state of individual and unmitigated evil. Thus, while joy may enhance the ethical ideal, it might also appear pathologically afflicted. What I wish to focus attention upon is the reflective nature of the joy that accompanies a realization of the responsive relation of caring: the sense of connectedness, of harmony—the combination of excitement and serenity—the sense of being in tune that is characteristic of receptive joy.[24] The occurrence of joy as a willing transformation of self under the compelling magic of other subjectivities points to a receptive consciousness, one that is energized by engagement and enlightened by looking and listening.

RECEPTIVITY AND JOY IN INTELLECTUAL WORK

Because joy comes to us unbidden as a real quality of the relational world, we might ask whether other benefits might appear in similar fashion. In particular, we might ask whether understanding and insight are products or signs of receptive consciousness. Receptive joy occurs when we are engaged as though possessed—when we are caught up in a relation. We may have ceased manipulative activity and fallen quiet; we are listening. We are not trying so much to produce a particular product or answer as we are trying to understand, to see. Whereas explanation is controlled, contrived, and constructed, understanding—like joy—comes unpredictably. At one moment we are baffled, stymied. Then, suddenly, the light dawns. C. S. Lewis speaks of being "surprised by joy" and, similarly, we may be surprised by understanding. It is not something we do that produces the light, although things we have done undoubtedly contribute to the event, but it is something that happens, something that is revealed to us. This is the beginning of creativity, the mode in which understanding begins and is completed. Again and again it is described as receptive.

We may recall our earlier mention of Mozart hearing melodies in his head, of Gauss being "seized" by mathematics, of Miró having his hand guided "by a magnetic force." In a series of interviews recorded in *The Creative Experience,*[25] creative thinkers in science, literature, music, drama, and other fields testify to the power of the receptive phase in their creative work. Again and again the voice of the object-turned-subject is heard. In the midst of an emphasis on craft and skill, Arthur Koestler says, "the thing develops to some extent by itself."[26] Speaking of the origin of ideas and his own tendency to avoid some of them, Sidney Lumet says

> the idea will hit and then without my knowing it another idea will wipe it out; then depending on its persistence, depending on its importance, depending on what role it's playing, it will keep intruding in little bursts, literally, and then depending on circumstances, either crash through or be wiped out.[27]

Selden Rodman testifies to the surprise inherent in creative work:

> I'm surprised at the moment of writing a phrase or a sentence that it worked out that way; and that it perhaps produced something that I hadn't anticipated at all.[28]

Yet despite a flood of testimony emphasizing both the joy and power of receptivity, schools are urged to teach more and more directly—to state exactly what students will do as a result of instruction and to prove that they can do whatever has been stated. I have no quarrel with those who would use direct teaching for instruction in well-defined skills. On the contrary, I would endorse direct instruction and drill on component routines where a lack of skill might incapacitate students in their struggle with new and difficult concepts. Common sense tells us that lack of background skills often keeps us from choosing to learn new material. Individual skills, many of which can be identified as crucial in working with significant concepts and which can be precisely stated, can and should be taught directly. We would be foolish to deny this. But the teaching and learning of such skills are only a part of the process. They serve to set learners free to explore. For students to engage a subject matter directly, they must be free of the mediation supplied by precise objectives. Subject matter should not always be a thing to be analyzed and mastered. It may be possible for almost all students to have at least occasional I-Thou relations with subject matter—occasions in which student and subject meet without prestated objective and in which the subject speaks to the student. The values to be realized are twofold; there is the instrumental value attached to learning more thoroughly when one is deeply engaged, and there is the consummatory value attached to the joy we feel in genuine relatedness to the object of the study.

Just as joy may arise without reference to a particular object, what-is-there may make itself known without our striving to define it. There are times when we must stop thinking in order to make sensible connections with the object field. Neither the joy nor the receptivity of which we have been talking is passive; both are active but not manipulative, not assimilative. They do not strive to impose structure, but they open all channels to perceive it. They represent an opening-up and a taking-in.

I have watched students under "stop thinking" directions suddenly "see," and the result is impressive. Advocates of direct teaching and specific objectives may make a parody of the suggestion and ask: What shall we do with our students—sit around and stare at the math problems? The answer is, of course not. Incubation and illumination do not come to the unprepared. But we need balance in our instructional efforts and far greater emphasis on affect and training of the senses. That the subject matter is worth looking at and listening to, that it can be played with, that it may respond unexpectedly, are messages worth conveying to our students.

JOY AS BASIC AFFECT

We began talking about receptivity in connection with intellectual tasks, and we shall continue that discussion in the next chapter. The joy that we experience in relation to things and ideas does not enhance the ethical ideal directly. Our relation to things and ideas is not an ethical relation. There is no other consciousness to receive our caring or to fill it out recip-rocally. But an important similarity in domains is apparent. We may still be receptive. The thing or idea may "speak" to us.

The occurrence of joy is a manifestation of receptive consciousness—a sign that we live in a world of relation as well as in one of instrumentality. That joy is sometimes an emotion—a nonreflective, direct contact with some object—is not denied. As emotion it is delightful. But joy is often different from the basic emotions. As basic affect, it accompanies our recognition of relatedness and reflects our basic reality. Its occurrence and recurrence maintain us in caring and, thus, contribute to the en-hancement of the ethical ideal.

7

CARING FOR ANIMALS, PLANTS, THINGS AND IDEAS

OUR RELATION WITH ANIMALS

AN ETHIC GROUNDED in the natural caring of ordinary life must consider our relation to animals. For us, there is no absolute source of life, meaning, and morality that separates the species neatly according to some preordained value hierarchy. We are not given dominion over the beasts of the land. Further, there are intellectual reasons for examining our relation to animals. The problems we struggle with as we do so shed further light on the questions we have already considered, and we may find deeper support for our contention that the ethical impulse or attitude is grounded in the caring relation.

A third reason for exploring our relation to animals is simply that many of us experience in our encounters with animals feelings very like those we are familiar with in genuinely ethical situations. We need to account for these feelings and come to grips with the question whether our relation to animals can ever be properly described as having an ethical aspect. Are we obliged to promote the welfare of animals? Are we obliged to refrain from inflicting pain upon them?

Finally, we live in an age when many in our society have become crusaders for animals rights. There are those who become vegetarians, fight to protect whales and seals, refuse to neuter their pets in order to protect their "rights" to natural sex lives, and act to prevent the building of dams, power plants, and roads in order to preserve odd creatures like the snail darter. Clearly, these people at least care about the creatures under discussion, and an ethic built on caring must consider the possibility that the ethical domain reaches beyond our relations with human beings to those we may establish with animals.

We behave ethically toward one another, I have suggested, because we carry with us the memories of and longing for caring and being cared-for. There is a transfer of feeling and an opportunity—an invitation of sorts —to commit ourselves to the recognition of this feeling and to the continuing receptivity that will bring it to us again and again. But we have already seen that our obligation to summon the caring attitude is limited by the possibility of reciprocity. We are not obliged to act as one-caring if there is no possibility of completion in the other. We must ask then about the possibility of reciprocity in our relations with animals. It seems obvious that animals cannot be ones-caring in relation to human beings but, perhaps, they can in some sense be genuine cared-fors. Is the form of their responsiveness sufficiently similar to that of the cared-for to require our adoption of an ethical attitude toward them?

As we discuss our relationships to animals, plants, things, and ideas, we shall observe a shading-off from the ethical into the sensitive and aesthetic. We shall see again that ethical caring is anchored in the feeling and recognition of relations that are integral to natural caring, but we shall see the role of choice and commitment emphasized. Reasons for the rejection of universalizability will become even clearer. Natural caring in the human domain is accessible to each of us; it is there at the very foundation of our continued existence. But affection for animals—even the opportunity for such affection to develop—varies greatly across persons. Recognition of this variance underscores the wisdom of a nonjudgmental ethic. I may indeed be called ethically to do that which I cannot judge you for omitting. But even if the quality of natural affection for animals varies enormously across persons and in the same person for different sorts of animals, there may be some feeling with respect to animals that is universally accessible or nearly so.

What can we receive when we encounter an animal as a conscious being? We do not have a sense of the animal-as-subject as we do of a human being as subject. But we really do not have this sense as we encounter a newborn human infant, either, and yet we have already acknowledged that the infant plays a vital part in the caring relation and contributes substantively as cared-for. Is the same true of animals? Of *all* animals?

Surely, we can receive—be aware of—pain in many forms of animal life. Pain crosses the lines between the species over a wide range. When a creature writhes or groans or pants frantically, we feel a sympathetic twinge in response to its manifestation of pain. With respect to this feeling, this pain, there does seem to be a transfer that arouses in us the induced feeling, "I must do something." Or, of course, the "I must" may present itself negatively in the form, "I must not do this thing." The desire to prevent or relieve pain is a natural element of caring, and we betray our ethical selves when we ignore it or concoct rationalizations to act in defiance of it. One does not have to justify not inflicting pain on creatures; one has to justify inflicting it. Thus, insofar as we can receive the pain of a creature and detect its relief as we remove the pain, we are both addressed and received. There is at least this much reciprocity in our contact and, therefore, at least this much obligation—that we must not inflict pain without justification.

Can the infliction of pain be justified? The one-caring cannot, logically, argue that there is no such justification. Her ethic springs from human caring. She might insist that animals be spared pain whenever possible, but if animal pain is inescapable in the investigation of ways to relieve human suffering, she must logically accept this. Still, she would ask: Is there some other way? She does not brush aside lightly what she is doing in, say, vivisection. She looks at herself: I am one inflicting pain upon this creature in order to reduce pain in these creatures. I am doing this. Must I? If there is another way, if, for example, that which she may learn is already known by others, she will turn to these other sources. Direct "hands-on" learning does not in itself justify ignoring the inner call to prevent pain.[1]

Before considering the question of whether we may ethically kill and eat animals, we should review the ethical apparatus and claims already made. This is the place to make clear—and to test—the basic notions on which an ethic of caring rests. I have been using relation as ontologically basic and the caring relation as ethically basic. We may think of relation as a set of ordered pairs generated by some rule. The sense in which I have used this term requires that the rule include some description of affect—that is, that the rule say something about the subjective experience of members in the relation. The caring relation, in particular, requires *engrossment* and *motivational displacement* on the part of the one-caring and a form of *responsiveness* or *reciprocity* on the part of the cared-for. It is important to re-emphasize that this reciprocity is not contractual; that is, it is not characterized by mutuality. The cared-for contributes to the caring relation, as we have seen, by receiving the efforts of one-caring, and this receiving may be accomplished by a disclosure of his own subjective experience in direct response to the one-caring or by a happy and vigorous pursuit of his own projects.

Peter Singer, who has also taken a practical approach to ethics, insists that we should reject ethics built on notions of reciprocity:

> These examples should suffice to show that, whatever its origin, the ethics we have now does go beyond a tacit understanding between beings capable of reciprocity, and the prospect of returning to such a basis is not appealing. Since no account of the origin of morality compels us to base our morality on reciprocity, and since no other arguments in favour of this conclusion have been offered, we should reject this view of ethics.[2]

In response, we may say, first, that the notion of reciprocity offered by contract theorists is too limited. It regards human beings as entirely separate entities drawn together in rational agreement to further the welfare of each separately. But our view begins with organisms in relation, striving to maintain the relation as a caring one or to transform it from non-caring to caring. The desire to be good is a natural derivative of the desire to be related. It springs from our experience of caring and the inevitable assessment of this relation as "good." What we seek in caring is not payment or reciprocity in kind but the special reciprocity that connotes completion.

Second, I have attempted to give an account of the origin of morality that does compel us to consider reciprocity as vital in our ethics. Clearly, on this view, our inclination to be moral rests upon and arises out of natural caring.

Now, the third point that will be important in arguing for an ethic of reciprocity and against Singer's utilitarian view is that an ethic of caring strives consistently to capture our human intuitions and feelings. We cannot accept an ethic that depends upon a definition of personhood if that definition diminishes our obligation to human infants. An ethic that forces us to classify human infants with rats and pigs is unsettling. We feel intuitively that something must be wrong with it. We can, certainly, accept criteria of personhood as guides to what we shall do—that is, as guides to the form our obligation must take—but even in this very difficult task it may be wiser to consider the form of response in the potential cared-for rather than some crystallized notion of personhood.

Because we are human and our human affections lie at the very heart of our morality, we inevitably consider response in relation to human response. We detect pain in animals when we perceive behavior similar to pained behavior in human beings and, when we attempt to move beyond behavioral indicators, we point to physiological similarities to human beings. Locating our primary obligation in the domain of human life is a logical outgrowth of the fact that ethicality is defined in the human domain—that the moral attitude would not exist or be recognized without human affection and rational reflection upon or assessment of that affection. It is not "speciesism" to respond differently to different species if the very form of response is species specific.

On Singer's view, there is a major difficulty in any ethic based on reciprocity, and that is that it necessarily invokes the idea of encounter. For him, an ethic is badly conceived if it allows us to escape obligation to future generations or to the needy in far regions of the earth. Now, I have already accepted and even urged this sort of constraint on our obligation. Let me try here to strengthen my earlier arguments. Singer suggests that we have an ethical obligation to future generations, and he uses the example of nuclear wastes and their accumulation as a problem involving such obligation. We, too, should want to find a way to consider future generations, but we cannot proceed as the consequentialist does.

First, we cannot be certain about consequences. What is likely today may not be likely years hence; what is waste today may be a resource tomorrow. Second, our attention is drawn consistently to the conscious nature of our acts. We cannot ignore possible consequences of our acts, but these do not entirely determine the ethical goodness of our acts. We would do better, then, to argue against the accumulation of nuclear wastes on grounds of present and imminent danger to organisms now living. But there is a way to be sensitive to those we cannot encounter or have not yet encountered, and we have already established the machinery to describe how this may be done. In our discussion of circles and chains, we established formal relations—those relations that link us to others in such a way that we are prepared to care. We may think of future generations in this fashion and, when we do so, we are prepared to live conservatively. But it is important to recognize that this preparation to care cannot tell us exactly what to do; it cannot prescribe the particular acts we must perform. We may live sensitively and reasonably, but obligation can only arise on encounter. Caring, natural or ethical, must be completed in the other.

We also found it painful to acknowledge that an ethic of caring limits our obligation to those so far removed from us that completion is impossible. But, again, this move seems intuitively right. It directs us to find what we must do in what we can do, and we are continually pulled back to the concrete, where we are challenged again and again not to justify our acts with reasons but to fulfill our obligations. Painful as it is to give up romantic notions of loving everyone, we see that we must in order to care adequately for anyone. Further, there is, again, a way in which we may respond to those too far removed for caring to be activated directly and completed. When human beings call out for help, it is obligatory for those in proximity to respond. Those in contiguous circles must respond. If they cannot find the material resources to respond adequately, they must address the next circle and entreat aid. Eventually, the cry for help may be heard directly in my own circle. Then I must respond, and I must then depend upon the one who seeks my help to be thoroughly honest and responsible, both in his translation of the initial cry for help and in what he does with the material aid I pass along through him. My obligation is met when my caring is completed in this other who entreats me in direct encounter. Only a chain of trust links me to the faraway other. I can have no obligation to him, although, of course, I may choose to abandon my life here and take up obligation by going to him and precipitating encounter.

Having reiterated and, possibly, strengthened my earlier arguments, I am now prepared to consider further our relation to nonhuman animals. I have already noted that when the form of response permits detection of pain, we are obligated to relieve it. Beyond this major obligation—in which I agree entirely with Singer—can our relation to animals be described as ethical?

Are we justified in killing and eating animals? Should the one-caring, logically, be a vegetarian? Here is another question that is often answered facilely and mistakenly through an odd transfer of principle: "Animals have a right to live, too!" Where does this "right" come from?, asks the one-caring.[3] I, we, must confer it. But consider what an odd predicament we get ourselves into when we decide to do this. We decide not to eat animals and to "let them live." Now here I am going to use a form of generalization for exploratory purposes. I have rejected universalizability, but generalizing, asking "What would happen if everyone did this?" is sometimes useful, because we may uncover a paradox. In the interest of preserving animal life, I decide to be a vegetarian. Now what happens to the animal life I wish to preserve if everyone makes a similar decision? It seems clear that we must surely arrive at a condition in which sharing the earth with large animals would be impossible.[4] We would either have to destroy them to relieve our mutual pain and hunger, or we would have to regulate their reproduction so stringently that they would become rarities in special preserves and zoos. My decision to "let them live," then, may lead to their certain destruction.

Now I am not going to advocate the utilitarian argument which Peter Singer calls "the replaceability argument."[5] On this view, we ought to kill animals (as painlessly as possible, of course) in order to allow space for animals reproduced and, thus, increase the total pleasure or happiness experienced by animals. We have already made an odd move when we talk this way. We are no longer considering how we shall meet the particular other but how we shall treat a vast group of interchangeable entities. We have assumed that we are somehow obliged to increase the total of animal pleasure by perpetuating animal life. Indeed, this argument—like so many others advanced by utilitarians—is conducted at a level of generality that renders it very nearly meaningless. What is animal pleasure? Is it the same for a snail as for a dog? Is there some indicator of "happiness" that will allow us to infer its presence in a large number of organisms?

I suggest that we make an error when we think of the moral good in terms of acts that produce the greatest good for the greatest number, even among human beings. Such thinking may be as close to the ethical as we can come in the contemporary political arena, but this seems to count against our political machinery rather than for utilitarian thinking in social life. It is presumptuous to suppose that we can determine the greatest good for large numbers of people with whom we have no direct contact, and it too easily passes over the assessment of the acts themselves. We are not behaving morally if we turn our backs on the present other in order to give some good to a large number of others. At best, we are behaving expediently.

Returning to the question of morality with respect to nonhuman animals, we see that we cannot preserve animal life in general by refusing to kill and eat animals, and we see also that considering animals as interchangeable "receptacles" for happiness somehow misses the point of meeting the other morally. Because I am not, and cannot be, obligated to the entire class of animals, I may decide either to be a vegetarian or to raise animals for food. What I must prevent, having made either decision, is pain to consciousness, even to the nonreflective consciousness of animals. Thus I must not allow my creatures to suffer terror and physical pain at the end of their lives. A sense of conflict and sadness stirs in the one-caring as she finds herself feeding a live chicken or duck one day and serving it to her family as food a few days later. She may even look forward to a day well beyond her own lifetime in which animals have mostly disappeared and none is eaten; but she lives today, and this is a conflict that cannot be resolved but only lived awarely and sensitively.

There is another point to be made as we look back over our discussion on the ethicality of preserving animal life. If one accepts the utilitarian "replaceability" argument for animals, why not use it also in considering human life? Why not destroy the aged, unfit, and hungry surplus in order to replace them with healthy human beings who can experience the maximum of human pleasure? Most of us would reject this option firmly. We would insist upon preventing surplus population by controlling birth and not by insuring an optimum number of deaths. It seems clear that, unless we perceive an important difference between human and non-human animals, we should do the same in our relation to animals. Indeed, if the ethical aspect of our conduct toward animals extends beyond the injunction against inflicting pain, we should have to act in this way. Most of us, however, place reflective consciousness over non-reflective, and this is another indication that ethicality belongs in the human domain.

We have so far been talking at a somewhat abstract and general level about our relation to animals. But we may also discuss receptivity and direct contact in connection with them. I have already presented a number of examples illustrating the one-caring's receptive attitude toward animals, and in a previous chapter we discussed ways in which caring for pets might serve to nurture the ethical ideal of a child who has opportunities for such caring in cooperation with a caring adult.

Just as there is natural caring when the one-caring loves the one-to-be-cared-for, so there can be natural caring when one has familiarity with animals. When one is familiar with a particular animal family, one comes to recognize its characteristic form of address. Cats, for example, lift their heads and stretch toward the one they are addressing. Receiving an animal as nearly as we are able to do so adds greatly to the pleasure we experience in its company. Its responsiveness helps to sustain us as ones-caring. When I enter my kitchen in the morning and my cat greets me from her favorite spot on the counter, I understand her request. This is the spot where she sits and "speaks" in her squeaky attempt to communicate her desire for a dish of milk. I understand what she wants, and it does not seem inaccurate to say that she expects to be given both milk and affectionate stroking. I have incurred an obligation and, as we shall see, this obligation rests on the establishment of a relation. Puffy is a responsive cared-for, but clearly her responsiveness is restricted: she responds directly to my affection with a sort of feline affection—purring, rubbing, nibbling. But she has no projects to pursue. There is no intellectual or spiritual growth for me to nurture, and our relation is itself stable. It does not possess the dynamic potential that characterizes my relation with infants. I must consider her welfare because we are in a relation where reciprocity is presently exhibited.

But must I receive the stray who calls at my door? Is there an ethical dimension to our caring beyond the one already discussed, that is, beyond refraining from inflicting pain? I think there is, in the very important sense of maintaining internal truth and serenity. If I have pleasant memories of caring for cats and having them respond to me, I cannot ethically drive a needy one away from my back door. A chain has been forged. A stranger-cat comes to me formally related to my pet. I have committed myself to respond to this creature.

But what if the creature at the door is a rat? I would certainly not invite it in, nor examine its body for wounds nor stroke it affectionately nor even feed it. Indeed, I might kill it with whatever effective means lay at hand. Now, we have an opportunity to explore something important. We are once again faced with the threat of capriciousness in our ethical conduct. I have suggested that the "I must" arises (for me) with respect to cats but that I feel no such stirring in connection to rats. Is this not pure sentiment of the most idiosyncratic form?

Sentiment is surely involved. Indeed, I have been trying throughout this work to show just how sentiment is involved in ethicality and why we cannot brush it aside or try to get "above" it in our ethical reasoning. It is sentiment, a feeling of sensual pleasure and affection, that has induced a relation between me and the cat family. The relation, in turn, gives rise to the genuine ethical "I must." But I was not obliged to enter the relation. There was no inevitable caring and being cared for with respect to cats. The first encounter was either an accident or a choice. Hence it is entirely reasonable for me to claim that I have an ethical responsibility toward cats and that you may not have such a responsibility. I shall claim, also, that while I have such a responsibility for cats, I have none, beyond refraining from the infliction of pain, for rats. I have not established, nor am I likely ever to establish, a relation with rats. The rat does not address me. It does not appear expectantly at my door. It neither stretches its neck toward me nor vocalizes its need. It skitters past in learned avoidance. Further, I am not prepared to care for it. I feel no relation to it. I would not torture it, and I hesitate to use poisons on it for that reason, but I would shoot it cleanly if the opportunity arose.

What we see clearly here is how completely our ethical caring depends upon both our past experience in natural caring and our conscious choice. We have made pets of cats. In doing so, we have established the possibility of appreciative and reciprocal relation. If we feel that the cat has certain rights, it is because we have conferred those rights by establishing the relation. When we take a creature into our home, name it, feed it, lay affectionate hands upon it, we establish a relation that induces expectations. We will be addressed, and not only by this particular creature but also by others of its kind. It seems obvious that we might live ethically in the world without ever establishing a relation with any animal, but once we have done so, our population of cared-fors is extended. Our ethical domain is complicated and enriched, and to behave uncaringly toward one of its members diminishes it and diminishes us. If we establish an affectionate relation, we are going to feel the "I must," and then to be honest we must respond to it. Farm people have a saying: "If you are going to eat it, don't name it." This is doubly wise. It is not only that it takes a certain stoicism to go on eating "Goldie" or "Henrietta" but naming a creature and eating it seem symptomatic of betrayal. By naming it, we confer a special status upon it and, if we would be ethical, we must then honor that status.

Now, we might wonder whether there are members of the animal kingdom with whom we should form relations of some friendly sort. This is a question typical of the instrumentalist position and, although that is not the position generally espoused here, it is worth asking. We might ask a similar question when we admit that the one-caring sometimes "scouts" alien territory, inviting or initiating relations in order to protect her inner circle more effectively. There is, of course, nothing sleazy or grubby about that sort of foray; the one-caring is prepared to behave as one-caring in her encounters. But we should carefully separate this second-hand "caring" (which is really a search for contractual reciprocity) from the real caring that might or might not follow. Similarly, we might recognize through observation or report that some members of the animal world are useful to us. Spiders, toads, and king snakes (if I ever see one) are welcome in my garden because they serve my purposes: they eat marauders. The ought that arises in connection with them, then, is the instrumental ought: I ought to protect them if I value their services. The one-caring agrees but she does so warily, because she knows that this instrumental ought is a product of cool knowledge. Contractual reciprocity may give way to genuine reciprocity. It may provide an impetus toward relation: spiders should be protected. She looks at spiders and their extraordinary work. She reads about or actually sees a "spider fall" in which the landscape is transformed into a shimmering network of webs. She recalls the legend of Robert Bruce and how he revived his courage by watching a spider build and rebuild. She reads "Charlotte's Web" to her small daughter. She is entranced by the African spider-man-spirit, Anansi, the trickster. What happens? A relation is established. She must forever after coax spiders onto paper towels so that they can be carried with some dignity (and safety) out of the house. She does not squash them, and no one in her household would think of doing so. There is no ethical escape from the obligation that arises in the caring relation.

What can we say about attempts to save the whales, the seals, or the condors? Do the persons engaged in these efforts actually care for the creatures in question? In cases where a relation has been established, we would have to answer affirmatively, but in many cases the effort seems very like campaigns to save valuable objects and works of art. Those promoting such campaigns are behaving sensitively toward future generations of human beings and not necessarily toward the creatures to be saved. If, for example, I care for a particular pair of condors, I may prefer to let them live out their lives in their own natural way rather than to protect them in the interest of perpetuating the species. Even if the animals in question are threatened by overt and deliberate destruction—as opposed to a gradual deterioration of their environment—I must, as one-caring, consider the possible effects of my recommendations on human welfare. It may not be as easy as it sounds for persons engaged in whaling to find other occupations. Thus, when I dare to make an ethical judgment of someone else's behavior, when I insist that he should behave as I would in a given situation, I must also offer my support and help. Otherwise, I forfeit myself as one-caring.

In all of these situations the one-caring is in some conflict. The appeal of intelligent, warm-blooded and attractive creatures is enormous. But the one-caring knows this. She sees clearly what her ethicality is built upon. The slaughter of baby seals brings revulsion, but the slaughter of moray eels might bring mere relief. We should not be accused of sentimentality when we recognize the role of sentiment in ethicality. Indeed, one who ignores the role of affection may be accused of "romantic rationalism." We can see clearly that animals are not capable of entering a mutually or doubly caring relation with human beings, but as their responsiveness or perceived responsiveness increases, our natural caring increases also. When I hear recordings of "whale songs" or look at the soft, lovely eyes of a baby seal, I am touched. Whether or not the creature is responsive, I am responsive to the possibility of its responsiveness. But then I must realize that the secondary sentiment, the "I ought," that arises differs from the true ethical sentiment. Toward those creatures with whom I have formed an actual relation—in which the creature recognizes me, displays "affection" for me, may even protect me—I feel an obligation; what arises is the ethical sentiment, and my denial of it diminishes my ideal. But as I move past those creatures with whom I have a relation, the feeling that arises is more nearly pure sentiment and I risk talking nonsense as I act upon it. I may not know enough about the creature's natural ways to ensure that my "caring" will be completed in the cared-for. I may ride roughshod over the needs and desires of human beings in my zeal to protect the creature. And, possibly worst, I may confuse raw, passionate feeling with the more gentle, considered, committed, and often conflicted state of ethical caring.

Again, we see that an ethic of caring is perceptive and creative rather than judgmental. I may, as an individual, be willing to enrich and complicate my ethical life by including some members of the animal kingdom in it but, aside from demanding justification for the infliction of pain, I cannot judge you if you do not decide to complicate your life in a similar fashion.

OUR RELATION TO PLANTS

Human life and animal life depend upon plant life. The instrumental ought arises, then, with dramatic force when we ask whether we should protect and enhance plant life. But, of course, we are not limited to or even primarily interested in the instrumental ought. We are interested in the possibility of relation, of caring and being cared-for.

The relation, if it is possible, is again one-sided. Plants serve me, but they cannot care for me. They are not potentially ones-caring. They are, however, responsive cared-fors. They grow vigorously and in their own distinctive ways in response to my caring, and they sustain me as one-caring. But do they respond to my caring or merely to my caretaking? Would they do just as well if I did the right things at the right time with no engrossment and no displacement of motivation? I do not know the answer to this. I, being scientifically educated, suspect that they would do quite as well whether I care or not. I am quite sure that my talking to them is not crucial. I do talk to them: *Aha, so you have mealy bugs again. . . . A bit chlorotic, eh? . . . Beautiful, beautiful.* But I remove the mealy bugs with an alcohol swab, and I apply iron to cure the chlorosis, and I provide food to maintain the beauty. The talk enlivens me, and I suspect that is what the caring does. I could just caretake, but in caring the responsive behavior of the cared-for adds something to me as one-caring that it cannot give to the perfunctory caretaker. Further, the engrossment of caring leads me to learn more about the plants in my care and to try harder to meet their needs. I am not convinced that a mere caretaker will do the right things at the right time.

The ethical shades off into the sensitive. I feel the "I must" in connection with those plants I have captured and confined in pots or garden beds. When the iresine droops, I see the effects of stress in the plant and respond with a sympathetic distress. Again, what happens to me is very like what happens in ethical caring. I have chosen to bring these plants into my home, I see or remember how lovely they can be at their best, and I feel that I ought to maintain them. But this is not, strictly speaking, the true ethical ought. I cannot receive a plant as I can a human being, or even as I can certain animals, and the relation can never be doubly caring. There is, so far as I can tell, no affective response in plants. I must remember this as I assess my natural caring for plants. These are my fascination. I shall not be pleased if you kill the plant I give you, but I cannot pass an ethical judgment on you.

It is another matter, of course, if one's behavior toward the plant world or the natural world in general affects human beings deleteriously. If I care for human beings, I must not defoliate their forests, poison their soils, or destroy their crops. Similarly, I may wish to preserve the delicate desert from the damage caused by dirt-bikes but, in doing so, I am not behaving ethically toward the desert. Rather, I am supposing that the aesthetic appreciation I feel for the landscape may be shared by other persons, and I feel that I ought to preserve that possibility for them.

Might I have an actual relation with the desert? This is not an easy question. It was not easy to answer questions concerning my relation to cats, and I may wonder about my relation (or its possibility) to the ferns, and orchids, and gesneriads I grow. The feelings aroused in me are the result of receptive and sensitive contact and the perceived responsiveness of the cared-for. This perceived responsiveness induces further engrossment and displacement of motivation. It may induce real joy. But the relation, of necessity, falls short of the human relation, and I must remember this as the protective feeling arises in me. I must not beat, or kill, or curse the one who destroys my orchids, or spoils the desert, or cuts down the redwoods. Rather, my approach must be that of one-caring toward the marauder. By gentle and persistent example and persuasion, I encourage him to enhance his life by joining me in caring.

There is another side to this. It may well be that you care deeply for some plant, animal, or environment in which I have no interest. My carelessness may shock and offend you. Now my obligation as one-caring is to listen, to receive you in all your indignation. I do not give way because of political pressure and the might of your lobbying, but I listen carefully because you address me. What matters to you is of interest and concern to me. We do not draw the line of principle, choose sides, and confront each other across it. Rather, we receive each other, we allow ourselves to feel what the other feels, and then we reason together. "All this is of variable importance, but you still matter more."

THINGS AND IDEAS

We have been moving steadily away from the ethical toward the sensitive and aesthetic. As we pass into the realm of things and ideas, we move entirely beyond the ethical. We may encounter a thing or an idea as "Thou"—it may "fill the firmament"—but we do not receive feelings from it in response to our Thou-saying. It may, indeed, reveal itself to us somehow; our engrossment is rewarded, but we do not usually suppose that the thing or idea is itself somehow subjectively enhanced by our caring. It develops under the effort we produce having succumbed to its spell; there is reciprocity, but no affective reciprocity or manifestation of feeling for us as ones-caring.

I am not going to say much about things, partly because I am not much interested in things except as they are the embodiment of ideas and partly because much that is useful has been said about them elsewhere.[6] My main reason for setting things aside is that we behave ethically only through them and not toward them. Further, our relation to them as things is stable. As we see beyond the things to the ideas that generated them and are generated by them, we encounter the possibility of dynamic relation, of growth. Hence, I shall concentrate on our relation to ideas but, even in this domain, our relation is not ethical.

We have spoken again and again of receptivity. We have looked at what characterizes it in the caring relation, at the joy it induces in relation, and at its various manifestations in human, animal, and plant domains. In the intellectual domain, this receptivity is sometimes labeled "intuition." As we move toward a discussion of education, intellectual intuition or receptivity will be of some interest. Every so often, educators are prodded into thinking about intuition and its role in education. In the sixties, Jerome Bruner urged us to consider two questions: What is intuitive thinking? What affects it?[7] While he and some curriculum workers explored the second question with some vigor, and Bruner himself looked at the first question with some care,[8] curriculum people and educators in general failed to bring the two questions together in a significant pedagogical exploration.

In this decade, discussion of intuition is often accompanied by talk about "two brains," and educators are being urged to "educate both halves of the brain," to educate for intuitive as well as for intellectual development.[9] But in much of this discussion, we find a sharp separation between intuition and intellect. The striving characteristic of Bruner's "intuitive thinking" is either missing entirely or directed at very different kinds of goals. Again, we feel the need to ask: What is intuition? How is intuition related to intellect? Exactly what are we trying to develop when we set out to educate "the other half of the brain"?

I want to explore intuition as direct contact, as a receptive faculty. For this discussion, "to intuit the other" will be to receive the other. Intuition has been a topic of some fascination for centuries. The earliest metaphysics was, of course, founded on intuition, and "seers" pronounced as truth what they saw, not what they derived by reason.[10] Indeed, the analogical identification of intuition with seeing remains prominent in contemporary descriptions of intuition. Fascinating as the exploration might be, we cannot undertake here a global or historical account of intuition. We are interested in what it means to make contact, to receive the object.

A quick glance at the literature on intuition reveals a multiplicity of views, some of them in at least superficial contention. Intuition is variously associated with the dark, mysterious and timeless and with the light, simple and direct. It is seen as a special instrument of women;[11] as an alternative way of knowing;[12] as nonverbal thinking;[13] as the special province of artists. It appears bound in endless dichotomies: intuitive/ analytic, feminine/masculine, Dionysian/Apollonian, dark/light, analogic/digital, nonverbal/verbal, indirect/direct, left/right, concrete/ abstract, synthetic/analytic, holistic/atomistic, parallel/sequential, spatial/linguistic, metaphoric/rational.[14] Not only are the views diverse but in some cases they are even contradictory. References to intuition as indirect and mysterious contrast sharply with descriptions of intuition as illuminating, direct, and primitive.

In philosophical views, we find similar diversity and even more striking contradiction. Intuition is described as a source of truth;[15] as the special tool with which life and all living are understood;[16] as art;[17] as the source of moral judgment;[18] as a capacity of the soul that connects reason and experience, making the latter meaningful;[19] as a means of achieving knowledge in introspection; as a mode of evidence;[20] as the source of mathematics;[21] even as a "force of habit rooted in psychological inertia."[22] The reader interested in the general topic of intuition will not run out of reading material quickly.

Even in the views we started with—Bruner's concept of intuitive thinking and the current notion of intuition as the domain of the minor hemisphere—we find certain incompatibles if not outright contradictions. When Bruner speaks of intuitive thinking in an educational setting, he leads us to think of a flashing mentality, one that arrives at "plausible but tentative formulations without going through the analytic steps by which such formulations would be found to be valid or invalid conclusions."[23] He very nearly equates the training of intuition with the "training of hunches." When Robert Ornstein talks about educating for the intuitive mode, he talks about "physiological self-mastery," "the ignoring of thought," "nonattachment," "magic words," and "oral language."[24]

Can these views be reconciled? If we restrict our attention to the domain of intellectual activity, I think there is a significant range of overlap that we might profitably study. It seems obvious that we are not ready to teach biofeedback in schools and that we cannot use the methods of Zen masters to send our students with a resounding slap from the analytic-verbal to the intuitive-nonverbal realm of knowledge. We have, on the one hand, an emphasis on problem solving, on a deep level of intellectual learning and understanding and, on the other hand, an emphasis on receptivity, on a cessation of manipulative striving. It will be a major point in this section that a receptive phase is absolutely essential to a quest for understanding. The engrossment of caring may be directed to objects and ideas, and to engage in this kind of caring, we need to be free to pursue where we are led by the objects and ideas.

There seem to be two general situations in which the intuitive faculty can be directly involved in producing intellectual results. In one, we may be confronted with a conceptualization of some sort—say, a verbal description of a phenomenon or a statement of principle—and we must, to understand it, find objects that can serve as representatives of the things referred to in the verbalization. In the other, we are presented objects in hazy context; we "see" the objects but, because we do not understand their possibilities, we can say nothing about them nor predict the result of anything we might do with them. We have already encountered such situations in caring for persons.

Let's start with the first problem. I am faced with a statement of principle or conceptual definition, let's say, "Every group is isomorphic to a permutation group." Now, presumably, this statement is not thrown to me out of the blue by a sadistic teacher. I have some preparation for it; I have some notion, although it may be vague, what is meant by "group," "isomorphic," and "permutation." Faced with this half-meaningful statement, I ask: *What shall I do?* This reaction is comparable to our ethical, "I must do something." Now this is, I think, important. Too often those interested in the relation between intellect and intuition entirely neglect the initial motivational factor. The Gestaltists, for example, leaped immediately to an examination of the intellectual question: *What is it?* and failed to see that a reason for their subjects' frequent failure in intellectual tasks might be that they never asked that question. If one's reaction to the initial internal question is, *Fake it!* or *Run!* or *Memorize!* one never really confronts the statement in a search for meaning. So first of all, there must be a feeling that it is safe to move on to the intellectual question, and there must be a will to do so. I must not be pressed for time, and I must not be made to feel foolish as I begin my exploration.

I say, *What does this mean?* and receive, perhaps, a storm of silence in reply. Then I return to the active question, *What shall I do to find out what it means?* I need objects that I can handle. I construct a simple group. I put beside it a permutation group with the same number of elements. I draw up a correspondence, matching identities and inverses. It works. I ask, *Is there a systematic way in which I can produce a permuta-*

tion group from any given group? What does the behavior of these objects tell me? What do I see here?

Now I think I am describing here what can be called an intuitive mode of working. I am working; there is effort expended. But I am alternately active (I'll try this) and receptive (What is happening here?). The active phase depends upon my store of knowledge and is partly analytic, but the receptive phase provides that which will be acted upon. I must let things come in upon me. I cannot be interrupted. I am watching, being guided, attentive as though listening. The idea "fills the firmament."

The nature and value of the receptive mood or phase is too often overlooked. Those who work from a philosophical base that accepts intuition as a faculty generally emphasize the activity of the subject, and that activity is not denied here. But manipulative or assimilative activity must cease in order that what-is-there may exercise its influence upon the situation. If we agree that an act of consciousness puts us into contact with the object, there is still the question: *How shall I act upon it?* One possible answer, critical at many stages of intellectual activity, is not to act upon the object in response to some decision about what I have seen, heard, or felt. I let the object act upon me, seize me, direct my fleeting thoughts as I scan the structures with which I may, in turn, act upon the object. My decision to do this is mine, it requires an effort in preparation, but it also requires a letting go of my attempts to control. This sort of passivity, it should be noted, is not a mindless, vegetablelike passivity. It is a controlled state that abstains from controlling the situation; it involves ongoing processes but not explicitly goal-oriented activities.

Now let's return briefly to the problem with which we started, that of bringing meaning to the statement, "Every group is isomorphic to a permutation group." I have labeled the mode in which we search for and observe representative objects as "intuitive." This is not to say that no analytic activity occurs. (In particular, the manipulative activities that intervene between search and observation may be analytic.) But the mood is dominantly intuitive. I am more often in a state of receptivity, allowing the world to come in upon me and only occasionally pinching down on my objects with particular structures. All of the action techniques that are usually described as part of intuitive approaches may be employed: I may draw pictures, use favorite symbols as object-representatives, concoct analogies, study hypothetical special cases;[25] but as soon as I have created a situation through the use of one of these techniques, I relax my controlling impulse and let the situation absorb and direct me.

Any teacher who has worked with students in mathematics knows that the present discussion reveals a matter of practical importance. Frequently, students employ the techniques of intuitive approaches, for example, drawing pictures, constructing tables, but they fail to see what is there. A working mode is not necessarily intuitive because certain techniques identified as "intuitive" are being employed. It is essential that the cast of mind be intuitive, and it is that cast of mind I have been trying to describe. It involves a dual orientation toward objects that are confronted in consciousness: I am subject, but then I am object. I relax my subjectivity. Again, we see the similarity between this sort of activity and caring for human beings.

We must observe, also, that the purpose of my intuitive search with respect to "Every group is isomorphic to a permutation group" is to understand, to create meaning. I may or may not succeed in constructing an actual proof. The quest for meaning is itself a creative endeavor and, thus, I must go through much the same process as I might in creating the proof. But there are differences. First, in one form of original creation, much of the play with concrete objects would have preceded the realization of the general statement. Indeed, one might stumble across the method of proof before the generalization itself. Second, I know, as I work, that I can refer to a text in which the proof is spelled out for me. That proof, which is at-hand, may be unintelligible to me, however, until I go through the process of constructing and observing objects. Reading the textbook proof after struggling at length with the problem and understanding what is needed—what will satisfy the requirements of the situation—I may have an "of course!" reaction. I should see clearly why certain moves are made, why certain objects are chosen. Although I may not have created a proof, I should have achieved insight with respect to an existing proof.

Let's move on to the second kind of problem, that in which intuition starts with given objects and moves toward an understanding of their possibilities. We encounter, now, a quest for background, for contextual structure. But it is important to realize that, again, there is a personal context that sets the stage for what is to follow. The question *What shall I do?* arises again and must be resolved in favor of an intellectual orientation before meaningful exploration can begin. The intellectual *What shall I do?* is comparable to the ethical *I must do something.* In each instance I must be free to explore and to choose, and I must make a commitment.

A graduate student recalls the first time he encountered the symbol

"⊃" in a logical exposition. He had expected the book in which it appeared to be difficult, perhaps beyond his comprehension, and when he saw the "⊃," he thought, "Oh, my, I knew it!" But he was not pressed; no one was awaiting a response from him. He moved on to ask: What is it? After examining the page in the alternately active-receptive way we have been discussing, he could see that "⊃" was just an alternative for the familiar " → ." A characteristic of this kind of seeing is its clarity. One cannot imagine, having achieved this insight, ever returning to a state of bewilderment.

The quest for structure is essentially an intuitive search. I must return again and again to confront, alternately, the object and its background features, to let first one and then the other be the focus of my attention. I put myself into the picture and allow myself to be moved about by what is there. When I think that I have discerned a structure, I pass into an analytic mode and impose that structure. If the object does not behave as I would have predicted, I withdraw my imposition and confront the situation again from another perspective. Again, I submit myself to the influence of the object.

There are, of course, intuitive modes that have no intellectual orientation at the outset and may or may not turn toward an intellectual stance as the mode continues. Such modes have a consummatory flavor. I may turn on the stereo to listen to *Tristan and Isolde*. I prepare for a delightful experience: glass of sherry, light reading material, comfortable chair, shoes off. I let the music flood all of my being. I am totally receptive. I may remain that way to satiety. Similarly, a devout Christian may prepare himself for Holy Communion with a rigorous intellectual search of conscience and an active quest for forgiveness. But when he turns to the communion rail, it is with an expectation of being filled. The spaces purged of willfulness and pride can be filled with Grace. The expression, "Be still, and know that I am God," illustrates the ultimate receptivity of the intuitive mode.

Robert Frost describes the creation of a poem as though he were seized by it:

> The figure a poem makes. It begins in delight and ends in wisdom. . . . It has an outcome that though unforseen was predestined from the first image of the original mood—and indeed from the mood. . . . It finds its own name as it goes.[26]

Later he contrasts the scholar and artist by way of how they acquire knowledge:

Scholars get theirs with conscientious thoroughness along projected lines of logic; poets theirs cavalierly and as it happens in and out of books. They stick to nothing deliberately, but let what will stick to them like burrs where they walk in the fields.[27]

We must add that scientist (or scholar) and artist are equally dependent upon intuitive modes for both the acquisition and creation of knowledge. The poet may begin in the intuitive and move to the analytic once his poem has come into being. The scientist often begins in the analytic and moves to the intuitive in order to understand the objects he has created conceptually.

Our justification for including here a brief description of intuitive modes in which there is no intellectual orientation is threefold: First, there may be, as there is in the creation of a poem, a turn toward the intellectual; second, there is a "storing up" of images that may be used in later intellectual endeavors. As Frost puts it:

The impressions most useful to my purpose seem always those I was unaware of and so made no note of at the time when taken, and the conclusion is come to that like giants we are always hurling experience ahead of us to pave the future with against the day when we may want to strike a line of purpose across it for somewhere.[28]

Third, there may be affective transformation, which itself changes the course not only of intellectual life but of everyday life for the subject experiencing it. If we value the beauty and fulfillment of such moods in adult life, if we feel that they enhance us as ones-caring, then we must grant their legitimacy in education. Just as joy may arise in human relation, it may arise in intellectual relation. It arises here as an accompaniment to our realization that we have received something, that we stand in a special relation to the object of investigation.

It may well be that the well-known phenomena of incubation and illumination represent a case of the receptive-intuitive phase. We strive mightily on a problem (the period of preparation), try every trick we can think of, wring the situation dry of all it will produce, and then we give up. It is important to note that we do not give up with the intention of abandoning the topic forever; we give up "for now." At this point, it is possible that the intuition can maintain an unconscious openness to a well-defined class of internal stimuli. This is the period of "incubation." Illumination, if it occurs, comes dramatically, accompanied by the characteristic "Eureka" reaction.[29]

I have dwelt on the receptive phase at some length because I believe it represents an area of pedagogical neglect and, perhaps, pedagogical helplessness. We see in it something of the unteachable and turn away without considering what we might teach or how we might teach in order to enhance it. We quite naturally turn to proof, which is complete in itself, and away from the sort of demonstration that reveals our seeing; we rely on explanation and shy away from an obligation to induce understanding.

In our examination of caring and ethical caring, we noted a quest for response; success in establishing caring is marked by completion in the form of affective response in the cared-for. In the intellectual domain, our caring represents a quest for understanding. When we understand, we feel that this object-other has responded to us. The quest for understanding establishes a direction in the intuitive mode, and this direction is both sure-and-clear and continually subject to minor changes. We know where we are headed but must tack constantly to stay on a course we cannot chart beforehand. Frost's comment about "giants hurling experience ahead of us" seems especially to the point, for that seems to be what we are doing in an intuitive mode: hurling ahead of us the very directional signs that will lead us. As Einstein described his experiences:

> During all those years there was a feeling of direction, of going straight toward something concrete. It is, of course, very hard to express that feeling in words but it was decidedly the case and clearly to be distinguished from later considerations about the rational form of the solution.[30]

What the object-other yields to us in nonconscious response is understanding.

The affective aspect of intellectual experience is entirely ours; it serves to increase both our engrossment and our vulnerability, for we fear—as we sometimes do in human relations—that this other may reject or desert us. As we turn to a discussion of education, we shall ask how we can legitimate engrossment in intellectual activity—how we can avoid punishing the student for failure to achieve a particular goal and allow him to experience the joy of relation and the quest for understanding.

SUMMARY

In this chapter, we have moved from the ethical into the intellectual and sensitive. We first considered our relation to animals, and found that an ethical dimension based on relation exists but that it gives rise to "ethical calls" that may vary with the nature of the relation. We then considered the plant world and found that, while caring occurs in the elliptical sense given by the "I care," there is no true ethical relation between humans and plants because the relation is logically one-sided and there is no other consciousness to receive the caring.

In a section on caring for things and ideas, we first considered the nature of aesthetical or intellectual caring. Here we found the common features of engrossment and displacement of motivation; we found a meaning for this displacement in terms of "being seized" or allowing ourselves to be seized as we relinquish control. Finally, an attempt was made to characterize intuitive modes.[31] In an important sense, this characterization parallels the description of the one-caring in human relations, but there is no suggestion of ethicality. Such intellectual caring, while not ethical in itself, may contribute to ethicality by giving rise to receptive joy and that joy, in turn, may increase our personal vigor and thus help to sustain us in our quest for ethicality.

8

MORAL EDUCATION

WHAT IS MORAL EDUCATION?

A DISCUSSION OF PRACTICAL ethics quite naturally involves a discussion of how we shall educate people to be ethical. From the view we have taken, such a discussion is of vital importance, for we all bear a responsibility for the ethical perfection of others. Moral education is, then, a community-wide enterprise and not a task exclusively reserved for home, church, or school. Further, it has for us a dual meaning. It refers to education which is moral in the sense that those planning and conducting education will strive to meet all those involved morally; and it refers to an education that will enhance the ethical ideal of those being educated so that they will continue to meet others morally.

As in development of the ethic itself, I shall refrain from the use of jargon often associated with moral education. I shall not, for reasons already made clear, discuss "stages" of moral development and, obviously, I shall not dwell on moral reasoning. Is my view, then, "affectivist"? I shall reject that label, although both the ethic and the resulting recommendations for moral education rest on a foundation of affective relation. I reject the label because such labels are often affixed simplistically, and the notion arises that one who insists on recognizing the affective base of morality must, therefore, minimize the role of cognitive activity. One cannot dismiss thinking and reasoning from ethical conduct, and I have made no attempt to do this. It is a matter of emphasis and of origin. When I have recognized the affective "I must," I must think effectively about what I should do in response to the other. I do not respond out of blind sentiment, but I put my best thinking at the service of the ethical affect. If I exclude cognition, I fall into vapid and pathetic sentimentality; if I exclude affect—or recognize it only as an accompaniment of sorts—I risk falling into self-serving or unfeeling rationalization.

171

As in other parts of the book, I shall accept the label "feminine" but only if we understand that all of humanity can participate in the feminine as I am describing it.

The one-caring has one great aim: to preserve and enhance caring in herself and in those with whom she comes in contact. This quite naturally becomes the first aim of parenting and of education. It is an aim that is built into the process itself—not one that lies somewhere beyond it. Everything that is proposed as part of education is examined in its light. That which diminishes it is rejected, that which casts doubt on its maintenance is postponed, and that which enhances it is embraced.

Clearly, from this point of view, rationality as "trained intelligence" is not the dominant and guiding aim of education, but that does not mean that it is not at all an aim to be valued. It means that rationality, while important and prized, must serve something higher. Joseph Junell describes and questions the view that insists on "trained intelligence" as the primary aim of education:

> Nor are present-day academicians espousing this view hard to find. In a provocative essay review of Arthur Schlesinger's book, *The Crisis of Confidence: Ideas, Power and Violence in America,* John Bunzel, president of San Jose State College, raises by implication the most nagging of all questions with which educators, since the days of Socrates, have ineffectually come to grips: To what part of man does public education owe its first obligation? Is it to his intellectual-academic world, or his emotional-social one? Which is more likely to insure him a measure of happiness and a reasonable chance of survival?[1]

The question has, for the most part, been cast in this form. Sometimes, a writer acknowledges the supreme importance of both human domains but assigns their nurturance to separate institutions. Thus, the school trains the intelligence, and the home and church train for morality and emotional well-being. We must reject this view emphatically. It is not that these functions cannot be separated theoretically. It is, rather, that the human being who is an integral composite of qualities in several domains is thereby shaped into something less than fully human by the process. The primary aim of every educational institution and of every educational effort must be the maintenance and enhancement of caring. Parents, police, social workers, teachers, preachers, neighbors, coaches, older siblings must all embrace this primary aim. It functions as end, means, and criterion for judging suggested means. It establishes the climate, a first approximation to the range of acceptable practices, and a lens through which all practices and possible practices are examined. Questions concerning the ethical arise in every aspect of human life, and nurturance of the ethical ideal cannot be assigned to any one or two institutions. All must accept responsibility.

If the primary aim of all educative effort is the nurturance of the ethical ideal, educational institutions may still differ in their secondary aims. The school, in particular, need not—because it is an educational institution and thus committed to fostering ethicality—abdicate its essential responsibility to train the intellect. This notion is pernicious and silly. Suppose we were to agree that a mother's first responsibility to her young child is to feed it nutritious food. Would it not be foolish to suppose that she could not also attend to dressing it warmly and attractively? But our priorities would be instructive. If the mother were to withhold certain fruits, soups, and beverages consistently on the grounds that the child's clothing might be soiled by these foods, we might suggest that her priorities had been confused. Similarly, when we deliberately pose tasks or suggest means that may promote the intellect but put the ethical ideal at risk, we have confused our priorities dangerously.

Junell, in the paragraph quoted, seeks an education that will ensure humankind a "measure of happiness and a reasonable chance of survival." This suggests that the aims of life are happiness and survival. Surely, we must agree that living things seek to preserve their own lives and, in the nonreflective mode, to perpetuate their kind. From a naturalistic viewpoint the aim of life is life. But life as survival, while an obvious prerequisite, is not a sufficient aim for reflective consciousness. One aims for more than mere survival, and many would rather die than accept perpetual mere life.

Is happiness, then, the aim of life? Many philosophers and educators assert that it is. A. S. Neill says it straight out: "I hold that the aim of life is to find happiness. Education should be a preparation for life."[2]

But most of us, while agreeing that happiness is important, want to define it. Some in the hedonistic tradition are very close to perfectionists, in their description of what constitutes happiness. They differ only in that which they identify as the aim of life. As we have wrestled with problems of ethicality, however, we have been led to identify something more basic—something from which both happiness and perfection spring, toward which they tend. For the one-caring, this "something" is the special relatedness of caring. To receive and to be received, to care and be cared-for: these are the basic realities of human being and its basic aims.

To be with another in time of trouble is better than to be permanently alone and trouble-free. Indeed, one cannot imagine being trouble-free and permanently alone. One loses both the "human" and the "being" when one is severed from all relation. The aim of life, then, is not primarily happiness in either the sense of fulfilling pleasure or avoiding pain and trouble; nor is it perfection in the sense of preparation for another life or of perfecting a separate entity such as the soul. The primary aim is, rather, caring and being cared for in the human domain and full receptivity and engagement in the nonhuman world. A life meeting this aim is—despite pain, deprivation, and trouble—filled at least occasionally with joy, wonder, engagement, and tenderness.

In pointing to the maintenance and enhancement of caring as the primary aim of education, I am drawing attention to priorities. I certainly do not intend to abandon intellectual and aesthetic aims, but I want to suggest that intellectual tasks and aesthetic appreciation should be deliberately set aside—not permanently, but temporarily—if their pursuit endangers the ethical ideal. We cannot separate means and ends in education, because the desired result is part of the process, and the process carries with it the notion of persons undergoing it becoming somehow "better." If what we do instructionally achieves the instructional end—A learns X—we have succeeded instructionally but, if A hates X and his teacher as a result, we have failed educationally. A is not "better" as a result of our and his efforts. He can receive neither the teacher nor the subject as one-caring.

Now, am I suggesting that an educator must retreat every time a student shows discomfort or disinterest in a topic? Some educational thinkers, Neill and Rogers possibly, seem to endorse such a suggestion. In their views, the teacher must wait for the student to display interest before working with him to establish and attain particular objectives. But I would not hesitate to teach that which I, as teacher, believe the student should know if he is to be credited with mastery of a particular set of topics. Throughout the process, however, I would accept his attitude toward the subject, adjust my requirements in light of his interest and ability, and support his efforts nonjudgmentally. He must be aware always that for me he is more important, more valuable, than the subject. In our discussion of teaching, we shall see that the teacher properly influences and, also, quite properly plays a role in evaluation.

The view to be expressed here is clearly different from the dominant view in contemporary education. The difference is revealed in the remarks of Louis Rubin in his introduction to a set of essays on moral education:

> Ethical behavior arises neither out of psychological predisposition nor instinct. Rather, moral quality stems from the cumulative development of appropriate beliefs regarding proper human conduct. The capacity and desire to make ethical decisions—perhaps the major goals of citizenship education—are therefore the product of commitment coupled with choice; one takes certain ideals as moral imperatives and chooses actions that are most likely to fit.[3]

I have been at pains to insist that ethical behavior does arise out of psychological deep structures that are partly predispositional (I would prefer to say "natural") and partly the result of nurturance. When we behave ethically as ones-caring, we are not obeying moral principles—although, certainly, they may guide our thinking—but we are meeting the other in genuine encounters of caring and being cared for. There is commitment, and there is choice. The commitment is to cared-fors and to our own continual receptivity, and each choice tends to maintain, enhance, or diminish us as ones-caring.

What would schools be like under an ethic of caring?

THE ONE-CARING AS TEACHER

Whatever I do in life, whomever I meet, I am first and always one-caring or one cared-for. I do not "assume roles" unless I become an actor. "Mother" is not a role; "teacher" is not a role.[4] When I became a mother, I entered a very special relation—possibly the prototypical caring relation. When I became a teacher, I also entered a very special—and more specialized—caring relation. No enterprise or special function I am called upon to serve can relieve me of my responsibilities as one-caring. Indeed, if an enterprise precludes my meeting the other in a caring relation, I must refuse to participate in that enterprise. Now, of course, an enterprise by its very nature may require me to care for a problem or set of problems. If I am a bus driver, or airline pilot, or air traffic controller, or surgeon, I may properly "care" for the problems and tasks presented. My major responsibilities focus on the other as physical entity and not as whole person. Indeed, as traffic controller, I do not even meet the other whose safety I am employed to protect. In such enterprises I behave responsibly toward others through proficient practice of my craft. But, even in such enterprises, when encounter occurs, I must meet the other as one-caring. It is encounter that is reduced and not my obligation to care. Clearly, in professions where encounter is frequent and where the ethical ideal of the other is necessarily involved, I am first and foremost one-caring and, second, enactor of specialized functions. As teacher, I am, first, one-caring.

The one-caring is engrossed in the cared-for and undergoes a motivational displacement toward the projects of the cared-for. This does not, as we have seen, imply romantic love or the sort of pervasive and compulsive "thinking of the other" that characterizes infatuation. It means, rather, that one-caring receives the other, for the interval of caring, completely and nonselectively. She is present to the other and places her motive power in his service. Now, of course, she does not abandon her own ethical ideal in doing this, but she starts from a position of respect or regard for the projects of the other. In the language of Martin Buber, the cared-for is encountered as "Thou," a subject, and not as "It," an object of analysis. During the encounter, which may be singular and brief or recurrent and prolonged, the cared-for "is Thou and fills the firmament."

When a teacher asks a question in class and a student responds, she receives not just the "response" but the student. What he says matters, whether it is right or wrong, and she probes gently for clarification, interpretation, contribution. She is not seeking the answer but the involvement of the cared-for. For the brief interval of dialogue that grows around the question, the cared-for indeed "fills the firmament." The student is infinitely more important than the subject matter.

The one-caring as teacher is not necessarily permissive. She does not abstain, as Neill might have, from leading the student, or persuading him, or coaxing him toward an examination of school subjects. But she recognizes that, in the long run, he will learn what he pleases. We may force him to respond in specified ways, but what he will make his own and eventually apply effectively is that which he finds significant for his own life. This recognition does not reduce either the teacher's power or her responsibility. As we saw in our earlier discussion of the cared-for, the teacher may indeed coerce the student into choosing against himself. He may be led to diminish his ethical ideal in the pursuit of achievement goals. The teacher's power is, thus, awesome. It is she who presents the "effective world" to the student.[5] In doing this, she realizes that the student, as ethical agent, will make his own selection from the presented possibilities and so, in a very important sense, she is prepared to put her motive energy in the service of his projects. She has already had a hand in selecting those projects and will continue to guide and inform them, but the objectives themselves must be embraced by the student.

Buber suggests that the role of the teacher is just this: to influence. He says:

> For if the educator of our day has to act consciously he must nevertheless do it "as though he did not." That raising of the finger, that questioning glance, are his genuine doing. Through him the selection of the effective world reaches the pupil. He fails the recipient when he presents this selection to him with a gesture of interference. It must be concentrated in him; and doing out of concentration has the appearance of rest. Interference divides the soul in his care into an obedient part and a rebellious part. But a hidden influence proceeding from his integrity has an integrating force.[6]

When, out of intrinsic interest or trust and admiration for the teacher, the student does embrace an objective, he may need help in attaining it. The teacher, as one-caring, meets the student directly but not equally. Buber says that the teacher is capable of "inclusion," and this term seems to describe accurately what the one-caring does in trying to teach the cared-for. Milton Mayeroff, for example, in his discussion of caring, emphasizes this duality in the one-caring:[7] the "feeling with" that leads the one-caring to act as though for herself, but in the projects of the other and the accompanying realization that this other is independent, a subject. In "inclusion," the teacher receives the student and becomes in effect a duality. This sounds mystical, but it is not. The teacher receives and accepts the student's feeling toward the subject matter; she looks at it and listens to it through his eyes and ears. How else can she interpret the subject matter for him? As she exercises this inclusion, she accepts *his* motives, reaches toward what *he* intends, so long as these motives and intentions do not force an abandonment of her own ethic. Inclusion as practiced by the teacher is a vital gift. As we saw earlier, the student's attempts at inclusion may result in a deterioration of the learning process.

The special gift of the teacher, then, is to receive the student, to look at the subject matter with him. Her commitment is to him, the cared-for, and he is—through that commitment—set free to pursue his legitimate projects.

Again I want to emphasize that this view is not romantic but practical. The teacher works with the student. He becomes her apprentice and gradually assumes greater responsibility in the tasks they undertake. This working together, which produces both joy in the relation and increasing competence in the cared-for, was advocated, we may recall, by Urie Bronfenbrenner in his discussion of cooperative engagement in tasks, and it was also implied by Robert White's discussion of competence as the desired end of "effectance motivation." The child wants to attain competence in his own world of experience. He needs the cooperative guidance of a fully caring adult to accomplish this. The one-caring as teacher, then, has two major tasks: to stretch the student's world by presenting an effective selection of that world with which she is in contact, and to work cooperatively with the student in his struggle toward competence in that world. But her task as one-caring has higher priority than either of these. First and foremost, she must nurture the student's ethical ideal.

The teacher bears a special responsibility for the enhancement of the ethical ideal. She is often in contact with the ideal as it is being initially constructed and, even with the adult student, she has unique power in contributing to its enhancement or destruction. In dialogue, she can underscore his subjectness—encourage him to stand personally related to what he says and does. He is not just part of the lesson, a response to be recorded as "move 15" or whatever. He is a human being responsible for his words and acts, and the one-caring as teacher meets him thus. Why he thinks what he thinks is as important as what. The domain to which he refers for justification is significant. How he relates to others as he does all this is important.

Besides engaging the student in dialogue, the teacher also provides a model. To support her students as ones-caring, she must show them herself as one-caring. Hence she is not content to enforce rules—and may even refuse occasionally to do so—but she continually refers the rules to their ground in caring. If she confronts a student who is cheating, she may begin by saying, *I know you want to do well,* or, *I know you want to help your friend.* She begins by attributing the best possible motive to him, and she then proceeds to explain—fully, with many of her own reservations expressed freely—why she cannot allow him to cheat. She does not need to resort to punishment, because the rules are not sacred to her. What matters is the student, the cared-for, and how he will approach ethical problems as a result of his relation to her. Will he refer his ethical decisions to an ethic of caring or to rules and the likelihood of apprehension and punishment? Will he ask what his act means in terms of the feelings, needs, and projects of others, or will he be content with a catalog of rules-of-the-game?

A teacher cannot "talk" this ethic. She must live it, and that implies establishing a relation with the student. Besides talking to him and showing him how one cares, she engages in cooperative practice with him. He is learning not just mathematics or social studies; he is also learning how to be one-caring. By conducting education morally, the teacher hopes to induce an enhanced moral sense in the student. This view was held, also, by John Dewey. Sidney Hook describes the relation in Dewey's thinking:

> How, then, does Dewey achieve the transition from what we have called the morality of the task to the task of morality? His answer—original for his time and still largely disregarded—is to teach *all* subjects in such a way as to bring out and make focal their social and personal aspects, stressing how human beings are affected by them, pointing up the responsibilities that flow from their inter-relatedness.[8]

Everything we do, then, as teachers, has moral overtones. Through dialogue, modeling, the provision of practice, and the attribution of best motive, the one-caring as teacher nurtures the ethical ideal. She cannot nurture the student intellectually without regard for the ethical ideal unless she is willing to risk producing a monster, and she cannot nurture the ethical ideal without considering the whole self-image of which it is a part. For how he feels about himself in general—as student, as physical being, as friend—contributes to the enhancement or diminution of the ethical ideal. What the teacher reflects to him continually is the best possible picture consonant with reality. She does not reflect fantasy nor conjure up "expectations" as strategies. She meets him as he is and finds something admirable and, as a result, he may find the strength to become even more admirable. He is confirmed.

The sort of relatedness and caring I have been discussing is often dismissed as impossible because of constraints of number, time, and purpose. Richard Hult, in his discussion of "pedagogical caring," notes that such requirements seem to require in turn close personal relationships of the I-Thou sort. He says: "While these may sometimes occur and may be desirable, most pedagogical contexts make such relationships implausible if not undesirable."[9] He concludes that caring as Mayeroff has described it, and as I have described it, "cannot be the kind of caring demanded of teachers." I insist that it is exactly the kind of caring ideally required of teachers.

I think that Hult and others who take this position misunderstand the requirement that Buber has described as an I-Thou encounter; that Marcel has described in terms of "disposability"; that Mayeroff has described as identification-with-recognition-of-independence; that I have described as engrossment and displacement of motivation. I do not need to establish a deep, lasting, time-consuming personal relationship with every student. What I must do is to be totally and nonselectively present to the student—to each student—as he addresses me. The time interval may be brief but the encounter is total.

Further, there are ways to extend contact so that deeper relationships may develop. If I know how my student typically reacts to certain topics and tasks, I am in a better position to guide him both sensitively and economically. Why can we not opt for smaller schools, for teachers and students working together for three years rather than one, for teachers teaching more than one subject? We are limited in our thinking by too great a deference to what is, and what is today is not very attractive. Our alternative is to change the structure of schools and teaching so that caring can flourish, and the hope is that by doing this we may attain both a higher level of cognitive achievement and a more caring, ethical society.

When we begin our educational planning, we may start with schools as they are, identify their primary functions, and ask how they may best be organized to serve their functions. Or we may start with our picture of caring and education and ask what sort of organization might be compatible with this picture. When James Conant made his influential recommendations concerning the organization of secondary education,[10] he began with the intellectual function of schools and, assuming a national need for high-powered curricula in mathematics and science, suggested that larger schools were required to support such programs. I have begun by identifying the maintenance and enhancement of the ethical ideal as the primary function of any educational community, and so I shall be interested first not in the establishment of programs but in the establishment and evaluation of chains and circles of caring. To establish such chains and circles, we may need to consider smaller schools.

I shall say more about how schools might be organized to support caring and, in particular, we should discuss, in the context of teaching, dialogue, practice, and confirmation. We should remind ourselves, before we leave this initial discussion on the one-caring as teacher, that there is another in the caring relation. The student also contributes to caring. The one form of mutuality that is excluded from the teacher-student relation is an attempt at inclusion on the part of the student. A focus of student attention on the teacher's instructional strategies is fatal to the relationship—and to the student's learning. The student may, however, care for the teacher as a person. He may be fascinated by her and hold her in the highest regard. He may be willing to help her with physical tasks and, indeed, to assist her in teaching other students. Nothing in our discussion was meant to preclude the possibility of the student's caring but, within the teacher-student relation, his caring is different from that of the teacher.

The student has his greatest effect on the relationship as the one cared-for. If he perceives the teacher's caring and responds to it, he is giving the teacher what she needs most to continue to care. As the infant rewards his caring mother with smiles and wriggles, the student rewards his teacher with responsiveness: with questions, effort, comment, and cooperation. There is some initiative required of the cared-for. Just as the one-caring is free to accept or reject the internal "I must" of caring, so the cared-for is free to accept or reject the attitude of caring when he perceives it. If the cared-for perceives the attitude and denies it, then he is in an internal state of untruth.

Many of our schools are in what might be called a crisis of caring. Both students and teachers are brutally attacked verbally and physically. Clearly, the schools are not often places where caring is fulfilled, but it is not always the failure of teachers that causes the lapse in caring. Many urban teachers are suffering symptoms of battle fatigue and "burn-out." No matter what they do, it seems, their efforts are not perceived as caring. They themselves are perceived, instead, as the enemy, as natural targets for resistance.

The cared-for is essential to the relation. What the cared-for contributes to the relation is a responsiveness that completes the caring. This responsiveness need not take the form of gratitude or even of direct acknowledgment. Rather, the cared-for shows either in direct response to the one-caring or in spontaneous delight and happy growth before her eyes that the caring has been received. The caring is completed when the cared-for receives the caring. He may respond by free, vigorous, and happy immersion in his own projects (toward which the one-caring has directed her own energy also), and the one-caring, seeing this, knows that the relation has been completed in the cared-for.

We see another cogent reason for insisting on relation and caring in teaching. Where is the teacher to get the strength to go on giving except from the student? In situations where the student rarely responds, is negative, denies the effort at caring, the teacher's caring quite predictably deteriorates to "cares and burdens." She becomes the needy target of her own caring. In such cases, we should supply special support to maintain the teacher as one-caring. Communities are just barely awakened to this need. But no indirect caring can fully compensate for the natural reward of teaching. This is always found in the responsiveness of the student.

What am I recommending? That students should be more responsive to their teachers? Can we command them to respond? This approach seems wrong, although parents might reasonably talk to their children about the difficulties of teaching and ways in which students can support and encourage their teachers simply by exhibiting a spontaneous enthusiasm for their own growth. But, realistically, such a recommendation seems unlikely to be productive. What I am recommending is that schools and teaching be redesigned so that caring has a chance to be initiated in the one-caring and completed in the cared-for. Sacrifices in economies of scale and even in programs might be called for. These would be minor if we could unlock our doors and disarm our security guards. Schools as institutions cannot care directly. A school cannot be engrossed in anyone or anything. But a school can be deliberately designed to support caring and caring individuals, and this is what an ethic of caring suggests should be done.

DIALOGUE

As we discuss the three great means of nurturing the ethical ideal—dialogue, practice, and confirmation—we must also bring together our major threads of thought. Our aim is to nurture the ethical ideal, and the ethical ideal strives to maintain and enhance caring. We are also concerned with making the voice of the mother heard in both ethics and education. Our ethic of caring springs from woman's conception of her ethical self as one-caring.

Of first importance to the one-caring is relatedness. She is not eager to move her students into abstraction and objectivity if such a move results in detachment and loss of relation. Indeed, at least one writer, Madeleine Grumet, suggests that the excessive efforts at abstraction, objectivity, and detachment in our schools are a manifestation of the father's psychological need to take possession of the child. Grumet begins by taking a position similar to that of Chodorow on the effects upon the male child of separation from his mother:

As mother is not him, so too objective reality becomes not him, and his own gender, more tentative than that of the female, is constituted by the symbolic enculturation of his culture's sense of masculinity, a conceptual overlay that reinforces his own sense that his subjectivity (that preoedipal maternal identification) and objectivity (that primary object, mother) are alien. Chodorow's point is that masculine identification processes stress differentiation from others, the denial of affective relations, and categorical, universalistic components of the masculine role, denying relation where female identification processes acknowledge it. Both as infants and as adults, males exist in a sharply differentiated dyadic structure, females in a more continuous and interdependent, triadic one.[11]

She then explores what this means for schools:

> Because schools are ritual centers cut off from the real living places where we love and labor we burden them with all the ornate aspirations our love and labor are too meager and narrow to bear.
> Contradicting the inferential nature of paternity, the paternal project of curriculum is to claim the child, to teach him or her to master the language, the rules, the games and the names of the fathers.[12]

We may have to struggle through a tremendous upheaval before mother and father are heard equally in the schools. The mother must actively resist having her children turned into a succession of roles. She must point out and question the foolishness that pervades current school practice and, at least initially, the dialogue she invites may be met with hostility.

If dialogue is to occur in schools, it must be legitimate to discuss whatever is of intellectual interest to the students who are invited into dialogue. God, sex, killing, loving, fear, hope, and hate must all be open to discussion. Many educators will insist that this openness is impossible— that we run the risk of indoctrinating particular religious values when we discuss God, that we shall surely offend parents if we discuss sex, that killing and hate are best discussed historically or in the context of faraway places. The attempt to separate that which may be spoken into legitimate domains strengthens those who would control our children and wrench them away from lives of attachment and caring. At present, values are rarely discussed in schools. The supposition is that they are, and should be, discussed at home and church. But even if this were so, it would not be enough. Both home and religious institution are often engaged in the deliberate inculcation of particular values, and these are sometimes in conflict with each other. The school, ideally, is a setting in which values, beliefs, and opinions can be examined both critically and appreciatively. It is absurd to suppose that we are educating when we ignore those matters that lie at the very heart of human existence.

Does it seem odd to suggest that we should talk about happiness and grief, about what makes life worth living, about conflicts of loyalties? Or does it seem odd that we do not talk about these things? In order to engage in true dialogue with our students, we educators will first have to engage in true dialogue with their parents. We will need trust and cooperation in a genuine attempt to educate. We may have to forsake our professionalism and take up our common humanity in extended caring relations.

It is not possible to discuss in depth how we might approach the host of controversial issues that will arise in true dialogue. But let us consider religion. I suggested in earlier chapters that women have no ethical need for gods. One might suppose, then, that my purpose in suggesting that schools discuss religion freely is ultimately destructive—to lead the way to a completely secular society. While such a society may one day be established, it is not necessary that we push strongly toward it. Do we not all embrace the notion of meeting the other morally? Here is the place to start—in caring for each other so that we may teach our children to live in the world as ones-caring and cared-for.

Small children are already permitted to share in various religious festivals, but we often strip away the religious qualities of these ceremonies before allowing children to observe them. Again, we introduce division and mere appearance into what should be educational experience. I am suggesting that all the religious groups in a community be represented in planning and presenting programs for the spiritual and ethical growth of the community's children, and that these programs be discussed openly and appreciatively. The fear arises, of course, that children will be lured away from the beliefs of their parents or that someone will treat what is dearly held with mockery or disdain. Are we not already guilty of the grossest mockery and disdain when we refuse to discuss these matters at all? Surely, teachers can be just as careful and sensitive in this area as they have learned to be in matters of socioeconomic status, race, and ethnic identity. If those sensitivities are not so well developed as we might wish, few of us would recommend that we cease talking about such matters.

What I am suggesting is that students be exposed not only to information about religions but to their affective accompaniments as well. They should read religious writings, view religious art, and hear religious music. They should have opportunities to feel what the other is feeling as a result of deeply held beliefs. They should be touched by the beauty, faith, and devotion manifested in the religious practices of others. Through such experiences—feeling with the other in spiritual responsiveness—they may be reconnected to each other in caring. The mother's hope is, of course, that this caring will be held above all particular religious beliefs and that young people devoted to each other will refuse to bayonet, shoot, and bomb each other. Will young people educated in this fashion "lose" their religions? Perhaps. If a particular set of beliefs is so fragile that it cannot stand intellectual examination, or so uncharitable that it cannot tolerate caring relations, then indeed it should be lost.

Just as the educator who is properly fascinated with her subject matter will put it aside temporarily for the sake of the student and his ethical development, so must the religious leader put aside the objects, and territories, and possessions he cherishes for the sake of the living other.

This sort of education is important in a special way for young women. They should know what the world's great modern religions have done to them and for them, and they should be aware that the feminine once played a far greater role in religious experience. They should be aware of how shabbily women have been treated by certain "saints" and how even the great-hearted have suffered under this abuse. Pearl Buck describes the loving charity of her mother and the terrible loneliness and self-doubt that afflicted her because of her "spiritual inferiority." Working side by side with her husband in a church dominated by St. Paul, she suffered from his misogynic doctrines. Buck writes of her father's attitude toward his wife:

> Strange remote soul of a man that could pierce into the very heavens and discern God with such certainty and never see the proud and lonely creature at his side! To him she was only a woman. Since those days when I saw all her nature dimmed I have hated Saint Paul with all my heart and so must all true women hate him, I think, because of what he has done in the past to women like Carie, proud free-born women, yet damned by their very womanhood.[13]

This woman who "hated" St. Paul founded both an adoption agency and a foundation for children whose fathers had created and left them. Indeed, she filled her home with such children. Along with exposure to the beauties and flaws of religion, students should learn what it means to embrace an ethic of caring.

From this discussion of religion and dialogue, we may abstract a general approach to the discussion of issues that affect us deeply. What I am advocating is a form of dialectic between feeling and thinking that will lead in a continuing spiral to the basic feeling of genuine caring and the generous thinking that develops in its service. Through such a dialectic, we are led beyond the intense and particular feelings accompanying our own deeply held values, and beyond the particular beliefs to which these feelings are attached, to a realization that the other—who feels intensely about that which I do not believe—is still one to be received. Watching another in prayer, or at communion, or even brandishing a holy sword, I may feel what he feels even though I reject what he believes. Then I am reconnected to this other in basic caring.

We have been talking about dialogue—about talking and listening, sharing and responding to each other. It is vital in every aspect of education. In teaching subject matter, the teacher must learn to listen as well as to talk. As the student thinks aloud, the teacher may direct and correct him, but he is thinking, initiating, trying things out. He may even have opportunities to meet the subject matter as "Thou"—that which seizes and directs his energies, that which responds to him.

School people talk incessantly about goals such as "critical thinking," and "critical reading," and "critical reasoning." So long as our critical skills and the exercises presented to develop them are confined to "Ps" and "Qs" and "P implies Q" our schools will have the absurd appearance of a giant naked emperor. We need to look with unclouded eyes on what we are doing. The purpose of dialogue is to come into contact with ideas and to understand, to meet the other and to care.

It is clear, I think, that instituting open and genuine dialogue implies a weakening of professional structures and an attempt to establish teachers and parents as cooperative educators. In order to establish the level of trust and understanding that is required for open dialogue, we might consider a reorganization of schooling that would provide extended contact between teachers and students. If, for example, elementary school teachers were to remain with a group of students for three years rather than for the traditional one year, there might be time to develop the sort of deep caring relationship that could provide the basis for trust and genuine dialogue. Similarly, high school teachers might assume responsibility for a group of students in their particular subject over the entire span of high school years. Such arrangements would make it possible for us to expect that teachers should act as counselors and advisors in their subject fields and not just as imparters of knowledge. The objection that is most often raised to suggestions for extended contact is that we should not want our children subjected to a bad teacher for an extended period—for, say, our suggested three years. But think what we are saying when we raise that objection! The appropriate reply is, surely, that we should not want our children exposed to a poor teacher for even one year. We have become too well adjusted to mediocrity, routine, and things-as-they-are.

PRACTICE

When we discussed construction of the ideal, we outlined a program for its nurturance. We noted then that children—indeed, all of us—need practice in caring. How may this practice be provided in schools? We can see, in a general way, that opportunities for shared efforts at caring must be provided. If legal structures were amended to make real work possible for students in schools, we could make many suggestions. Students might be expected to participate in regular service activities. Some might work with a custodial master, learning how to replace window panes, repair damaged furniture and appliances, and keep the physical surroundings clean and comfortable. Others might work outdoors, learning how to plant, groom, and maintain the grounds. Some might work in the kitchen, some in offices, some in classrooms as aides to teachers. Some might work off campus in agencies designated as appropriate by a school committee constituted to oversee the apprenticeships in caring. Wherever students might be assigned—to hospitals, nursing homes, animal shelters, parks, botanical gardens—a definite expectation would be that their work be a true apprenticeship in caring. There would be no demand that the student learn the occupation-as-occupation, although, of course, vocational choices might emerge in such a program. I am not suggesting that there would be no expectation for the learning of skills; there would, of course, be such an expectation. But the emphasis would be on how the skills developed contribute to competence in caring, and not on the skills for vocational ends.

I have purposely included in the initial list of tasks both opportunities to care for humans and animals directly and opportunities to care for people indirectly through maintenance of the environment. An interesting and important by-product of this sort of program for caring would be the involvement of adults in all kinds of occupations with students. Everyone in the program would function as teacher in his or her own area of expertise and take special responsibility for nurturing the ethical ideals of the young people working with him or her. In making this recommendation, I am consciously rejecting the prevailing notion that persons engaged in the moral education of students must be specially trained in moral reasoning. I think such persons do need to be included in the continuous dialogue of planning, reviewing, and emphasizing commitment. They need to know what they are about, but their usefulness and moral worth as models do not depend on an understanding of the forms of syllogism or of the principles of moral philosophy.

Again, I am recommending that we carefully, deliberately, and generously dismantle the professional structures that separate us into narrow areas of specialization. Such a move will almost certainly be resisted strongly and, among those who welcome the suggestion, there will be many who do so for destructive or self-serving reasons. We may find ourselves with strange bedfellows. Nevertheless, we should explore the possibilities in deprofessionalization. Education is an enterprise in which all of us should be engaged. I want to return to the matter of deprofessionalization shortly, but first let's pursue the recommendation for establishing opportunities for students to care.

The recommendation is not a warmed-over suggestion for elaborate work-study programs. I am not recommending that students be paid for their opportunities to care, nor am I suggesting that only nonacademically oriented students engage in such work. All students should be involved in caring apprenticeships, and these tasks should have equal status with the other tasks encountered in education. I suspect we teach an unfortunate lesson when we suggest that geometry is worth learning for itself, but that caring—for the elderly or for children or for animals or, indirectly, for everyone by maintaining the environment—must be "paid work." This special service is more properly conceived as a significant component of the educational program. The practical difficulty involved in welcoming so many unpaid learner-workers to the occupational domain can be solved if we are willing to commit ourselves to the education of our children as ones-caring. If we continue to insist that all work —at whatever stage of expertise—is dignified only to the extent that it is paid, then we really are lost as a caring community. We can only be a self-seeking set of individuals engaged in caretaking for whatever monetary rewards that effort will bring.

We meet, again, a dilemma for modern women. In order to achieve equality with men in the public world, we must insist that much of the work we have traditionally done as unpaid volunteers now be paid work. Pay, it seems, gives dignity to our efforts. This is another case of working against ourselves, and our deepest longings for a world in which affect and relation count, by pursuing a supposedly neutral "equality." An alternative, as we properly move into the professional world of paid work, is to insist that what we did in the past has such value that all of us should be engaged in it. Working from this alternative requires an expansion of the volunteer domain and a steady, responsible contraction in the domain of professional "helpers." No one helps so well as one-caring when he or she is reasonably well trained in the requisite skills.

I have already suggested, however, that skill training for our apprentices-in-caring ought not to become an end in itself. With this in mind, I suggest that students should not always be assigned to areas in which they have shown special talent. Such a decision could only lead to a reestablishment of status hierarchies and increased separation among those we are trying to initiate into the caring community. I suggest that both the student and the placement committee be involved in selecting the student's service program. In some study intervals, the student might elect his service; in others, he might accept the committee's suggestion that he try something for which he has shown little aptitude. Thus the math whiz might struggle to complete a mechanical task, and the youngster who has trouble with math himself might work with small children who are just starting their adventure with numbers. The idea, here, is to induce a genuine respect for the multiplicity of human talents and abilities and to make it safe for students to risk themselves in new and difficult situations. When we share our tasks, our successes, our failures, we care more easily and naturally, because we gain some understanding of what the other is trying to do.

We see in this suggestion another form of dialectical growth. As we engage alternately in tasks at which we excel and in those at which we must struggle somewhat clumsily, we move to a greater appreciation for both skilled work and the individuals who perform it. We move beyond pride in this particular task and fear of that particular task to a state in which we are, again, reconnected to the other in appreciative relation.

Now, clearly, when we consider seriously the establishment of opportunities to care, we must look not only at special programs but also at the structure of schools and classrooms. If we value genuine caring encounters, then our classrooms will be cooperatively organized for many tasks.

Children will be encouraged to learn from each other as well as from teachers and books. The research literature on what is learned in cooperative groups as contrasted to what is learned individually is ambiguous,[14] but we must keep in mind that I am not claiming enhanced individual cognitive development as an outcome of this new structure. It may occur; indeed, I suspect it will occur. But the aim is enhancement of the ethical ideal, of the sense of relatedness, of renewed commitment to receptivity. With that aim clearly in mind, we will not give up when the first rash of studies produces "no significant differences" in academic achievement. The purpose in talking about aims is to keep our priorities straight.

In structuring the schools longitudinally over the grades K–12, we must again consider which arrangements support or are likely to support caring and which might work against it. We will be wary of sharp age separations, because these separations may induce a selfish in-turning toward the problems unique to particular ages. This does not mean that we should ignore developmental needs when we plan our programs and physical facilities, but it does mean that we must consider the development of the ethical ideal as we make our plans. If we had considered seriously the development of children as ones-caring, I suspect we would never have established junior high schools. To separate these youngsters, just as their social consciousness is developing—just as they are becoming capable of reflection on their natural sympathies—is to risk their potential as ones-caring. And to force them all through the same graded experience, when they are developing unevenly intellectually, is to risk their intellectual potential as well.

Might it not be better to organize K–7 and 8–12? This suggestion is not meant to be a hard and fast recommendation, but let me supply a rationale for it. First, youngsters would encounter only two school environments and would remain in each long enough to develop a sense of participation, of belongingness or ownership. Second, the grades seven and eight, under this rationale, would serve the particular needs of young adolescents differentially. What I suggest is that grade seven serve as a "finishing experience" for the elementary years. Many youngsters would skip it entirely. But many others would spend this year polishing intellectual skills, or working out social and emotional problems, or just growing bigger and stronger physically before moving on. Parents, teachers, and students should all be involved in the decision. The decision itself should be entirely separated from any consideration of the student's eventual academic course of study; that is, it should not be considered a sorting out or variation of tracking. It is, rather, a decision aimed at optimal development and not at academic acceleration. That academic acceleration for some students would result is not, on balance, an undesirable outcome. Grade eight, as an introductory year for high school studies, might also be optional. Again, careful consideration of the needs of each youngster should determine placement. In both of these crucial years, service activities should be handled with exquisite sensitivity, and much time should be given to talking about the work that is done.

It should be made clear that whether a child participates in or skips over grades seven and eight, he or she will be continually involved in service activities. Allowing differential movement is one way—and other, perhaps better, ways might be suggested—of helping students to stay in touch with the intellectual objects of their schooling.

We have already discussed receptivity and the intuitive mode in intellectual work. It seems right to say that we can make direct contact with the objects of knowledge, although, we must remind ourselves, this direct contact does not necessarily result in either truth or dependable knowledge. When we allow ourselves to come under "the gaze of the object," so to speak, we enter relation. Joy or elation may accompany our recognition of relatedness, and a deep knowledge of the object and its relation to other objects of our knowledge may also emerge. Taking intellectual receptivity seriously, we should say something about the organization of subject matter.

If we want students to enter a relation with subject matter—to make direct, receptive contact with it—it seems reasonable to suggest that the scope of subject matter be very broad. Now, I am not suggesting that there must be a great many subjects in the curriculum. Rather, I am suggesting that each subject be laid out along the entire range of human experience so that students may make multiple and potentially meaningful contacts with it. This does not imply, either, that subjects must somehow be "integrated" or clustered together around some common theme or organized from a problem solving approach.[15] Laid out along the entire range of human experience, both personal and cultural aspects of the subject are revealed.

To lay out a subject along the entire range of human experience means, at least, to consider its history and applications, its potential personal and recreational uses in both child and adult life, its epistemological problems and typical modes of resolution. It means, also, an increased emphasis on biography and the meaning of the subject in individual lives.

To make it possible for students to encounter the subject as "Thou"—as that which will seize and delight them—we need to include experiences in all subject areas that will be offered freely with no demands for specific achievement and no attempt at systematic evaluation. Our attitude in offering such experiences is this: Here is something I find delightful, and I would like to share it with you. Stories, puzzles, poems, songs, films—all sorts of things that the educator cherishes—may properly be included in a curriculum that is aimed at receptivity and relatedness.

Along with cultural and personal dimensions of the subject, we should consider the psychological dimension. As students engage in a variety of practical experiences, they will experience a variety of affects. So far I have emphasized the possibility of receiving joy or delight in intellectual experience. We may also discuss motivation, anxiety, working styles, and mental blocks.

Possibly no subject inspires greater fear in more people than does mathematics. Yet, we rarely train our mathematics teachers to act as mathematics counselors. There are ways to reduce fear and anxiety physically (breathing and relaxation exercises), but we may also reduce anxiety by talking about it and revealing how universal it is. We can help, as teachers, by providing multiple opportunities for students to demonstrate that they have learned the material we judge to be essential. Why should a student be penalized for not learning something on the first attempt? Think about it. What is it we are trying to accomplish? If a student has difficulty the first (or second or nth) time with a topic, both teacher and student have a job to do: Try again with renewed support and, perhaps, more imaginative techniques. Do we really want our students to learn mathematics, or do we want to sort them into those who have learned quickly and will therefore be labeled "successes" and those who have not learned and are, thus, righteously declared to be failures? The effort, if learning really is our goal, is a mutual one. Teacher and student contribute significantly to what is achieved.

It should be clear, again, why some of us see traditional curriculum as a masculine project, designed to detach the child from the world of relation and project him, as object, into a thoroughly objectified world. In this part of our discussion of practice in caring, I have emphasized that an alternative feminine approach allows the child to remain in relation and also to grow intellectually. So many of the practices embedded in the masculine curriculum masquerade as essential to the maintenance of standards. I suggest that they accomplish quite a different purpose: the systematic dehumanization of both female and male children through the loss of the feminine.

CONFIRMATION

When we attribute the best possible motive consonant with reality to the cared-for, we confirm him; that is, we reveal to him an attainable image of himself that is lovelier than that manifested in his present acts. In an important sense, we embrace him as one with us in devotion to caring. In education, what we reveal to a student about himself as an ethical and intellectual being has the power to nurture the ethical ideal or to destroy it. In this section I shall say something about the confirmation of both students and teachers.

Even a tiny child, obviously incapable of formal reasoning, has a nuclear ethical ideal. A two-year-old may shout, "No! No hurt baby," at another child who threatens a third. She shows her distress at the infliction of pain. Already the fundamental sympathy reveals itself. The educator does not want to diminish this incipient ideal but to enhance it. It is fragile. If the teacher or parent inflicts pain on the child for whatever reason, the child learns that the infliction of pain can be justified. It is for this reason that the young child must be treated gently and lovingly. He must be shown what it means to be one-caring and to be cared-for. There is no assumption here that the young child is innately wise and good and that, therefore, our best course is to abstain from intervention. It is not suggested that a three-year-old is fully ethical but, rather, that he can become ethical only if the sympathy and tender awareness of which he is already capable are encouraged and enhanced, and, eventually, confirmed with reflection and commitment. So we do intervene. We intervene perceptively and creatively, attributing the best possible motive, and offering our help and our example in caring.

For the one-caring as teacher, the sort of attributions that are made in evaluating raise difficulty. The teacher as one-caring and the student as cared-for both have difficulty in the matter of evaluation. The teacher has no unusual difficulty in evaluating the student's work for the sake of the student and his progress. Problems that arise here arise everywhere in caring; they require appropriate thought, sensitivity, and open communication. The great difficulty is in grading, which is an intrusion upon the relationship between the one-caring and the cared-for. Here is a demand that both know to be an intrusion. The teacher does not grade to inform the student. She has far better, more personal ways to do this. She grades to inform others about the student's progress. Others establish standards, explicitly or implicitly, and they charge her to report faithfully in observance of these standards. Now the teacher is torn between obligation to the employing community and faithfulness to the student. Is this conflict resolvable? Am I making too much of it?

I think the conflict is real and that most attempts to settle it are mistaken. Some say that there is no real conflict, that it is in the best interest of the student to be graded fairly according to openly established and uniformly applied standards. But this is mere glibness. What is a fair standard for student achievement? What is or should be measured to the standard? How? And how can such a standard be "uniformly applied"? Even if the processes (which are so easy to talk about) could be effectively carried out, we would still experience conflict. We are asked to look at the student as object—as a thing to which some measuring stick can be applied. Even if we execute the procedures as carefully and fairly as we can, we must still explain our decisions to the cared-for. After considering all this, we must say, I have decided thus-and-so. This is demeaning and distracting. It violates the relationship.

There are ways to relieve the conflict, to make the situation more livable, but they do not resolve it entirely. One way is to concentrate on whatever learning or achievement is to be attained and not on when it is attained. Under such a plan, the teacher encourages students to retake tests and redo papers and other projects until they are content with the teacher's decision on grade. Students learn something about themselves and their own motives when they are thus allowed to persist and, of course, they usually feel that the process is more honest and fair, more properly aimed at learning, than the usual one-chance forms of grading. This approach also allows the teacher to maintain "standards" and to insist on whatever degree of excellence seems appropriate. But time runs out in our public schools. After six weeks or eight weeks or whatever interval constitutes a marking period, a grade must be assigned.

Some teachers use a contract method. Under this plan, students must accomplish so much for an "A," so much for a "B," and so on. This, too, relieves the conflict a bit but, obviously, it places great emphasis on quantity and almost none on the quality of work submitted. There are modifications in which points can be added or subtracted for quality, but by and large quantity is the criterion.

This is a dilemma that goes to the heart of teaching. Teaching involves two persons in a special relationship. Usually, there is a fairly well-defined "something" in which the two engage, but this is not always true. Sometimes teacher and student just explore. They explore something, of course, but this something is not always prespecified; nor need it remain constant or, for that matter, even lead somewhere definite. The essence is in the relationship. In the relationship, the teacher has become a duality: she shares a view of the objects under study with the student. Then suddenly, grindingly, she must wrench herself from the relationship and make her student into an object of scrutiny. When I doubt my own position on grading, I have only to think of this fundamental violation to be convinced anew that grading—summative evaluation of any kind—should not be done by teachers. If it must be done, it should be done by external examiners, persons hired to look at students as objects. Then teachers and students would be recognized as together in the battle against ignorance. Are there problems with this solution? Of course there are. Now both teacher and student are in a battle against the examiners; they are partly controlled by outside agents. The "regents" or SATs" or "GREs" or "inspectors" become a controlling force. Still, it seems to me that this sort of plan is preferable. In subjects or skills for which an external set of criteria can be applied—and there are, surely, many such areas—it would seem right to work toward them. Airline pilots, doctors, lawyers, teachers, plumbers, electricians, architects all surely need to have mastery of at least some well-defined concepts and skills. Where we can say what must be learned, it seems reasonable to do so. The teacher must help the student toward the prescribed mastery. She must do much more than this, of course, but this she must do also. As it is, her effort is always subsumed and even distorted in the grading process.

How much better it would be if teachers could simply say to students: *You are not yet ready to move along. Stay with me a while and we shall work on these problems.* Or, of course, the teacher might gently suggest that the student try another area of concentration, saying: *It will take a very long time. Are you sure you want to spend your life doing this?* The point is that the caring teacher does not shrink from evaluating her student's work along all the dimensions proper to the field she is teaching; but she feels no need, and no right, to sum it up with a report to the world. At this point the relationship crumbles; it is altered. In many cases, it is utterly destroyed.

When the teacher works with the student toward cooperatively constructed goals, any evaluation is an evaluation of both student and teacher, and it is best carried out cooperatively. The teacher who values her student as subject will be concerned with his growing ability to evaluate his own work. She seeks to confirm him in his intellectual life as well as in his ethical life. In both domains she points him toward his best possible self. From this point of view, neither has a need for grades, and both may see what is lost when they must be given.

The discussion of evaluation has revealed another dramatic split between the masculine world of objectness and the feminine world of subjectness. For whose sake do we make our children into objects? What structures are held together by the cement of grading and evaluating for the purpose of distributing educational goods?

Confirmation, the loveliest of human functions, depends upon and interacts with dialogue and practice. I cannot confirm a child unless I talk with him and engage in cooperative practice with him. It is not confirmation to pronounce someone better than he is at something if he has no inclination toward that something or cannot achieve the goals we expect of him. Simply to have high expectations for our students in general is not confirmation. It is just another form of product control. To confirm, I must see and receive the other—see clearly what he has actually done, and receive the feelings with which it was done. Out of what may be a mixture of feelings and motives, I choose the best to attribute to him. Thus, we are realistic; we do not hide from what-is-there. But we are also idealistic, in the important sense that our attention and educational efforts are always focused on the ethical ideal, on its nurturance and enhancement.

Teachers, also, need confirmation in order to nurture their own ethical ideals. We have already discussed the central role played by the cared-for as he responds to the one-caring through both pursuit of his own goals and attribution of caring motives. The response of students remains at the heart of confirmation for teachers.

But teachers as whole persons need confirmation in the larger world of education, and it may be that such confirmation is necessary in order that the natural confirmation of students may be received without conflict. If, on one hand, teachers are told that what they are doing is wrong, or old-fashioned, or not good enough, they may fear that the confirmation of their students is mere liking and not a genuine pointing upward. If, on the other hand, they are praised or defended generally as a matter of policy by some organization, they find themselves thrown into a crowd, many of whom do not deserve either praise or defense.

We know that teachers are, with students, the heart of the educational process. We know, also, that all sorts of changes and innovations have been effectively blocked, ended, or distorted behind the classroom door.[16] But we still persist in asking how we can crash through this block-ade—how we can get teachers to adopt the methods and practices we think they should use. Perhaps we should try more seriously to find out what they are doing, and to work cooperatively with them toward per-fecting the methods to which they are devoted and in which they reveal their talent. As in every other area of our discussion, this does not mean that we should accept and approve shoddy practices, and we should never allow practices obviously motivated by meanness—what might be termed *anti-caring*. But, surely, we should cease coercing teachers to adopt particular philosophical, psychological, or pedagogical positions and should, instead, talk with each other about the methods we have chosen, the ends we seek, and the pleasure we experience in knowing each other.

It seems obvious, once again, that a feminine approach to education requires a change in the structure of schooling.

ORGANIZING SCHOOLS FOR CARING

What will happen to schools if we take seriously the possible benefits of a movement toward deprofessionalizing education? First, it seems obvious that other adults in the community will have to take an interest in and become more actively involved in educational matters. Second, for this to occur in a way that supports caring, the structure of schools would have to change. Before we consider a form for reorganization, I should say more clearly what is meant by "deprofessionalization." It certainly does not mean a reduction of emphasis on quality, nor a loss of pride and distinction. It means, rather, an attempt to eliminate the special language that separates us from other educators in the community (especially par-ents), a reduction in the narrow specialization that carries with it reduced contact with individual children, and an increase in the spirit of caring—that spirit that many refer to as "the maternal attitude."

A move toward deprofessionalization would be accompanied by a careful look at credentialing. A teacher, I have claimed, must be one-caring. A teacher must also be knowledgeable in her subject field if she is to practice inclusion. If the teacher does not know her subject matter very well, she cannot give her full attention to the students who are approaching it in a variety of ways. She must, instead, maintain absolute control so that things are done her way—the only way with which she is familiar and comfortable. Further, if teachers are to take full responsibility for, say, three or four years of their students' mathematical education, they must know their subject in some depth. Subject matter expertise, however, is rarely what we are concerned with in credentialing. Rather, we allow all sorts of organizations to press for the inclusion of their subjects in the preservice curriculum for teacher education. Many of the skills we associate with teaching are, if they are skills at all, skills whose need is induced by the peculiar structure of modern schooling. If we were to change that structure, many of the skills we now underscore would become unnecessary. Many so-called "management" or "disciplinary" skills would be unnecessary in schools organized for caring.

Assessing the subject matter expertise of aspiring teachers seems a fairly straightforward task, although we would want to allow retests, alternative evaluations, and all the other supports we have recommended for students in general. But how are we to judge whether the apprentice teacher measures up as one-caring? How can we assign caretaking with a reasonable expectation that caring will be present? If we follow the guidelines already laid down, we might recommend that a new teacher work with a master teacher for her first three years. This need not be an expensive program, for two teachers working together with volunteer adults and, perhaps, older children can handle almost the equivalent of two classes. During this extended apprenticeship, the master teacher—who will already have shown herself as one-caring through a prior three-year period with a set of students—will provide the young teacher with powerful practice in caring. Further, in schools organized for caring, parents and other adults would be frequent and welcome visitors to classrooms: supervising small groups, leading discussions, playing with children on the playground, eating with youngsters. No teacher would be alone with students for extended periods of time, or solely responsible for the welfare and progress of her charges. Ideally, caring will extend well beyond the circle of teacher and students to embrace all those interested enough to make themselves known and available in the school.

It is not my purpose to propose a plan for the complete reorganization of schools, but I shall offer a suggestion illustrative of the view we have taken throughout our discussion. Instead of the usual hierarchical order, we would use the idea of circles and chains. Circles would define sets of actual relation, and chains, as before, would describe formal relation—

those places to be filled eventually by persons for whom we are prepared to care, as we do now for those within our circles. We might also employ the notion of cycles: Career teachers might teach for three years and then spend a year in administrative work or study.

Under an extended contact plan, for example, a teacher might see one group of students through three years of their schooling and spend the fourth as a supervisor, or curriculum planner, or disciplinary counselor, or personnel administrator. At the high school level, arrangements might be made for administrator-teachers to meet one advanced class so that their students would not be deprived of their presence in the final year of study. The details of such a plan will not concern us here, but the idea may induce fresh thinking on the sort of structure that might support a caring community within the school.

A plan of this sort would, clearly, displace many career administrators. Many I have talked to, however, profess a longing for the classroom and insist that they would not have "left" it if it had been possible to "advance" within it. Teaching, it is well known, is a "flat" profession; year one and year thirty look much alike. If we were to organize in circles and cycles, teachers could look forward to advances in both financial status and responsibility as they gained experience. Those who have expertise in business, for example, would bring experience to the business office, and would take from their year at that task a host of practical applications and a fuller understanding of the financial problems facing the district. Further, with the enemy—the professional administrator— removed, teachers might be more receptive to innovation and, having a hand in its creation, might implement that which is promising.

Such a plan is thought by many to be inherently inefficient. Specialization is perceived as the solution for efficient operation. There may be some organizations that really do their best work organized bureaucratically and hierarchically, but these may be organizations in which caring is not crucial to the enterprise by its very nature. There is no reason to believe that the existing mass of principals, deans, supervisors, assistants, directors, counselors, and consultants has really contributed to either efficiency or effectiveness. The enterprise can be organized differently, and it should be if we want to establish a community of caring. Clearly, we would face many problems, and some plan for continuity would have to be generated, but reorganization is not impossible.

Now, why is it likely that the kind of thinking I am engaged in will lead nowhere? Is it impractical? It obviously is not; on the contrary, it is hard-headed. Would it be expensive? My guess is that it would *save* money. Well, why will we not at least consider such reorganization? Consider, again, the orientation characterized by hierarchy, specialty, separation, objectification, and the loss of relation. Who is it who climbs the hierarchical ladder and accepts the loss of relation? Who is it who insists on the constant round of testing, labeling, sorting, credentialing? Those who have succeeded in the traditional masculine structure may not easily or graciously give up their hard-won power.

One must keep in mind, finally, that many important and relevant objections might be made against the specific suggestions I have offered. One might, for example, argue that teachers are not competent to conduct the administrative and supervisory work of schooling. That seems a crucial objection. We might, however, respond in two ways. First, teachers could learn these functions, and the requirement that such competencies be mastered might raise the level of aspirant in teaching. Second, many teachers today are incompetent as teachers, and the present system of organization has been unable to change this condition. We have very little to lose and much to gain by trying something different.

The most fundamental answer to specific objections, however, is this: The suggestions are illustrative. They represent an invitation to dialogue, to join in a dialectical conversation between men and women that will embody dialectics between feeling and thinking, between concrete and abstract, between present and future, between community and school. Women, by our very nature, are unlikely to seek domination in education; our circles will be circles of support and not of power. But it is time for the voice of the mother to be heard in education.

We should not leave the topic of school structure without some discussion of the role of rules and penalties. In congruence with the position already set forth, it is obvious that one under the guidance of an ethic of caring would interpret rules as guidelines toward desirable behavior. We might very well state as general expectations that teachers and students should be on time to class, be regular in attendance, and turn in work as promptly as good work will allow. But we need not enforce these rules with penalties. Indeed, an ethic of caring counsels that we should not assign penalties for infractions of these rules. If we post such guidelines, we should monitor relevant behavior, of course, but this may be done out of concern for one who does not meet the guidelines as well as for others who may be affected. If a student is consistently late, we should want to know why this is so. We stand ready to offer help if the difficulty can be remedied. But we do not give zeros for work missed because of unexcused absences, nor do we subtract points for late work, nor assign detentions or other punishments. All of these punitive moves work against the development of subjective responsibility that is required for continuous construction of the ethical ideal. They give the wrong message about both intellectual work and our relations to each other.

Will our students learn to respect law and order if we treat rules in this way? The one-caring really does not want her students to respect law and order for themselves, but for their contribution to the maintenance of caring. We in this century have seen sufficient horror induced in the name of obedience. What we should unceasingly work toward is a thorough examination of laws and rules that will allow us to sort ethically among them. Some we shall accept as valid and appropriate constraints on our behavior; some we shall regard but interpret and reinterpret in the light of caring; and some we shall ignore as unfit for one-caring to obey. Our students should come to understand that this last decision is not one to be made cavalierly and, clearly, it is not made by one-caring out of selfish interest. They will need to hear, also, that they will sometimes find themselves in very wicked company when they decide to reject a law and that their rejection may enrich persons who break the law for their own material gains. But they should also come to understand that one who obeys the law may find himself in very bad company indeed. Obedience to law is simply not a reliable guide to moral behavior.

One must meet the other in caring. From this requirement there is no escape for one who would be moral.

NOTES

1: *Why Care About Caring?*

1. Gauss's remark is quoted by Morris Kline, *Why Johnny Can't Add* (New York: Vintage Books, 1974), p. 58.

2. See Carol Gilligan, "In a Different Voice: Women's Conception of the Self and of Morality," *Harvard Educational Review* 47 (1977), 481-517. Also, "Woman's Place in Man's Life Cycle," *Harvard Educational Review* 49 (1979), 431-446. Also, *In a Different Voice* (Cambridge, Mass.: Harvard University Press), 1982.

3. Milton Mayeroff, *On Caring* (New York: Harper and Row, 1971), p. 1.

4. See David Brandon, *Zen in the Art of Helping* (New York: Dell Publishing Co., 1978), chap. 3.

5. Søren Kierkegaard, *Concluding Unscientific Postscript,* trans. David F. Swenson and Walter Lowrie (Princeton: Princeton University Press, 1941).

6. Ibid., p. 322.

7. See Mary Anne Raywid, "Up from Agape: Response to 'Caring' by Nel Noddings," *Journal of Curriculum Theorizing* (1981), 152-156.

8. Martin Buber, *I and Thou,* trans. Walter Kaufmann (New York: Charles Scribner's Sons, 1970), p. 69.

9. See Richard E. Hult, Jr., "On Pedagogical Caring," *Educational Theory* 29 (1979), 237-244.

10. See H. J. Blackham, *Six Existentialist Thinkers* (New York: Harper and Row, 1959), p. 80.

11. Ibid., p. 80.

12. T. E. Lawrence, *Seven Pillars of Wisdom* (New York: Garden City Publishing Co., 1938), pp. 549, 562-566.

13. Søren Kierkegaard, *Either/Or,* I, trans. David F. Swenson and Lillian M. Swenson (Princeton: Princeton University Press, 1959).

14. See the account in Jacques Hadamard, *The Psychology of Invention in the Mathematical Field* (New York: Dover Publications, Inc., 1954), pp. 16-17.

15. See E. T. Bell, *Men of Mathematics* (New York: Simon and Schuster, 1965), p. 254.

16. Quoted in Hadamard, *The Psychology of Invention in the Mathematical Field,* pp. 16-17.

17. On NBC's *Prime Time Sunday* (July 8, 1979).

18. Ralph Waldo Emerson, "Self-Reliance," in *Essays,* First Series (Boston and New York: Houghton Mifflin Company, 1903), pp. 45-90.

19. Ralph Linton, "An Anthropologist's Approach to Ethical Principles," in *Understanding Moral Philosophy,* ed. James Rachels (Encino, Calif.: Dickenson Publishing Company, Inc., 1976), p. 8.

20. Fred Feldman, *Introductory Ethics* (Englewood Cliffs, N.J.: Prentice-Hall, Inc., 1978), p. 2.

21. See, for example, Joseph Fletcher, *Situation Ethics* (Philadelphia: The Westminster Press, 1966).

2: *The One-Caring*

1. Martin Buber, *I and Thou,* trans. Walter Kaufmann (New York: Charles Scribner's Sons, 1970).

2. Jean-Paul Sartre, "The Emotions: Outline of a Theory," in *Essays in Existentialism,* ed. Wade Baskin (Secaucus, N.J.: The Citadel Press, 1965), pp. 189-300.

3. Paul Tillich, *The Courage to Be* (New Haven and London: Yale University Press, 1952), p. 52.

4. Buber, *I and Thou,* p. 66.

5. Carol Gilligan cites D. McClelland as interpreting the myth as a description of the feminine attitude toward power. See Gilligan, "Woman's Place in Man's Life Cycle," *Harvard Educational Review* 49 (1979), 445.

6. Thomas Bulfinch, *Mythology: The Age of Fable* (New York: The New American Library, Inc., 1962), p. 86.

7. The legend of Ceres has been variously interpreted. The ancient myth clearly referred to the conferral of special gifts on young males by creative and powerful female figures. In this sense, we find a long-standing tradition for the interpretation of Ceres as one-caring, bestowing the gifts of competence and usefulness on her protégés. See Erich Neumann, *The Great Mother* (Princeton: Princeton University Press, 1955). On p. 321, Neumann states: "This investiture is not an 'agricultural' rite, although in the earliest primordial age it was probably bound up with such a rite. In the mysteries at least, it has a far more profound significance. It is the investiture of the male with his chthonic and spiritual fecundating function, which is transmitted to him by woman."

8. See the account in Bulfinch, *Mythology: The Age of Fable.*

9. For a fascinating account of the dark and light in feminine thinking and legend, see M. Esther Harding, *Woman's Mysteries* (New York: Harper and Row, Publishers, 1971).

10. See Lawrence Kohlberg and R. Kramer, "Continuities and Discontinuities in Childhood and Adult Moral Development," *Human Development* 12 (1969), 93-120.

11. Genesis 22: 9, 10.

12. Søren Kierkegaard, *Fear and Trembling,* trans. Walter Lowrie (Princeton: Princeton University Press, 1941), p. 81.

13. Robert Frost, "Home Burial," in *The Complete Poems of Robert Frost* (New York: Henry Holt and Company, 1949), p. 71.

14. Pearl S. Buck, *Fighting Angel* (New York: Pocket Books, Inc., 1964), p. 38.

15. Ibid., p. 2.

16. Joseph Fletcher, *Situation Ethics* (Philadelphia: The Westminster Press, 1966).

17. John Steinbeck, *The Red Pony* (New York: The Viking Press, Inc., 1945).

18. Robert Frost, "The Death of the Hired Man," in *The Complete Poems of Robert Frost,* p. 53.

19. George Orwell, *Nineteen Eighty-Four* (New York: Harcourt, Brace and World, Inc., 1949), p. 289.

3: *The Cared-For*

1. Urie Bronfenbrenner, "Who Needs Parent Education?," *Teachers College Record* 79 (1978), 773-774.

2. Ibid., p. 774.

3. Robert W. White, "Motivation Reconsidered: The Concept of Competence," *Psychological Review* 66 (1959), 327.

4. See Martin Buber, "Education," in *Between Man and Man* (New York: Macmillan Publishing Co., Inc., 1965), pp. 83-103.

5. Martin Buber in "Dialogue Between Martin Buber and Carl Rogers," in *The Worlds of Existentialism,* ed. Maurice Friedman (Chicago: The University of Chicago Press, 1964), p. 487.

6. Margaret Sanger, ed., *The Sixth International Neo-Malthusian and Birth Control Conference,* Vol. 4: *Religious and Ethical Aspects of Birth Control* (New York: American Birth Control League, 1926).

7. M. F. Ashley Montagu, *Prenatal Influences* (Springfield, Ill.: Thomas, 1962).

8. Fritz Wengraf, *Psychosomatic Approach to Gynecology and Obstetrics* (Springfield, Ill.: Thomas, 1953).

9. Edward Pohlman, *The Psychology of Birth Planning* (Cambridge, Mass.: L. Schenkman Publishing Company, Inc., 1969).

10. Gregory Zilboorg, "The Clinical Issues of Postpartum Psychopathological Reactions," *American Journal of Obstetrics and Gynecology* 73 (1957), 308.

11. See, for example, R. R. Sears, E. E. Maccoby, and Harry Levin, in collaboration with E. L. Lowell, *Patterns of Child Rearing* (Evanston, Ill.: Row, Peterson, 1957).

12. See E. S. Schaefer and R. O. Bell, "Patterns of Attitudes Toward Child Rearing and the Family," *Journal of Abnormal Social Psychology* 54 (1957), 391-395.

13. John Holt, *How Children Fail* (New York: Dell Publishing Co., Inc., 1964), p. 80.

14. Donald W. MacKinnon, "The Nature and Nurture of Creative Talent," in *Readings in Managerial Psychology,* ed. Harold J. Leavitt and Louis R. Ponti (Chicago: The University of Chicago Press, 1964), p. 104.

15. Martin Buber, *I and Thou,* trans. Walter Kaufmann (New York: Charles Scribner's Sons, 1970), p. 60.

16. Ibid., p. 58.

17. Ibid., p. 59.

4: *An Ethic of Caring*

1. David Hume, "An Enquiry Concerning the Principles of Morals," in *Ethical Theories,* ed. A. I. Melden (Englewood Cliffs, N.J.: Prentice-Hall, Inc., 1967), p. 275.

2. Friedrich Nietzsche, "Mixed Opinions and Maxims," in *The Portable Nietzsche,* ed. by Walter Kaufmann (New York: The Viking Press, Inc., 1954), p. 65.

3. See, for example, William F. Frankena, *Ethics* (Englewood Cliffs, N.J.: Prentice-Hall, Inc., 1973), pp. 63-71.

4. The argument here is, I think, compatible with that of Philippa Foot, "Reasons for Action and Desires," in *Virtues and Vices,* ed. Philippa Foot (Berkeley, Los Angeles, London: University of California Press, 1978), pp. 148-156. My argument, however, relies on a basic desire, universal in all human beings, to be in relation—to care and be cared for.

5. The question of "summonability" is a vital one for ethicists who rely on good or altruistic feelings for moral motivation. Note treatment of this problem in Lawrence R. Blum, *Friendship, Altruism, and Morality* (London: Routledge & Kegan Paul, 1980), pp. 20-23 and pp. 194-203. See, also, Henry Sidgwick, *The Methods of Ethics* (Indianapolis: Hackett, 1981), and Philip Mercer, *Sympathy and Ethics* (Oxford: Clarendon Press, 1962).

6. Friedrich Nietzsche, *The Will to Power,* trans. Walter Kaufmann (New York: Random House, 1967), pp. 476, 670. For a contemporary argument against strict application of universalizability, see Peter Winch, *Ethics and Action* (London: Routledge & Kegan Paul, 1972).

7. W. D. Ross, *The Right and the Good* (Oxford: Clarendon Press, 1930). See also Frankena, *Ethics.*

8. Paul Ramsey raises this concern in *Fabricated Man* (New Haven and London: Yale University Press, 1970).

9. See the discussion in James Rachels, ed., *Understanding Moral Philosophy* (Encino, Calif.: Dickenson Publishing Company, Inc., 1976), pp. 38-39.

10. See Lawrence Kohlberg and R. Kramer, "Continuities and Discontinuities in Childhood and Adult Moral Development," *Human Development* 12 (1969), 93-120. See also Lawrence Kohlberg, "Stages in Moral Development as a Basis for Moral Education," in *Moral Education: Interdisciplinary Approaches,* ed. C. M. Beck, B. S. Crittenden, and E. V. Sullivan (Toronto: Toronto University Press, 1971).

11. Carol Gilligan, "Woman's Place in Man's Life Cycle," *Harvard Educational Review* 49 (1979), 440.

12. See Nancy Chodorow, *The Reproduction of Mothering* (Berkeley, Los Angeles, London: University of California Press, 1978).

13. Luke 16: 24-26.

14. Søren Kierkegaard, *Fear and Trembling,* trans. Walter Lowrie (Princeton: Princeton University Press, 1954), p. 129.

15. For a lovely exposition of this view, see A. S. Neill, *Summerhill* (New York: Hart Publishing Company, 1960).

16. Willard Gaylin, *Caring* (New York: Alfred A. Knopf, 1976), p. 115.

17. Gene Outka, *Agapé: An Ethical Analysis* (New Haven and London: Yale University Press, 1972), pp. 300-305.

18. Immanuel Kant, *The Metaphysics of Morals,* Part II: *The Doctrine of Virtue* (New York: Harper and Row, 1964), pp. 44-45.

5: *Construction of the Ideal*

1. For a discussion of this point with respect to "conscience," see James F. Childress, "Appeals to Conscience," *Ethics* 89 (1979), 315-335.

2. Friedrich Nietzsche, *Beyond Good and Evil,* trans. Walter Kaufmann (New York: Vintage Books, 1966), p. 205 (§260).

3. Martin Buber, *The Way of Response,* ed. Nahum N. Glatzer (New York: Schocken Books, 1966), pp. 17-18.

4. The research of Marian Radke Yarrow and that of Stuart Westerlund are reported in the popular press. See "Kind Kids are Nice to Know," *Parade* (October 21, 1979), pp. 16-19; "Baby Altruists," *Family Weekly* (October 14, 1979), p. 11. See also Marian Yarrow, P. Scott, and C. F. Waxler, "Learning Concern for Others," *Developmental Psychology* 8 (1973), 240-260. For a comprehensive review on the development of caring, see Paul Mussen and Nancy Eisenberg-Berg, *Roots of Caring, Sharing, and Helping* (San Francisco: W. H. Freeman and Company, 1977).

5. C. S. Lewis, *Surprised by Joy* (New York: Harcourt, Brace, Jovanovich, 1955), p. 184.

6. This is pointed out also by Richard E. Hult, "On Pedagogical Caring," *Educational Theory* 29 (1979), 237-244.

7. See Nancy Chodorow, *The Reproduction of Mothering* (Berkeley, Los Angeles, London: The University of California Press, 1978).

8. Philip Wylie, *Generation of Vipers* (New York: Rinehart, 1942).

9. See Chodorow, *The Reproduction of Mothering;* Jessie Bernard, *The Future of Motherhood* (New York: Penguin Books, 1974).

10. See Matina S. Horner, "Toward an Understanding of Achievement-Related Conflicts in Women," *Journal of Social Issues* 28 (1972), 157-174.

11. See, for example, Carol Gilligan, "Woman's Place in Man's Life Cycle," *Harvard Educational Review* 49 (1979), 431-446; Nel Noddings, "Women and Power," in *Philosophy of Education 1980,* ed. C. J. B. Macmillan (Normal, Ill.: Philosophy of Education Society, 1980), pp. 98-100.

12. The "redemptive" function of motherhood in the political domain is discussed by Jessie Bernard, *Future of Motherhood,* pp. 351-355. See also Jane Alpert, "Mother Right: A New Feminine Theory," *Ms.* (August, 1973).

6: *Enhancing the Ideal: Joy*

1. See Jean-Paul Sartre, "The Emotions: Outline of a Theory," in *Essays in Existentialism,* ed. Wade Baskin (Secaucus, N.J.: The Citadel Press, 1965), p. 235.

2. Ibid., pp. 198-199.

3. Joseph P. Fell, *Emotion in the Thought of Sartre* (New York: Columbia University Press, 1965), pp. 229-232.

4. Hazel B. Barnes, *An Existentialist Ethics* (Chicago: The University of Chicago Press, 1967).

5. See K. T. Strongman, *The Psychology of Emotion* (Chichester, Great Britain: John Wiley & Sons, 1978), pp. 13-50.

6. William James, "What is an Emotion?," *Mind* 9 (1884), 188-205.

7. See the account in Strongman, *The Psychology of Emotion,* and in Jean-Paul Sartre, "The Emotions: Outline of a Theory."

8. Carroll E. Izard, *Human Emotions* (New York: Plenum Press, 1977), p. 4.

9. R. S. Peters, "Emotion, Passivity and the Place of Freud's Theory in Psychology," in *Brain and Behavior,* ed. K. H. Pribram, 4, *Adaptation* (Middlesex, England: Penguin Books, LTD, 1969), pp. 373-394.

10. Sartre, "The Emotions: Outline of a Theory," pp. 244-245.

11. Magda Arnold, ed., *Emotion and Personality* (New York: Columbia University Press, 1960); *The Nature of Emotion: Selected Readings* (Baltimore: Penguin Books, 1968); "Brain Function in Emotions: A Phenomenological Analysis," in *Human Action,* ed. T. Mischel (New York: Academic Press, 1970).

12. S. Asch, *Social Psychology* (Englewood Cliffs, N.J.: Prentice-Hall, 1959). See also S. Schacter, "A Cognitive-Physiological View of Emotions," in *Perspectives in Social Psychology,* eds. Otto Klineberg and Richard Christie (New York: Holt, Rinehart & Winston, 1965), pp. 75-105; D. M. Armstrong, *A Materialist Theory of the Mind* (London: Routledge & Kegan Paul, 1968).

13. Izard, *Human Emotions.*

14. Karl H. Pribram, "The New Neurology and the Biology of Emotion: A Structural Approach," in *Brain and Behavior,* ed. K. H. Pribram, p. 463.

15. Sartre, "The Emotions: Outline of a Theory," p. 236.

16. Ibid., p. 246.

17. Fell, *Emotion in the Thought of Sartre,* p. 191.

18. Martin Buber, *I and Thou,* ed. Walter Kaufmann (New York: Charles Scribner's Sons, 1970), p. 55.

19. Peters, "Emotion, Passivity and the Place of Freud's Theory in Psychology."

20. Ibid., pp. 392-393.

21. Paul Tillich, *The Courage to Be* (New Haven and London: Yale University Press, 1952), pp. 14-15.

22. See B. S. Moore, B. Underwood, and D. Rosenhan, "Affect and Altruism," *Developmental Psychology* 8 (1973), 99-104.

23. Izard, *Human Emotions,* pp. 239-276.

24. See C. M. Meadows, "The Phenomenology of Joy: An Empirical Investigation," *Psychological Reports* 37 (1975), 39-54.

25. Stanley Rosner and Lawrence Abt, eds., *The Creative Experience* (New York: Dell Publishing Co., Inc., 1970).

26. Ibid., p. 137.

27. Ibid., p. 190.

28. Ibid., p. 339.

7: *Caring for Animals, Plants, Things and Ideas*

1. See the discussions in Theodore Roszak, *The Making of a Counter Culture* (Garden City, N.Y.: Doubleday and Company, Inc., 1968), and in Peter Singer, *Animal Liberation* (New York: The New York Review, 1975), chapters 2 and 3.

2. Peter Singer, *Practical Ethics* (Cambridge: Cambridge University Press, 1979), p. 71.

3. See the essays in T. Regan and Peter Singer, eds., *Animal Rights and Human Obligations* (Englewood Cliffs, N.J.: Prentice-Hall, Inc., 1976).

4. See the argument in John and Sally Seymour, *Farming for Self-Sufficiency* (New York: Schocken Books, 1973), pp. 19-21.

5. Singer, *Practical Ethics,* p. 100.

6. For discussion of the problems involved in deciding upon what objects and qualities we should appreciate, see Harry S. Broudy, *Enlightened Cherishing* (Urbana, Ill.: University of Illinois Press, 1972).

7. Jerome Bruner, *The Process of Education* (Cambridge, Mass.: Harvard University Press, 1960).

8. Jerome Bruner, *On Knowing: Essays for the Left Hand* (Cambridge, Mass.: Harvard University Press, 1962).

9. See, for example, Robert E. Ornstein, *The Psychology of Consciousness* (San Francisco: W. H. Freeman and Company, 1972).

10. See the account in William Ernest Hocking, *Types of Philosophy* (New York: Charles Scribner's Sons, 1939).

11. See, for example, M. Esther Harding, *Woman's Mysteries* (New York: Harper & Row, 1971).

12. See, for example, Carlos Castaneda, *The Teachings of Don Juan: A Yaqui Way of Knowledge* (New York: Ballantine, 1968).

13. See Ornstein, *The Psychology of Consciousness.*

14. For an extended list of dichotomies and the sources in which they appear, see Ornstein, *The Psychology of Consciousness,* p. 67. For a similar list, see Joseph Bogen, "The Other Side of the Brain: An Appositional Mind," in *The Nature of Human Consciousness,* ed. Robert E. Ornstein (San Francisco: W. H. Freeman and Company, 1973), p. 120.

15. For an account of intuition as a source of knowledge and truth (and for a critique of this position), see Roderick M. Chisholm, *Theory of Knowledge* (Englewood Cliffs, N.J.: Prentice-Hall, Inc., 1966). See also Hocking, *Types of Philosophy.*

16. See Henri Bergson, *Creative Evolution,* trans. Arthur Mitchell (New York: Liberal Arts Press, 1955).

17. See Benedetto Croce, *Aesthetic,* trans. Douglas Ainslie (New York: Farrar, Strauss and Giroux, 1972).

18. See G. E. Moore, *Ethics* (New York: Oxford University Press, 1965); Henry Sidgwick, *The Methods of Ethics* (London: Macmillan and Co., Ltd., 1907); Joseph Butler, *Five Sermons* (New York: Liberal Arts Press, 1949).

19. This, of course, is Kant's position. See Immanuel Kant, *Critique of Pure Reason* (Garden City, N.Y.: Anchor Books, 1966).

20. See Edmund Husserl, *Ideas* (New York: Collier Books, 1962).

21. See Hermann Weyl, "The Mathematical Way of Thinking," in *The World of Mathematics,* ed. James R. Newman (New York: Simon and Schuster, 1956), pp. 1832-1849.

22. Hans Hahn, "The Crisis in Intuition," in *The World of Mathematics,* ed. James R. Newman (New York: Simon and Schuster, 1956), p. 1976.

23. Jerome Bruner, *The Process of Education* (Cambridge, Mass.: Harvard University Press, 1960), p. 13.

24. Robert E. Ornstein, *The Psychology of Consciousness* (San Francisco: W. H. Freeman and Company, 1972), pp. 143-179.

25. These techniques are characteristic of the intuitive mode as described by Morris Kline, *Why Johnny Can't Add* (New York: Vintage Books, 1974).

26. Robert Frost, *The Complete Poems of Robert Frost* (New York: Henry Holt and Company, 1949), p. vi.

27. Ibid., p. vii.

28. Ibid.

29. See the description in Jacques Hadamard, *The Psychology of Invention in the Mathematical Field* (New York: Dover Publications, Inc., 1954).

30. Quoted in Max Wertheimer, *Productive Thinking* (New York: Harper and Brothers, Publishers, 1945), pp. 183-184.

31. This notion is developed more fully in Nel Noddings and Paul J. Shore, *Awakening The Inner Eye: Intuition in Education* (New York: Teachers College Press, 1984).

8: *Moral Education*

1. Joseph S. Junell, *Matters of Feeling: Values Education Reconsidered* (Phi Delta Kappa Educational Foundation, 1979), p. 2. See also John H. Bunzell, "What's Happening to Democracy?," *Saturday Review* (May 17, 1969), pp. 28, 29.

2. A. S. Neill, *Summerhill* (New York: Hart Publishing Company, 1960).

3. Louis Rubin, Introduction to *The School's Role as Moral Authority* (Washington, D.C.: Association for Supervision and Curriculum Development, 1977), p. 2.

4. For the opposite view, see Jessie Bernard, *The Future of Motherhood* (New York: Penguin Books, Inc., 1974).

5. Martin Buber discusses the teacher's "selection of the effective world" in "Education," in *Between Man and Man* (New York: Macmillan Publishing Co., Inc., 1965), pp. 83-103.

6. Ibid., p. 90.

7. Milton Mayeroff, *On Caring* (New York: Harper & Row, Publishers, 1971), pp. 3, 5, 10, and passim.

8. Sidney Hook, Preface to John Dewey, *Moral Principles in Education* (Carbondale: Southern Illinois University Press, 1975), p. xi.

9. Richard E. Hult, Jr., "On Pedagogical Caring," *Educational Theory* (1979), 239.

10. See James B. Conant, *The American High School Today* (New York: McGraw-Hill, 1959); also, *The Comprehensive High School* (New York: McGraw-Hill, 1967).

11. Madeleine Grumet, "Conception, Contradiction and Curriculum," *Journal of Curriculum Theorizing* 3 (1981), 292.

12. Ibid., p. 293.

13. Pearl S. Buck, *The Exile* (New York: Triangle Books, 1939), p. 283.

14. See David W. Johnson, et al., "Effects of Cooperative, Competitive, and Individualistic Goal Structures on Achievement: A Meta-Analysis," *Psychological Bulletin* 84 (1981), 47-62.

15. For a full and careful discussion of the problems involved in curricular integration, see Richard Pring, "Curriculum Integration," in *The Philosophy of Education,* ed. R. S. Peters (Oxford: Oxford University Press, 1973), pp. 123-149.

16. See Larry Cuban, "Determinants of Curriculum Change and Stability," in *Value Conflicts and Curriculum Issues,* ed. Jon Schaffarzick and Gary Sykes (Berkeley: McCutchan Publishing Corporation, 1979), pp. 139-196.

INDEX

Designer: UC Press Staff
Compositor: Janet Sheila Brown
Printer: Vail-Ballou
Binder: Vail-Ballou
Text: English Times 10/13
Display: English Times